"We Jews have beautiful teachings about kindness to animals, as well as inspiring stories about great rabbis and teachers who put them into action. These teachings should be studied and taught more often, not because of PETA or animal rights or the anti-*Kapporos* protests, but because they are an essential part of our own tradition. If you really believe that *all* of the mitzvahs are important, then you should not neglect this area of study and practice. 'Be as careful with a minor mitzvah as with a major one, for you do not know the value of a mitzvah." *(Pirkei Avot)*
— from *Kapporos Then and Now*

* * *

"Rabbi Gershom has a very clear, conversational style of writing, scholarly yet very readable, and he explains complex issues very well. He is careful to put issues in context. He is not a polemicist, but seeks common ground and solutions. He uses examples from his own personal experience and also cites authorities."
— Richard H. Schwartz,
Professor Emeritus, College of Staten Island

Books by Yonassan Gershom

49 Gates of Light: A Course in Kabbalah

Beyond the Ashes:
Cases of Reincarnation from the Holocaust

From Ashes to Healing:
Mystical Encounters with the Holocaust

Jewish Tales of Reincarnation

Eight Candles of Consciousness:
Essays on Jewish nonviolence

Jewish Themes in Star Trek

Kapporos Then and Now:
Toward a More Compassonate tradition

Books co-authored with:

Richard H. Schwartz, *Who Stole my Religion? Applying Jewish Values to Help Heal Our Imperiled planet*

William C. Barnes, *The Legend of Running Brook* and the soon-to-be published sequel, *Redemption*

Works in progress:

Allergic to the Light: A novel

Comrades in the Universe:
Jewish Stories about Animals, Nature, and the Environment

KAPPOROS THEN AND NOW

Toward a More
Compassionate Tradition

by

Rabbi Yonassan Gershom

with a Foreword by Richard H. Schwartz, Ph.D.

Peace & blessings!
Rabbi ayGershom
2018/5779

Lulu Press, Inc.

2015

FIRST EDITION

ISBN 978-1-329-18940-9

Published by Lulu Press, Inc.
Raleigh, South Carolina, USA

More copies available at Lulu.com
or through your favorite bookstore

Cover photo by Caryl Gershom

Layout and cover design by Yonassan Gershom

Dedication

In memory of Rabbi Aryeh Leib (Leo) Tessler, an old school Vizhnitzer Hasid who ate no meat except for a little bit on Shabbos, never used a chicken for *Kapporos,* and taught his students not to because of *tsa'ar ba'alei chaim* (cruelty to animals). Surely he now dwells among the shining souls in the spiritual Garden of Eden.

* * *

And to all Jews (and others) seeking to balance our traditions with compassion for all of God's beloved creatures.

Table of Contents

Chapter 3: The rise of modern Kapporos centers

Chapter 4: Kapporos and Jewish mysticism

Chapter 5: The question of suffering and cruelty

Chapter 6: Using money instead

Chapter 7: Beyond kapporos

Appendices

Foreword

by Richard H. Schwartz, Ph.D.

Kol hakavod (kudos) to Rabbi Yonassan Gershom for writing this splendid, much needed book, arguing that Jews should practice the ritual of *Kapporos* using money rather than chickens. He is the ideal person to write such a book for many reasons:

1. He is very knowledgeable on Jewish teachings, especially with regard to those about the proper treatment of animals. These include:

> Jews are to be *rachmanim b'nei rachmanim* (compassionate children of compassionate ancestors), emulating God, Whose compassion is over all His works (Psalms 145:9).

> Compassion to animals is a test for righteousness because, as Proverbs 12:10 indicates, "The righteous person considers the life of his or her animals."

> Compassion to animals is so important in Judaism that it is part of the Ten Commandments, which indicates that animals, as well as people, are to be permitted to rest on the Sabbath day.

A Jew must feed his or her animals before sitting down to a meal. The great Jewish heroes Moses and King David, were deemed suitable to be leaders because of their compassionate treatment of sheep during the time they were shepherds. In short, Jews are to avoid *tsa'ar ba'alei chaim,* causing sorrow to animals.

2. Rabbi Gershom is a Breslov Hasid, so he is very familiar with the thinking of Hasidim about the use of chickens for *Kapporos.* He is not an outsider who feels he can and should tell practitioners of *Kapporos* that their practice is irrational and has no redeeming positives. He recognizes that one cannot change a traditional practice without first understanding what it is, where it came from, and what it means to the practitioners. So he carefully explains the history of the rite and why Hasidim and other religious Jews find it meaningful. Most importantly, he eloquently explains how the purpose of seeking compassion from God during the "Ten Days of Repentance" between the start of Rosh Hashanah and the end of Yom Kippur can better be carried out using money rather than chickens.

3. He and his wife have long lived on a hobby farm where they raise chickens and other animals, consistent with the powerful Jewish teachings on compassion mentioned above. Hence he is sensitive to how serious the mistreatment of chickens is, before and during the *Kapporos* ritual. He explains that while initially the ritual was carried out using chickens that were raised and treated with care by the practitioners, nowadays massive numbers of chickens in cages are transported long distances by trucks, are often not given sufficient food and water, and mishandled during the ritual by people who are not used to handling chickens. As Rabbi Gershom explains, holding chickens by the wings during the ritual is very hurtful to the birds and they only appear calm because they are playing dead, as they instinctively do when they are attacked by another animal.

4. He properly sees his role as a bridge between animal rights activists, most of whom are secular and/or non-Jewish and often act in ways that are counterproductive, and practitioners of *Kapporos,* who do not recognize that they are performing a cus-

tom based on transgressing Jewish teachings about compassion to animals, and thereby committing an act that is not recognized as positive in the Jewish tradition.

5. Rabbi Gershom has a very clear, conversational style of writing, scholarly yet very readable, and he explains complex issues very well. He is careful to put issues in context. He is not a polemicist, but seeks common ground and solutions. He uses examples from his own personal experience and also cites authorities.

In summary, he is the ideal person to argue that Jews should use money rather than chickens for *Kapporos* and he does it splendidly in this groundbreaking book. I strongly recommend it, hope it will be widely read, and that his message will be heeded.

Richard H. Schwartz, Ph.D.
Professor Emeritus, College of Staten Island
Associate producer of the 2007 documentary film,
A Sacred Duty: Applying Jewish Values to Help the World

Author of:

Judaism and Vegetarianism
Judaism and Global Survival
Mathematics and Global Survival
Who Stole My Religion? Revitalizing Judaism and Applying Jewish Values to Help Heal Our Imperiled Planet
And over 200 articles and at JewishVeg.com/schwartz

Kapporos Then and Now

Author's Introduction

It has been said that one should not criticize another person until one has walked in his (or her) shoes. That sounds easy enough, but it is very difficult to do in real life. What if the shoes are way too small? Or what if the other person goes barefoot?

On the surface, my task in writing this book would seem easy: Explain to animal rights people the reasons why some Orthodox Jews use chickens in a religious ceremony, and explain to Orthodox Jews why animal rights people find this offensive and cruel in modern times. But there is much more to it than that. Beyond this specific ritual lies a vast chasm between two very, very different worldviews.

On both sides of the issue I have found sincere, caring people who, in all good faith, believe in what they are doing. But at the same time, each side is appallingly ignorant of the other. Could I possibly write a book to bridge the gap?

My methodology was to approach the subject as a combination of theologian, cultural anthropologist, and participatory journalist, examining the issue from the perspectives of both sides. In doing so, I found it necessary to make some compromises in style, in order to be understandable to readers from diverse backgrounds.

If this were a book for Orthodox Jews only, my writing would be much more "yeshivish," with a plethora of Hebrew and Yiddish terms left undefined. But for this project, I used the English terms with Hebrew translations in parentheses (or vice versa) where there is a need to clarify. Although there is a Glossary for these terms, this method reduces the need for constant page-flipping.

I have also included birth and death dates after the names of many rabbinical authorities. We don't normally do this in Jewish books, because the persons in question are familiar. However, in the public mind there is a 1900-year gap between the beginnings of Christianity and the Nazi Holocaust, during which the average person is often clueless about who or what was happening in the Jewish world. Providing secular dates gives some cultural context and helps to place the teachings and commentaries on the world's historical timeline.

If it seems that I am over-explaining the obvious sometimes, keep in mind that what is "obvious" in the yeshiva world is a mystery to outsiders. The same goes for concepts and terminology in the secular world that might not be familiar to religious Jews. My goal is to be accessible to the general reader on both sides. To that end, the Glossary also defines some animal rights terms and cross-cultural references used in the book.

Regarding the name of the ritual in question, I prefer to transliterate it with the Ashkenazic pronunciation as *Kapporos* (with a double "P" because in English a single "P" renders the "A" into a long vowel.) For the sake of consistency, I have used this spelling throughout the book, including within direct quotations where it was originally spelled otherwise. I feel this is easier for the reader than for him or her to constantly stumble over *Kaporos, Kaparos, Kapporos, Kapparos, Kaparot, Kaporot, Kapparot, Kapporot, etc.* The only exceptions are with "The Alliance to End Chickens as Kaporos" because it is the name of an organization, and the titles of books and articles so they can more easily be found in searches.

Similarly, I prefer "Hasidic" to "Chassidic" because many English readers cannot make the "CH" guttural and/or misread it as the "CH" in "church." There may be times when I appear to use "Hasidic" and "Orthodox" interchangeably. Sometimes they are indeed the same, since Hasidic Jews are also Orthodox Jews in terms of religious observances. At other times there are philosophical differences, and in those cases I differentiate. Although I dislike the term "ultra-Orthodox," I do sometimes use it to distinguish between the Modern Orthodox and groups like Neturei Karta. For specific Hasidic groups I use the name of the group: Chabad, Breslov, Bobov, Lelever, Ger, etc.

I decided to call God "He" throughout, not because I believe God is male (in Judaism God has no body or gender) but because this is still the common convention in the Orthodox Jewish world, as well as much of society at large. Calling God "She" or "It" or some other "non-sexist" name would introduce an area of gender politics that I wish to avoid here.

Similarly, I have used the term "biblical" at times, but never "Old Testament" or "New Testament," because that is offensive to Jews. For biblical quotations, I simply give the name of the book cited. In direct quotations where "Man" appears as the name of the human species, I left it as is, but in the narrative text I used "people" or "humanity."

On the other hand, there are some concessions to the animal rights style. I say "the chicken who" rather than "the chicken that" in referring to a live bird, (with a nod to Lilian Jackson Braun and her "Cat Who" mystery books), because animals are living beings, not inanimate things. I also refer to hens as "she" and roosters as "he." But I do not call a baby animal a child, nor do I speak of "non-human animals" or people as "human animals." This blurs the line between humans and animals too much and might be misunderstood in some circles. Mother hens in my book have chicks, not children.

"Animal rights" and "animal welfare" are often used interchangeably in the media, but they are two different movements, as defined in the Glossary. In general I tried to use them as specific technical terms. In places where I was not consistent in this, the context should make my meaning clear.

It is my hope that readers on both sides will not get hung up on these semantic details, and will look beyond them to try and understand what I am saying. To that end, I have used a more informal style than for an academic paper, with numerous true anecdotes from my life and the lives of others. Storytelling is a time-honored Hasidic tradition that often succeeds where preaching fails. Regarding references, I footnoted direct quotations, but not every academic detail. Since most people now have access to the Internet, it is relatively easy for readers to check the facts for themselves. For the same reason, I have provided Internet links where possible.

And now for the usual acknowledgements. To begin, I wish to thank my Creator for giving me the opportunity to write this book. And I also thank God for having made me autistic. Although some people view this as a curse, in my case it has given me a brilliant mind with an excellent, detail-oriented memory and enough emotional detachment to study this topic objectively. My autism is the secret of my writing skill. It also plays a very big role in my empathy for animals.

Next I am most grateful to my wife Caryl (pronounced "Carol") who supported me throughout this difficult project. Unlike my last book (*Jewish Themes in Star Trek*), this work was in no way fun to write. There were times when the subject was pure agony for me. And yet I felt driven to complete it and get it out there before the next Yom Kippur. (Hence the decision to self-publish.) For Caryl it was even more emotionally draining, because she is very tenderhearted and normally avoids watching or reading materials about animal abuse. In spite of the emotional trauma, she was supportive of the project in every way. Not only did she discuss the manuscript and give me excellent suggestions, she reminded me to stop and eat and provided food for me to do so. That's no small thing for an obsessive hyper-focused autistic writer like me!

I am also thankful to live where I can keep chickens and other animals. Without them, the book would lack the personal experiences that take my thesis beyond mere theory. I am therefore grateful to all the chickens who allowed me to look in on their lives – including my childhood pet, a White Leghorn rooster named Henry, who has long since crossed the Rainbow Bridge; and Big Bird, the yellowish-white rooster who appears with me on the cover.

The following people (in alphabetical order) read all or part of the manuscript and/or made various suggestions: Karima Bushnell, Rina Deych, Charles Foster, Caryl Gershom, Richard H. Schwartz, Rabbi Dovid Sears, Rabbi Shmuly Yanklowitz, and Lee Weissman. I did not always heed your suggestions, but I do appreciate your feedback. Any errors lurking in these pages are entirely my own.

Yonassan Gershom
Lag B'Omer, 5775
May 5, 2015

Chapter 1:

A Clash of Cultures

Every year, right before Yom Kippur, the Day of Atonement, there is a cultural war in certain Jewish neighborhoods over a ceremony called *Kapporos,*[1] in which a chicken is slaughtered just before the holy day. The animal rights people show up claiming that "Meat is murder!" while the Orthodox and Hasidic Jews who practice this ceremony accuse the activists of antisemitism and violating their freedom of religion. Epithets fly and confrontations occur across the barricades, but nobody is really listening to each other.

I am in the rather unique position of being caught between these two warring camps. On the one hand, I am opposed to using chickens for the *Kapporos* ritual and have publicly spoken out against it, bringing down the wrath of certain segments of the Hasidic community. But on the other hand, I am a Hasid myself and I believe in the mystical teachings behind this ceremony: the kabbalistic doctrine of "raising holy sparks" *(netzotzot)* to repair the universe. (I will explain these teaching in detail in Chapter 4.)

In fact, it is that very mysticism – which lied at the core of my personal belief system – that has led me *not* to use chickens for the ritual – a stance that the animal rights people not only do not understand or respect, they consider it self-centered

---

[1] Also spelled *Kaporos, Kaparos, Kapparot,* or *Kapporot,* as well as other variants, depending on Hebrew and Yiddish dialects. My preference is "Kapporos." For consistency I have used that spelling throughout, including in quotations cited, except for the names of organizations and in titles of articles. As it is a foreign term in English, I have italicized it throughout.

and "specie-ist." In neither case do most people understand how I can reconcile these two worldviews.

While this conflict has sometimes been very frustrating, it has also put me in the position to be able to write this book. Precisely because I understand both sides, I hope to build a bridge that will enable some respectful dialogue. Although I am a vegetarian, this will not be a vegetarian manifesto. But neither will it be a "Torah-true" religious tract. I intend to approach the subject both as a theologian and a cultural anthropologist, putting myself inside both cultures and examining them from within their own worldviews.

I am also going to assume "good faith" on both sides. While there have been accusations of fraud, deception, insincerity, hypocrisy, intellectual dishonesty and worse thrown back and forth, I see no point in re-hashing those things over and over. If we are to have any useful dialogue, then we must start with the assumption that people are sincere in their actions and beliefs. This does not mean we must agree with everything the other side says. It may even be that their beliefs are unfounded or wrong. But if so, then we must educate, not castigate.

All I ask of both sides is that you be open-minded enough to read about things you may not personally agree with, but which are important for understanding the opposing viewpoints. As things stand now, both sides are viewing each other as negative stereotypes, seeing only the most extreme examples of what they think "the enemy" is. Very often, these stereotypes are not only wrong; they are getting in the way of finding any real solutions to the controversy.

This is why I intend to present both sides of the argument with the assumption that both sides are sincere in their beliefs, and the hope that both sides can learn something from each other. It may well be that reading about how the opposition views you will cause you to re-examine your own assumptions about them. Such honest self-examination can often lead to better understanding and cooperation. Not an easy task, but one that I challenge you to try.

In the end, it will be up to each individual to decide for him/herself what to believe about this ceremony. That said, let us now begin the journey together.

What is Kapporos?

Kapporos is an atonement custom in which, some people believe, the sins of a person are symbolically transferred to a fowl (or a substitute object — as we will discuss in more detail later.) After reading certain biblical passages,[2] the fowl, usually a chicken, is held above the person's head. (Men use a male bird, and women use a female bird.) The bird is moved slowly[3] in a circle three times, like the "wave offering" in the biblical Temple, while the practitioner recites the following: *"This is my exchange, my substitute, my atonement; this rooster (or hen) shall go to its death, but I shall go to a good, long life, and to peace."*

The bird is then slaughtered and either eaten at the pre-Yom Kippur meal or given to the poor. The hope is that the death of the fowl and donation to charity will atone for the sins of the participant, thereby averting any punishment or misfortune in the coming year.

The origins of this custom are obscure. It is not mentioned in either the Torah or the Talmud. Jewish scholars first discuss doing *Kapporos* with chickens in the ninth century, with some rabbis supporting the custom and others condemning it as a pagan superstition adopted from the surrounding gentile culture. We shall discuss this in more detail in chapter 2. For now, it is enough to know that there was never agreement in the Jewish community about whether to do *Kapporos* with a chicken, or whether to do it at all. Even today, Orthodox rabbis do not speak with one voice on the issue.

Until recently, these controversies remained within the Jewish community, as debates among learned rabbis and scholars of Jewish law. In the outside world, *Kapporos* was relatively unknown. But all that changed with the advent of modern media and the Internet.

---

[2] Isaiah 11:9, Psalms 107:10, 14, and 17-21, and Job 33:23-24

[3] Some older English-language commentaries (and many Internet sites) have "swung" but this is a mistranslation. The bird is not supposed to be whirled around as if winding up to throw a fastball. Unfortunately it is true that some people are now literally swinging the chickens, possibly due to this very mistranslation. However, such swinging could cause pain or injury to the bird, which would violate the prohibition against cruelty to animals.

3

How Kapporos became a public controversy

Three generations ago, it was still possible to go to the market, buy a live chicken, take it to the *shochet* (kosher butcher) for slaughter, then bring the carcass home to pluck, clean, and prepare it yourself. This was done not only for the *Kapporos* ritual, but also for chickens in general, and was a skill that every Jewish housewife was expected to know. But as the kosher meat industry became more industrialized, the convenience of buying fresh or frozen chickens at the supermarket began to take over. In some neighborhoods there are still local kosher butcher shops, but by and large, most Jewish cooks today no longer process their own chickens.

In the United States, *Kapporos* had largely fallen into disuse among most Jewish groups. Those who still practiced it held the ceremony privately, either at their homes or in local kosher butcher shops. But outside of a few very Orthodox communities, the majority of American Jews had either relegated the ceremony to something left behind in the Old Country, or never heard of it at all.

But gradually, due mostly to the efforts of the Hecht family in the Chabad Hasidic community (more on that in chapter 3), the ritual was not only revived in America, it began to be promoted publicly. Hundreds of chickens were trucked into warehouses, where Hasidim gathered to do the ritual and have their birds slaughtered on the spot. This, in turn, attracted the attention of the media as well as animals welfare groups.

In 2007, People Against the Ethical Treatment of Animals (PETA) began to protest and posted videos of *Kapporos* rituals on their website. The kosher industry responded with an article in *Kosher Today,* acknowledging that there were problems but relegating them to a few "sidewalk operations." New York rabbis were responding, they said, by setting regulations for the operation of these sites, requiring humane treatment of the birds and rabbinical supervision. Other Orthodox groups responded with outrage, accusing PETA of antisemitism and of violating their religious freedom rights.

That same year, Karen Davis of United Poultry Concerns (UPC), an animal rights organization she founded in 1990,

4

sent out a news release protesting the practice, which was published by Jewish Vegetarians of North America (JVNA) in their newsletter[4] and elsewhere. Both JVNA and UPC began calling for action to stop using live chickens and substitute money instead – a practice that is acceptable under Jewish law.

Then in 2008, the ASPCA confiscated 200 chickens that had been abandoned and left to die in a warehouse on the evening of Yom Kippur. These were unsold birds left over at a *Kapporos* center. The organizers had made no provisions for caring for them, and neighbors who heard their anguished cries had called the police. This incident received national news coverage, which led to an interview with Rabbi Shea Hecht, public promoter of the ritual, on National Public Radio in 2009. From there, it went viral. Thus began the cultural war over this ritual that continues to this day.

My involvement in the anti-Kapporos movement

I first heard about the *Kapporos* controversy through the above-mentioned JVNA newsletter. Living in Minnesota, where Hasidic Jews are few and far between, I was not aware of what was happening in New York. Not long after that, Richard H. Schwartz, then president of JVNA, contacted me about helping with a pamphlet called "A Wing and a Prayer: the Jewish Chicken-Swinging Ritual," to be published by Karen Davis' UPC org. This was a well-written full-color handout based on a previous essay by Schwartz. It gave a brief history of the ritual, cited rabbinical authorities that opposed using chickens, and advocated using money instead. I was impressed, and wholeheartedly endorsed the project.

In 2010, Karen Davis and a number of other activists formed a spin-off organization called The Alliance to End Chickens as Kaporos (hereafter called the Alliance). Its logo featured an Orthodox-looking Jew gently holding a chicken, with a city skyline in the background. I was among the early founders of the Alliance – I even helped think up the name. Al-

---

[4] See http://jewishveg.blogspot.com/2007/08/82207-jvna-online-newsletter.html#a082207a8

though I could not attend the rallies and protests due to responsibilities at home, I tried to help from afar, writing articles on my blog and giving advice behind the scenes.

The first protests were held in 2010 in New York City only, guided by local activist Rina Deych, who had been protesting *Kapporos* in her Brooklyn neighborhood for over 20 years. These early protests were respectful of Jews and Jewish tradition. Participants dressed modestly and the signs were appropriate to the cause. At that time I had assumed – wrongly – that Davis was Jewish and that the keystone for the campaign would be Judaism. Only later did I learn otherwise.

In 2013, I wrote and narrated a one-minute slide show for the Alliance called "A Heartfelt Plea for Mercy," with the following text:

> Shalom, fellow Chasidim! My name is Rabbi Gershom, I live on a farm, and I have been around chickens all my life. You have been told that holding a chicken by its wings that way will make the bird calm and relaxed. This is not true! The bird is terrified, it is playing dead, the way it does if it is grabbed by a dog or a wolf. It is hoping you will let go so it can escape. Imagine somebody pulling your arms back, then hanging you up by the elbows. You would stop struggling, but you would NOT be calm or relaxed! You would be in terrible fear and pain, the same as these poor chickens are now. Please do not torture a bird this way – this is not a mitzvah, our Torah does not require this, it will not cancel your sins. I beg you, please give money instead of hurting one of God's living creatures.

This video was posted on YouTube[5] and the link was included in the Alliance news releases about the protests. It was widely re-distributed on activist sites, as well as quoted in several major newspaper articles. In New York, the sound track was also broadcast from a truck that displayed the slides on video side panels.

---

[5] View it at: https://www.youtube.com/watch?v=E3LKLwQ8lPA

The video truck attracted a lot of attention and was judged by all of us to be a successful effort. It definitely got the attention of Rabbi Shea Hecht, spearhead of the pro-*Kapporos* movement, who sarcastically told *The Brooklyn Brief* in 2014: "They hire some rabbi who wants to make a name for himself, and they tell us to raise a piece of tofu over our heads."[6] (For the record, nobody paid me anything for this. All my work with the Alliance was voluntary. But the fact that he felt a need to ridicule me says that I was having an impact.)

2013 was also the first year that protests were held outside of New York. I did not attend these rallies, but I certainly read about them, both in the national media and on activist websites. And that was when I began to see serious problems developing. Protesters in Los Angeles, many of whom were hearing about *Kapporos* for the first time, were far less respectful than those in New York. These groups were not officially sponsored by the Alliance, although Davis did publicize their events and distributed follow-up articles about their protest actions. Therefore, in my opinion, she and her organization do bear some responsibility for what happened next.

Many of the new groups jumping into the fray had neither the background nor the sensitivity to the Jewish community as in New York. They mixed in radical vegan themes, carrying signs declaring that meat is murder and comparing the slaughter of chickens to Jews in the Holocaust. "Genocide is wrong whether against Jews or against chickens," read a sign held by one protestor picketing at a Beverly Hills synagogue.[7] Not only was this inflammatory, it was grossly inaccurate regarding the definition of "genocide." Nobody is trying wipe out the entire chicken species – which is what a real genocide would be. In fact, the factory farm system, as horrific as it may be, has greatly *increased* the number of chickens on the planet.

---

[6] Taub, Matthew, "Animal Cruelty Protests, Legal Actions Continue Over Jewish Kapporos Ritual," October 1, 2014. http://brooklynbrief.com/animal-cruelty-protests-continue-jewish-Kapporos-ritual/

[7] Rodman, Edmund J., "Sunday's Protesters sought Kaparot concessions," September 9, 2013, *Jewish Journal,* http://www.jewishjournal.com/los_angeles/article/sundays_protestors_sought_kaporot_concessions

These were tactics that I knew were counter-productive in traditional Jewish communities. As I will explain later in this chapter, comparing animals to Holocaust victims is as offensive to most Jews as waving a noose would be to African Americans. The reactions were predictably negative. "I'm trying to keep kids off drugs, and they are calling me a murderer," said Rabbi Moshe Nourollah, whose Jewish outreach organization, Bait Aaron, organized the *Kapporos* ceremony behind Young Israel of Beverly Hills, where they had rented the space. "They were screaming at little kids," said Meir Nourollah, the rabbi's son. Some Jews, in return, screamed insults back. In general, the 2013 California protests were loud and disorderly, causing the police to eventually step in.

From then on, "meat is murder" became the watchword against *Kapporos* across the online activist networks. In vain did I try to explain why this was not an argument that Orthodox Jews would ever listen to. I suggested to Davis that we should produce some educational materials for protest organizers about Hasidic culture, and lay down some ground rules for content of signs and slogans at future protests. I also wrote a wrap-up article on my blog called "Kapporos Protests: What Works and What Doesn't,"[8] which Davis linked to the Alliance website. However, she showed little interest in setting rules for future protests through her own org or educating the other groups that her campaign was now inspiring. The offensive slogans continued to go viral, and the communications gap widened.

I leave the Alliance – but not the movement

During the summer of 2014, Rina Deych and I discussed the cultural gap between the Hasidic community and the mostly secular activists. We also talked about independently producing some handout materials that were geared specifically toward Hasidim and other Orthodox. I wrote a flyer that focused on the doctrine of "raising holy sparks," a kabbalistic idea that is absolutely central to Hasidic beliefs about eating meat and relating

---

[8] http://rooster613.blogspot.com/2013/10/kapporos-protests-what-works-and-what.html

to the world in general. I told two short stories, one of which was how the Baal Shem Tov,[9] who at one point in his life was a *shochet,*[10] used to whet the sharpening stone with his own tears.

Deych thought the flyer was great and would be effective, but Davis refused to use it because it was not 100% vegan in approach. She stated that, in her opinion, the Baal Shem Tov could not possibly have had compassion if he was willing to kill animals at all – thereby writing off the founder of Hasidism and with him the whole Hasidic movement. This brought to a head all of the behind-the-scenes frustrations I had felt over the past year and a half. So I self-published the flyer as a downloadable PDF that people could print for themselves.[11]

Davis and I continued to bump heads over doctrine, with me trying to convince her that mixing in militant veganism was counter-productive to doing outreach in Orthodox Jewish communities, because it linked the issue to PETA in the minds of the people – and PETA has a very bad reputation among religious Jews. In the same *Brooklyn Brief* article where Rabbi Hecht made the tofu remark, he also claimed that many of the protestors were "not being intellectually honest" because most of them were vegans or vegetarians associated with PETA but would not admit it publicly.

In a way he is right. The Alliance is a separate organization from PETA, but there is a lot of crossover among members, who often belong to many different groups at the same time and subscribe to each other's newsletters. This does not mean everybody agrees with everybody else on everything, but there is a lot of cross-fertilization. And it is true that although Davis never insisted I had to become a vegan (I am an ovo-lacto vegetarian), she also would not use any of my materials that did not pass the vegan litmus test – even if they were effective. In fact,

---

[9] Rabbi Israel ben Eliezer (1699-1760), known as the Baal Shem Tov ("Master of the Good Name") or "Besht" for short, was the founder of Hasidism, a mystical revivalist movement that began in Eastern Europe. For a brief history and explanation of Hasidism, see Appendix B.

[10] *Shochet:* A Jewish slaughterer trained in *shechita,* the laws and methods of kosher slaughter. He must be a religious Jew, usually Orthodox.

[11] Available on my blog at http://JewishThoreau.com

Davis goes *way beyond* PETA in her insistence upon pure veganism.[12]

The Mission Statement of UPC, parent organization of the Alliance, states: "Promoting the Compassionate and Respectful Treatment of Domestic Fowl." I took this at face value, reading "compassion" as including the Baal Shem Tov's love of animals and his tears shed over the necessity of slaughtering them so that the people could eat. Only later did I learn that "compassionate" to Davis is a code word for "vegan," and "never kill anything." Veganism, not Judaism, is the basis for the Alliance campaign, *even though veganism is nowhere mentioned on the Alliance website.* That, to me, is deceptive.

As the conflict between Davis and I escalated during the fall of 2014, she tightened her grip on the Alliance and made it very clear that she was in charge and veganism would prevail. The media began referring to her as "president" of the Alliance, although, to my knowledge, no election was ever held. Meanwhile, she made some offensive public statements about Hasidic culture and theology that she refused to retract.

Because she had become the primary spokesperson for the opposition to the ritual, this was not merely a matter of personality conflicts. It had reached a point where I, as a rabbi, felt the need to distance myself from her blatantly inaccurate statements about Hasidism. And so we parted ways.

However, I did not withdraw my permission for the Alliance to use the materials I had helped to produce, including the slide show and a poster with a photo of me holding a rooster. There was nothing in these materials that I would retract. As of this writing, there is still a link to the slide show on the Alliance homepage. Some may criticize me for this, but I am not a revisionist. I said what I said and I meant it. I still do.

I next turned my attention toward addressing the issue in the language of Hasidic thought. My *Kapporos* blog article that year was called "The Baal Shem Tov did it with a chicken, so

---

[12] For example, PETA has affirmed that kosher slaughter, if done properly, is humane. Davis, on the other hand, condemns all slaughter as cruelty. PETA is an animal welfare org, while Davis is in the animal rights camp. (See Glossary.)

why are you telling me not to?"[13] I expanded the "holy sparks" theme from the PDF flyer, arguing that the cruelties of modern conditions canceled out any merit that the ceremony once had, and that using money instead avoids the possibility of committing any new sins. I still maintain that this is the most effective way to argue against using chickens.

The positive responses I have received to my blog articles seem to indicate that I am right. Those articles, in turn, inspired me to write this book. It had become painfully obvious to me that the protests, although they received a lot of publicity, were ineffective in convincing anybody to give up using chickens. If anything, they were causing the practitioners to "circle the wagons" and hold on even tighter to the tradition. Insults and accusations were flying left and right, people where shouting at each other across the barricades, but nobody was really listening. Education was badly needed on both sides.

Let me be very clear that I still respect the work that Karen Davis is doing on behalf of domestic fowl in the secular world. Her groundbreaking book, *Prisoned Chickens and Poisoned Eggs,* is included in the bibliography. I recognize that she has worked tirelessly toward sensitizing the public to the suffering and exploitation of chickens, ducks, geese, turkeys and other domestic birds. I also acknowledge that the Alliance has done a lot of good in terms of bringing the *Kapporos* issue to the public eye, and in addressing the legal and health concerns evident at the mass *Kapporos* centers. If Davis would just stick to science and secular animal issues, everything would be fine. But when it comes to Jewish theology, she is simply out of her league. She lacks the knowledge and cultural sensitivity to deal with a Jewish religious ceremony.

Which brings us to the crux of this chapter: How do we communicate across the great chasm between the Jewish and non-Jewish worldviews? Between the beliefs of vegetarians and those who eat meat? Between those who see *Kapporos* as a sacred ceremony and those who see it as needless cruelty? Is it even possible for the two sides to respectfully communicate?

---

[13] http://rooster613.blogspot.com/2014/09/on-Kapporos-baal-shem-tov-did-it-with.html

To answer that question, we must first learn how each side "sees" the other.

How Kapporos practitioners view the activists

Jews who practice *Kapporos* with chickens are people who eat meat. Although there are many Jewish vegetarians, even Orthodox and Hasidic ones, these are not the people who slaughter chickens for this ritual. And because they are meat-eaters, the practitioners are genuinely puzzled as to why the activists are protesting the slaughter of chickens. The Torah permits eating meat, they argue. Moses ate meat, The Baal Shem Tov ate meat, the Hasidic Rebbes ate meat – and these were holy, God-fearing people. So what is wrong with eating a chicken?

In a telephone interview with the *Brooklyn Brief,* Rabbi Hecht explained it this way: "We kill animals to eat, we use their skin for household goods, for the clothes we wear, for *mezzuzot,* to make phylacteries. Why can't we use it for this sacrifice?"[14]

The vegan activists would counter that it's morally wrong to kill animals – but this is not what the Torah says, and for religious Jews, the Torah trumps modern ideas about "ethical veganism." The "meat is murder" argument makes no sense to them, because "murder" in the Torah is a specific term that applies to human beings, not animals.[15] Jewish law mandates that slaughtering animals must be done humanely, and lays down details for how it is to be done, but the slaughter itself is not forbidden nor is it murder. And if killing something for food is the issue, the practitioners ask, then don't we also kill plants when we harvest them? How then would human beings survive, if they were forbidden to kill anything?

Many practitioners also see the activists as antisemites trying to take away their religious rights. Keep in mind that in

---

[14] *See Brooklyn Brief* article cited earlier.

[15] In the Ten Commandments, for example, The King James Version says "Thou shalt not kill," which some vegetarians interpreted as a prohibition against killing anything. Newer translations render it as "You shall not murder" which is more correct. This, in turn, has caused some animal rights activists to say that "meat is murder" although that is not, and never was, the original intent of the Commandment.

12

past history there were indeed groups and governments who passed laws to forbid Jewish religious practices. From the Hellenistic Greeks, who made it punishable by death to circumcise, right down to the Nazis who outlawed all kosher slaughtering, such restrictions are often first steps toward stronger measures intended to destroy the Jewish people. Therefore many Jews, even non-Orthodox or secular ones, are immediately suspicious of any group that tries to outlaw a Jewish practice.

This perception of persecution has been increased by several very insensitive actions by PETA. As mentioned earlier, PETA has a bad reputation among Jews. In my opinion, that reputation is well deserved. Let us look at two PETA actions that not only "used" Jews for their own agenda, but also did it in very offensive ways.

First there was the infamous "Arafat Donkey Letter." On February 26, 2003, some Palestinians sent a donkey laden with explosives into a Jerusalem street, then blew the donkey up. PETA president Ingrid Newkirk was horrified, and wrote an open letter to Yassar Arafat, protesting the use of animals in warfare. "If you have the opportunity," she wrote, "will you please add to your burdens my request that you appeal to all those who listen to you to leave the animals out of this conflict?" She also made reference to cats fleeing under fire, but said nothing about human victims on either side of the war.

This letter enraged the Jewish community (as well as others throughout the world), because it seemed to be saying, "Go ahead and blow up the Jews, just don't hurt the animals."

To put this in perspective, in January 2003 – the same month in which the donkey died – terrorists killed 21 Israelis and eight foreign nationals in Israel, and 127 others were injured. Yet Newkirk felt no responsibility to protest this. When asked by the *Washington Post* if she had "considered asking Arafat to persuade those who listen to him to stop blowing up people as well," her response was, "It's not my business to inject myself into human wars."

At the time, *The Jewish World Review* ran a headline asking if PETA stands for "People Excusing Terrorist Atrocities." And this is still the perception of PETA in large segments of the Jewish community, eclipsing many of the good things that the organization has done for animals.

The Donkey Letter is also one source for the belief, common among Orthodox Jews, that animal rights activists care *more* about animals than they do about people. The letter is often mentioned in the same conversation with stories about Nazis who spent all day killing Jews, then went home to cuddle and play with their dogs. In 2014, Rabbi Eliezer Melamed, the *Rosh Yeshiva* (headmaster) of Har Bracha in Israel, took this even further. In an article entitled "The Significance of Eating Meat," he claimed that the animal rights movement *causes* people to be callous toward humans. He writes:

> Here in Israel, quite a few vegetarian activists support the terrorist organizations of the P.L.O. and Hamas, while at the same time, claiming that the settlers are the biggest culprits, hindering peace of the world. Incidentally, this type of evil is the most serious and dangerous, because it wraps itself in the guise of righteousness. In the same way that some of the greatest villains in history took pride in their compassion for animals.[16]

This is an extreme example, and Rabbi Melamed certainly does not represent all Orthodox Jews, heaven forbid. Nevertheless, we can see in this statement indirect references to both the Donkey Letter and Hitler, one of the "greatest villains in history" who was very fond of his dog, Blondi.

The linking of kindness to animals with Nazis is probably the source of a strange statement that I found numerous times while researching this book, namely, the claim by certain rabbis that kindness to animals actually *causes* cruelty to human beings. This is a patently absurd assumption that turns psychology on its head. Kindness to animals does not lead to violence towards humans. The opposite is true: cruelty to animals leads to cruelty toward humans.

One of the first signs of a developing psychopath is a tendency toward torturing animals. Part of the initiation into

---

[16] "The Significance of Eating Meat," June 8, 2014 online at:
http://blogs.timesofisrael.com/the-significance-of-eating-meat/# We should note that Rabbi Melamed is not Hasidic; he is a Haredi. See Glossary.

Hitler's Death's Head SS squads was to be given a puppy to love, raise and train, then later be ordered to shoot it. The purpose of this cruelty being, to teach the young soldiers to follow orders and have no compassion whatsoever, nor even for their best friends. It was not *kindness* to the dogs that hardened their hearts; it was *the act of betraying those dogs* in order to be accepted into the group. The same kind of callous behavior can be seen in gang initiations today.

Unfortunately, many rabbis are not very conversant in modern psychology, and some are openly hostile to it. In ultra-Orthodox circles, modern science in general is suspect. Partly this is because of the conflict between evolution and creationism, and partly it is because of secular hostility toward religion in general. Within the Jewish community itself, especially in Israel, there is a huge divide between the religious and the secular worlds. This is why I urge activists not to attack Hasidic beliefs as "medieval, "primitive," or "unscientific." All this does is cause people to shut down and ignore your message.

Also by PETA in 2003, there was "Holocaust on Your Plate," a traveling photographic exhibit that graphically paralleled Jews in concentration camps with animals on factory farms. The display consisted of seven large outdoor posters with juxtaposed pictures of farm animals confined and mistreated, then piled up after slaughter on one side, while on the other side were pictures of humans confined and mistreated, then piled up after slaughter during the Holocaust. Each poster included a short caption that drew an analogy between the subjects in the two pictures.

PETA's intention was to show that animals in modern agricultural facilities suffer the same kinds of abuse as Jews did during the Holocaust. Which, in terms of physical pain, fear, thirst, and starvation may well be true. But the Jews did not see it that way. *They saw the display as saying that the life of a Jew was not worth any more than the life of a chicken or cow.* Rather than increasing awareness of animal suffering, the exhibit lowered the value of human life – so much so, that it was

15

banned in Germany, a decision upheld by the European Court of Human Rights.[17]

Previously, in a 1989 interview with *Vogue,* PETA's president, Ingrid Newkirk, had said, "Animal liberationists do not separate out the human animal, so there is no rational basis for saying that a human being has special rights. A rat is a pig is a dog is a boy."[18] The Holocaust exhibit now reinforced this perception that PETA equated the lives of people with those of animals. Especially offensive was a poster showing Jewish children in the camps next to a photo of caged piglets, with the caption, "Baby Butchers." Comparing Jewish children to pigs evoked memories of Nazis calling Jews "swine."

These two incidents are by no means the end of offenses by PETA and others toward Jews, but they will suffice to illustrate why many *Kapporos* practitioners react negatively to the suggestion by activists that the practice is cruel to the chickens. They often point to the widespread belief that Hitler was a vegetarian (in fact, he was not)[19] and use that to prove that vegetarians are no better than the carnivores, so what right do the activists have to point fingers?

Using Hitler in this way is a classic example of false logic that I actually saw in a math book once: "Hitler was a vegetarian; Hitler was evil; therefore all vegetarians are evil." Stated that way, it sounds as ridiculous as it is. Even if Hitler were a vegetarian, that does not negate the entire diet and/or lifestyle for everyone. If Hitler had enjoyed baseball, would that mean we should condemn all baseball players?

Activists reading this section are probably saying to themselves, "But that's not me! I don't hate Jews, I love peo-

---

[17] http://verdict.justia.com/2012/11/28/the-european-court-of-human-rights-upholds-german-ban-on-petas-holocaust-on-your-plate-campaign

[18] *Vogue,* September 1, 1989. Newkirk later backpedaled on this statement, claiming she had only meant it in terms of feeling pain. (Wikipedia) However, the original statement is what people remember, and it resurfaced with the Holocaust exhibit. Many animal rights activists today, especially those in the "deep ecology" movement, do indeed believe that there is no difference between humans and animals.

[19] Hitler's vegetarianism is a myth. Although he sometimes refrained from meat for health reasons, he was also fond of liver, ham, sausage, turtle soup and roast pigeon – hardly a true vegetarian! Google "Hitler and vegetarianism" for more on this.

ple, and I'm not a Nazi." Which is probably true. But remember: my intent here is to show you *what the other side thinks,* not what you think of yourself.

How activists view the Kapporos practitioners

The majority of people in the animal rights and animal welfare movements sincerely care about animals and other living things, including people. A high percentage are vegans or vegetarians, but not all. There are some people who, although they eat meat, still care about how animals are treated. Animal welfare organizations like the ASPCA fall into this category. Although the ASPCA has confiscated *Kapporos* chickens and investigated allegations of cruelty, most of their members are not vegetarians. My point here is, that it is possible to care about animal issues without going all the way to become a vegan.

Both vegans and carnivores are genuinely horrified by what they see at *Kapporos* centers, partly because most people do not actually know how animals are treated in the meat industry. The general public still thinks in terms of "Old McDonald's Farm" and has no idea how chickens are raised and transported today. They do not realize that the only real difference between *Kapporos* and the chicken dinner on their own plates is that commercial slaughter takes place behind closed doors. So they see those stacks of cages with chickens crammed inside and, not knowing that this is how *all* chickens are treated on the way to the slaughterhouse, perceive it as some sort of "Jewish cruelty."[20] This, in turn arouses antisemitism, often expressed in vehement comments on the Internet.

The protesters are usually more educated about factory farms than the general public. They are also aware that chickens are living, breathing, sentient beings, with an intelligence level of at least a 3-year-old child,[21] certainly aware enough to know what is happening to them. While intelligence per se is

---

[20] See "Singling out Jewish kapporos for criticism" by Sherry F. Colb, Professor of Law and Charles Evans Hughes Scholar at Cornell Law School at: http://verdict.justia.com/2014/10/01/singling-jewish-kaporos-criticism

[21] See "The Startling Intelligence of the Common Chicken," by Caroline L. Smith and Sarah L. Zierlinski, *Scientific American,* Volume 310, issue 2.

not a moral criterion for humane treatment of animals, people should know that the chickens they see in the cramped cages are not "dumb clucks." They are severely traumatized birds in a state of physical and emotional shock.

Even worse, the activists sometimes see children poking at the chickens with sticks, handling them roughly, or laughing if the birds try to get away – and the adults don't seem to much care about this misbehavior. (There are videos of this on You-Tube. We will address the question of humane education in chapter 7.) Activists are also appalled at the casual, even callous way that the practitioners stand around chatting, while holding their chickens dangling by the wings as if they are nothing more than packages or shopping bags. Everywhere there is the smell of blood, with chickens crying, bleeding, dying, and feathers all over the place. In many cases, the mess left behind offends even meat-eating neighbors in the area.

None of this seems to the activists like "religion." Karen Davis, on several occasions, has referred to it as "a carnival atmosphere" and sees it as cruelty "in the guise of religion." She herself is not Jewish, and was raised in the Methodist church, where "religion" means sitting quietly with hands folded, listening to hymns and sermons. The same goes for Reform Jews, whose synagogue services are more church-like than the Orthodox, who often pace, shout, and rock back and forth during prayers. (I can only imagine what Davis would make of our dancing and drinking on Simchat Torah.)

To many activists, true religion is by definition vegan; otherwise it's not religion. The Jains of India, who refrain from killing even fleas and mosquitoes, are often held up as the ideal. At one point, Davis told me to "get in touch with the God of Genesis" as opposed to the God who permits slaughter. (She apparently meant the Garden of Eden, not Genesis per se, since God permits Noah and his descendants to slaughter animals in Genesis.) The idea that killing animals could be "religious" is abhorrent to Davis and others like her. She sees herself as the opposite of Rabbi Hecht, who considers *Kapporos* a religious act. Regarding Hecht, she states:

> Rabbi Hecht, and probably many (though not all) other
> Kapparot practitioners who use chickens, enjoy the ex-

perience of making and watching a helpless creature suffer and die "for them" (be punished in their stead for their sins). They like the control and are gratified by the pain and suffering they can inflict with impunity in the guise of religion... there is a liking for the slaughter, the power, the blood... [22]

An Orthodox Jew reading this would probably say, "Whoa! That's not what it's all about. I'm not a sadist, this isn't me, I don't get off on seeing blood." And he would be right. The Jews who practice this ceremony are not psychopaths; they do not get up in the morning and say to themselves, "I'm going to go out and torture chickens today so I can get rid of my sins." They sincerely believe that kosher slaughter is humane and that holding a chicken by the wings is not painful. (We shall return to the issue of suffering in chapter 6.)

There is *nothing* in Hasidism, or Judaism in general, about "enjoying" the suffering or being "gratified by the pain and suffering" as Davis interprets it. In fact, according to Jewish law, if a *shochet* (ritual slaughterer) ever does get to the point of enjoying the kill, he is disqualified as a *shochet.*

This perception of *shochtim* as bloodthirsty, perverted sadists has entered the vegan world through a short story called "Blood" by Nobel Laureate Isaac Bashevis Singer. Because Singer was vegetarian, he is practically canonized by the animal rights movement. Many of Singer's stories do deal with the question of eating meat, but it is important to keep in mind that they are *fiction.* Singer's writing is often anachronistic; he places his characters in 18th century Polish villages but deals with current issues. They are not historical documents or anthropological studies of Jewish s*tetl* life! Nevertheless, Singer is where many activists get their ideas about Judaism. [23]

---

[22] Mehta, Hermant, "The Kapparot Problem" October 1, 2014 at http://www.patheos.com/blogs/friendlyatheist/2014/10/01/the-kapparot-problem/

[23] Charles Patterson, Ph.D., in his 2002 book, *Eternal Treblinka: Our Treatment of Animals and the Holocaust,* devotes an entire chapter to Singer, with synopses of several stories and novels that deal with the question of slaughtering animals, including "Blood," "The Slaughterer," and "The Estate."

Kapporos is not done "in the guise" of religion. Those who do it are sincere and regard it as a form of worship, however alien it may seem to outsiders. Nevertheless, this is how Davis honestly views it, and this harsh judgment is a common perception of *Kapporos* among animal rights activists. From their perspective, *Kapporos* is a primitive, bloody, barbaric ceremony that is a waste of life and in no way religious or spiritual. One can find even stronger condemnations on the Internet, but I will spare you the details. Once again, remember: I am presenting *how the other side sees it.*

The need for respectful dialogue

As we have seen, each side is seeing the other only in the harshest, most negative terms. Each side is judging the other to be 100% wrong, and regarding their own side as 100% right. It is likely that, as you just read these last two sections, you were fully in agreement with the description of the side you oppose, but were horrified by what the other side thinks of you. But keep in mind that the other side probably agrees with the harsh description of you. Which is why, in my opinion, nothing is accomplished by shouting insults across the barricades.

Neither of these descriptions really fits the group that it attempts to describe. Both are negative stereotypes. And that is precisely my point. In order to have any kind of meaningful dialogue, both sides must begin to see the good in each other. Hasidic Jews are not a bunch of chicken murderers, and activists are not a bunch of raving antisemites. Each group has both good and bad points; each has things they can teach the other; and each has things they can learn from the other. For the rest of this book, please keep that in mind.

Chapter 2:

Sacrifice and Kapporos

The origin of *Kapporos* is shrouded in history. It is not mentioned in either the Torah or the Talmud, but this does not necessarily mean it is a modern invention. In addition to written history, Judaism has a vast oral tradition, passed down from parents to children and from teachers to students, that very often is not committed to writing until many centuries later. Therefore, it has been argued, *Kapporos* might be much older than the written traditions we now have.

Although anti-*Kapporos* activists frequently use the argument that "it is not required by Jewish law" and therefore assume it is something "just made up," this is a simplistic approach that carries no weight with the practitioners. There is also a process called *minhag*, whereby customs shared within a community over a long period of time take on the force of law for that community, even if not officially legislated. In the case of *Kapporos*, it has been practiced for at least a thousand years, which gives it far more weight than something "made up."[24]

---

[24] It is also counter-productive to call it "medieval" in the sense of uncivilized or barbaric, because the word does not carry this connotation to Jews. Some of the greatest Jewish scholars, who are still studied and revered today, wrote during the Middle Ages, including Rashi, Maimonides, Nachmanides, Saadia Gaon, Ibn Ezra, Isaac Luria, Chaim Vital, and other major Torah personages. In fact, it has been argued that the rise of scholasticism in the Christian community had its roots in contact with Jews. At any rate, insults never work to change people's beliefs.

It is important to remember that just because something is not found in a written text until after certain date, that does not mean it didn't exist before then. Oral traditions and customs can be passed down for many generations before they are put into books. Usually that happens when there is a danger of losing them due to a war, plague, or other disaster. Even today, ethnologists are still collecting songs, folktales, and customs from before the Holocaust – in some cases, remembered by only one or two survivors.

To fully understand how the *Kapporos* ceremony came to be practiced in modern times, it is necessary to understand the role of sacrifices in Jewish history and tradition. This will be a difficult chapter for animal rights activists to read, but a necessary one if there is to be any real dialogue between the two camps. Most people are not born vegetarian or vegan, so keep in mind that your ancestors, too, probably ate meat and offered sacrifices. As someone once said, you cannot understand where you are now unless you know where you have been.

Sacrifice in ancient times

Before the invention of money and other forms of token value, all payments for goods and taxes were accomplished through bartering the actual items, and this carried over into worship. Not only Jews, but all ancient peoples practiced some form of sacrifice, if not of animals then of food, incense, artwork or a "labor of love." Even today, we find people who bring gifts of various sorts to their houses of worship or spiritual leaders.

To understand *Kapporos,* we must try to understand the original concept of sacrifice – no easy task for a 21st-century person. Putting ourselves into the mindset of the ancient world is indeed difficult, as noted by Rabbi Abraham Joshua Heschel in his classic work, *The Prophets:*

> It is hard for us to imagine what entering a sanctuary or offering a sacrifice meant to ancient man. The sanctuary was holiness in perpetuity, a miracle in continuity; the divine was mirrored in the air, sowing blessing, closing gaps between the here and the beyond. In of-

fering a sacrifice, man mingled with mystery, reached the summit of significance: sin was consumed, self abandoned, satisfaction was bestowed upon divinity. Is it possible for us today to conceive of the solemn joy of those whose offering was placed on the altar?[25]

Heschel does not answer his own question, but leaves it open for us to ponder: Can we really put ourselves into the numinous mindset of our distant ancestors? Can we understand – even intellectually – how animal sacrifices were once seen as something holy? But before we go any further, we need to define what "sacrifice" actually means.

In the common wisdom of modern English-speaking people, "to sacrifice" means "to give something up," as in parents sacrificing their own needs for the sake of their children. However, the word itself comes from the same root as "sacred." To sacrifice something is to make it sacred. It may well be that, in accomplishing a higher, nobler task, we must also give something up, as in "everyone must make sacrifices for peace." But the original meaning was not about the "giving up" per se; it was about the sanctification of the gift.

The Hebrew word commonly translated as "sacrifice" is *korban,* which comes from the root K-R-B meaning "to come close." A *korban* was seen as a way for the worshipper to come close to God, both in the literal, physical sense of entering the sanctuary, and in the spiritual sense of connecting with a mystical reality or soul-consciousness. Jewish mystics would later argue that the sacrifice itself was also brought nearer to God through its participation in the rituals, in a process known in kabbalah as "raising holy sparks," which we will discuss in more detail in Chapter 4.

The Holy Temple was seen as a microcosm of the universe, laid out in the universal symbolism of the six directions (north, south, east, west, above and below), with the fire on the altar as the seventh point where the six directions meet. It was a place where the mineral, vegetable, animal and human levels of existence were bound together through ceremony and prayer.

---

[25] Heschel, Abraham Joshua, *The Prophets,* Harper & Row, New York, 1962, p. 197.

23

Jerusalem, location of the Temple, was the *axis mundi,* the spiritual center of the world that connected Heaven and Earth.

Maimonides: sacrifice as a transitional stage

The destruction of Solomon's Temple by the Babylonians in 586 B.C.E. was a major crisis for the Jewish people. As we have already noted, sacrifice was the normal mode of worship in ancient times. But how could sacrifices be offered if the Holy Temple no longer existed? "How shall we sing the Lord's songs in a strange land?" the psalmist lamented. (Psalm 137:4).

A people without their Holy Center was a people without a connection to God – which is precisely why temples were so often destroyed in warfare. The ancient pagans believed that their gods literally lived in the houses of worship built for them; to destroy a temple was to drive the enemy's god out of the land, and, by extension, take away the people's earthly power.

It appears that many Jews thought this way also. "Make me a sanctuary, that I may dwell among them," says God to Moses (Exodus 25:8). There is no reason to believe that Jews of the time did not take this literally, that God needed a physical house for His presence. Sacrificing in a "sacred space" was very important to all ancient peoples.

According to Maimonides, Jews of that time were so used to sacrificial forms of worship that God could not have abruptly ended them without it being a total shock to the people's faith. He writes:

It is impossible to go from one extreme to the other suddenly. Therefore man - according to his nature - is not capable of abandoning suddenly that to which he was deeply accustomed... As it was then the deeply-ingrained and universal practice that people were brought up with to conduct religious worship with animal sacrifices in temples... God in His wisdom did not see fit to command us to completely reject all these practices - something that man could not conceive of accepting, according to human nature which inclines to habit... He therefore left these practices but trans-

24

formed them from their idolatrous associations... that
their purpose should be directed toward Him.
(*Guide for the Perplexed*, Section III:32)

In other words, God took the familiar practices from paganism and adapted them to His own worship. But at the same
time, He also limited the sacrifices to one central place: first the
Tabernacle in the wilderness, later the Holy Temple in Jerusalem. There were to be no more local altars erected on every
"high place" in the land. This greatly limited the number of
sacrifices. God also prohibited abusing or torturing the animals
as some pagan cults had done. All sacrifices had to be perfect
specimens without any scars or blemishes (See Exodus 22),
which meant that they must have been treated gently. We can
therefore see that already in biblical times, there were major differences between pagan and Jewish practices.

A commonly held Jewish tradition states that had the
people not fallen back into idolatry with the worship of the
Golden Calf, there would have been no need for the sacrifices.
The first set of Tablets given to Moses, according to this teaching, contained only the Ten Commandments. But after Moses
came down the mountain, found the people worshipping an idol
and smashed the Tablets, it was obvious that the Israelites were
not ready for a complete break with familiar rituals. So God
had Moses go back up the mountain and get a second set of
Tablets, along with precise instructions on how to build the
Sanctuary and offer the sacrifices.

From blood sacrifices to verbal liturgy

Although God did permit sacrifices, there are early indications
that He was preparing the people, through the prophets, for a
time when they would no longer need such ceremonies. There
are numerous references in the prophetic writings to sacrifices
that were an "abomination" to God because they were offered
without any change of heart or improved behavior.

Already in the time of King Saul, the prophets had begun to question the importance of sacrifices. When Saul was
ordered by God not to take any plunder in the battle against the

25

Amalekites, he disobeyed and took flocks for sacrifices anyway. Saul claimed he would offer them at the Tabernacle (I Samuel: 19-22). Such sacrifices would probably have been thanksgiving or peace offerings *(shlamim),* which were to be eaten at a victory feast by the soldiers. This would have been the normal course of things during warfare, and Saul sincerely believed he was honoring God. But Samuel strongly rebukes him, saying:

> Does the Lord delight in burnt offerings and sacrifices
> As much as in obedience to the Lord's command?
> Surely obedience is better than sacrifice,
> Compliance better than the fat of rams...
> (I Samuel 14:22)

Even before Samuel's birth, the priests officiating at the Tabernacle were getting corrupt and not respecting the sacrifices or the people who brought them. Eli the High Priest was a pious, God-fearing man, but his sons, who would inherit the hereditary priesthood, were greedy scoundrels. They would demand their share of the meat even before the fat of the offering was burned on the altar, sometimes taking it by force from the worshipper (I Samuel 2:12-17). Eli took his sons to task for this blasphemy, but they ignored him and continued in their evil ways. So a "man of God" came to prophesy that the priesthood would be taken away from Eli's line and given to someone else (I Samuel 22-26). As indeed eventually happens.

At the same time, there is a hint of a purely verbal form of prayer developing. When Hannah, the mother of Samuel, went to the Tabernacle to pray, she did not bring a physical sacrifice. Instead, she sat by the doorway, quietly praying in her heart for God to bless her with a child. "Only her lips moved, but her voice could not be heard," the Book of Samuel tells us (I Samuel 2:13). Offering words alone, without a physical offering, was such a radical way to pray that Eli the Priest did not even recognize it as worship. He thought Hannah was drunk, and ordered her to sober up!

This biblical story tells us how much things have changed in the past 2500+ years. Nowadays, if you enter a house of worship, of any religion anywhere, and you see someone quietly moving their lips, you know they are praying. But in Hannah's day, it was a radical new idea to pray without offering a sacrifice – so much so, that Jewish tradition credits Hannah with being the first to teach us this quiet form of prayer.

Hannah explained to Eli that she was not drunk, but pouring out her heart to God. Eli then blessed her, and eventually Hannah did conceive, giving birth to the prophet Samuel. He, in turn, grew up to eventually anoint King David, the "sweet singer of psalms." One is tempted to wonder if Samuel's mother had taught him her verbal method of prayer, which he then passed on to his line of prophets. Did this influence his choice of the poetic David as the king to replace Saul?

Be that as it may, by the time of the destruction of the First Temple, the idea of verbal liturgy was firmly established in the Jewish community. This gave the prophet Hosea an answer to the question of how the people could worship without the Temple: "Take words *(dvarim)* and return to the Lord; instead of calves we will offer the words of our lips" (Hosea 14:12).

In Hebrew, the word *dvarim* means both "words" and "things." Hosea is making a connection that gets lost in translation: Instead of physical objects *(dvarim)*, one can bring verbal words *(dvarim)*. It was lip service in the truest, most sincere sense of the term: serving God with the words of one's mouth. The *Amidah* prayer, which Jews recite three times a day, ends with: "May the words of my mouth and the meditation of my heart be pleasing in Your sight, O Lord..." (Psalm 19:14)

According to Jewish mysticism, the Hebrew letters have a cosmic vibration or "energy," which is how God "speaks" the universe into existence. Words *(dvarim)* are the essence of things *(dvarim)*. This is the inner meaning of the line in Deuteronomy 8:3: "Man does not live by bread alone, but by every *word* proceeding out of the mouth of God does man live." The "word" is the spiritual essence of the physical thing, and it is this word – this divine energy – that sustains the world.

There could be no more physical sacrifices without the Temple but, as Hosea taught, "Instead of calves we will offer the words of our lips." To this day, the appropriate sacrificial passages are read as part of the Orthodox Jewish liturgy. In kabbalah, such recitations are considered as if one had actually offered the sacrifices themselves. This is how the rabbinical

27

Jews solved the problem of worship without sacrifices, and it has remained so to this day.

The Temple was rebuilt under the decree of Cyrus in 516 B.C.E, and animal sacrifices resumed, but the verbal tradition survived and continued to grow. When the Second Temple was destroyed by the Romans in 70. C.E., the basics of today's synagogue worship were already well established. Sins would still be forgiven on Yom Kippur, the Day of Atonement, even without the scapegoat or other animal sacrifices. Repentance, prayer, and charity would avert the harsh decree.

The Christian interpretation of sacrifice

Early Christians, who at the time of the Second Destruction were basically a minority Jewish sect, also struggled with the loss of blood sacrifices, but they solved the question in a completely different way. Instead of focusing on Hosea's teaching about bringing words instead of calves, they focused on a line by Paul of Tarsus in his letter to the Hebrews: "Without the shedding of blood there can be no forgiveness of sins" (Hebrews 9:22). Given this line of reasoning, Paul taught that even though the Temple was destroyed, even though there were no more sacrifices, sins could still be forgiven. How? By making Jesus into the last and final sacrifice, effective for all eternity. Thus, Christianity never completely gave up the idea of a blood sacrifice as being necessary for atonement.

In addition, Christianity also focused strongly on the *suffering* of Jesus on the cross as part of the atonement process. There was nothing equivalent to this in the Jewish sacrificial system. The Temple sacrifices were never tortured. They had to be perfect unblemished specimens, and the slaughter itself was done with one quick stroke of a very sharp knife – the same as in kosher slaughtering today. Nevertheless, the idea of "sacrifice" as including "pain and suffering" is part of the dominant culture in America, and has caused animal rights activists to wrongly assume that Jews *want* the *Kapporos* chickens to suffer in agony, and are purposely causing them pain. We shall address this question in more depth in chapter 5.

It is important to remember that this line about the necessity for "the shedding of blood" comes from the *Christian Scriptures,* notably the mind of Paul, and is not mainstream Judaism. In fact, the idea of a human sacrifice taking on one's sins is *pagan* and completely contrary to Jewish thought. Nevertheless, it is relevant to discuss this non-Jewish belief here, because it might be among the influences that eventually led to the custom of *Kapporos,* as well as misunderstandings today.

Possible origins of Kapporos

We come now to the question of how the ritual of *Kapporos* got started in the first place. As I noted earlier, there is no direct reference to it in either the Torah or the Talmud, and we do not read about it until the 9th century C.E. There are, however, some early hints that we can explore.

Although there could be no real sacrifices after the destruction of the Temple, many people still felt the need to do something physical as atonement. Judaism is essentially an experiential, hands-on religion, using physical things such as wine, bread, candles, spices, sukkah booths, prayer shawls, palm branches, ram's horns, etc. in the observances. It must have been very difficult for people to go from offering physical sacrifices in the Temple to merely reading words about them.

It is perhaps in this context that we can better understand why modern *Kapporos* practitioners like Rabbi Hecht feel the need to continue using chickens instead of the perfectly acceptable substitute of money. It is not, as some protesters have charged, a matter of enjoying power and blood; rather, it is an attachment to something familiar handed down for many generations. This is the way it was always done; to change suddenly is difficult, not only for Jews but for most people.

In my own household, going vegetarian meant major changes that were not always smooth and easy. For a long time my wife Caryl and I had been "flexitarians," keeping to a basically vegetarian diet but still eating fowl and fish on occasion. Then one Thanksgiving we decided to go all the way – and that meant no more turkey. It also meant the end of my eldest stepson and his family coming over for dinner. To him, Thanksgiving meant turkey and, in his own words to me, "I'm not going to deprive my children of that."

Here in Minnesota there are no big Thanksgiving Day parades or other festivities like I grew up with on the East Coast, where people feel closer to the historical event. American history for most Minnesotans begins in the late 1800s when the Norwegian settlers arrived (unless you are from a Native tribe), so the big turkey dinner is the main event. That's how it was when Caryl was growing up and when she was raising her three boys (my stepsons) in Minneapolis. So we pretty much lost the whole holiday when Caryl and I went vegetarian – a loss I still feel every year. A Thanksgiving turkey is not a sacrifice, but it is similar in terms of an ingrained custom.

A possible forerunner of *Kapporos* is mentioned by Rashi (a major tenth century scholar) in his commentary to the Talmud (Shabbat 81b). He describes a custom of growing a potted seedling, then waving it over one's head seven times before Rosh Hashanah (Jewish New Year). Each member of the household used their own plant, and it was done with a prayer very similar to the one now used for *Kapporos* before Yom Kippur, asking that "this is my redemption, this is my substitute," implying that the sins of the person were transferred to the sprout. The potted plant was then thrown into the river.

Rabbi Jacob Emden (1697-1776) reasoned that since the Torah says, "Man is a tree of the field" (Deuteronomy 20:19), then humanity shares a connection with the souls of plants. Therefore, a plant can substitute for a person. Emden also taught that if someone could not afford chickens or money to perform *Kapporos,* then he or she should use the planted seeds. Based on this, some modern Jews have revived this custom.

Rabbi Moses Sofer (1762-1839) had a different explanation. He explained that the seeds planted in the soil represented one's "seed" or children. People in talmudic times prayed that if there was a heavenly decree against their own "seed" then it should fall on the plants instead. The ritual was, in essence, a form of sympathetic magic to ward of a fatal breathing disease (tuberculosis?) that was killing many children at the time.[26]

---

[26] *Siddur Shaar Shomayim* 112b. Bacteria and the germ theory of disease were not discovered until the mid-1800s, so ancient peoples did not understand how diseases

This "vegetarian *Kapporos*" indicates that such ceremonies were not always done with a chicken or other fowl. It also resembles *Tashlich,* a ceremony still done today, where people symbolically "cast their sins into the sea" by going to a natural body of water and reciting certain prayers and biblical passages on the first day of Rosh Hashanah – but without actually throwing in a potted plant. However, many people do turn their pockets out to symbolically empty their sins into the water.

The custom of using chickens

Jewish scholars first discuss using chickens for *Kapporos* in the ninth century. They explain that since the Hebrew word *gever* means both "man" in Hebrew and "rooster" in Aramaic, a bird can be substituted for a person. This idea of substituting one word for another is common in the interpretation of many Jewish texts. Recall my previous example from Hosea, where *dvarim* is read as both "things" and "words." A similar type of interpretation is being used here.

From the beginning, there were hot debates about the validity of this ritual. Maimonides in the 12th century makes no mention of it in his many writings. Either he had never heard of it or he disapproved and chose not to discuss it. Rabbi Solomon ben Abraham Aderet (known as the Rashba), one of the foremost Jewish scholars of the 13th century, considered *Kapporos* to be a heathen superstition or *darchei ha'Emori,* "the ways of the Emorites" – a category of "occult" or idolatrous behavior that Jews are supposed to avoid. The Emorites were an ancient people who were considered to be especially superstitious. *Kapporos,* according to Rabbi Aderet, therefore fell into a category similar to modern folk practices like knocking on wood or rubbing a rabbit's foot.

The opinion of *Kapporos* as a superstition was shared by Nachmanides, which is all the more significant because he disagreed with Maimonides about the importance of animal sacri-

---

were spread. Even today the spread of disease is often misunderstood, which is one reason why Ebola spread so quickly during the recent outbreak in Africa. The "doctrine of signatures" – a belief that the shape of a plant indicated what it would cure – was commonly accepted even into relatively modern times.

fices. As we noted above, Maimonides was a rationalist who believed that sacrifices were a concession to the times and not really necessary. Nachmanides, on the other hand, was a mystic who upheld the spiritual value of sacrifices. Nevertheless, he opposed *Kapporos* as a superstition.

Rabbi Joseph Caro, the major 16th-century codifier of Jewish law, called it "a foolish custom" that Jews should avoid. Rabbi Hezekiah de Silva (1659-1698, known as the Pri Chadash) felt that all forms of *Kapporos* should be abolished, whether with chickens or with substitutes like money and potted plants. These rabbis all felt that *Kapporos* was a pagan custom that had mistakenly made its way into Jewish practice.

Central to the debate was whether such a ceremony could really atone for one's sins. In the early 20th century, Rabbi Israel Meir Hakohen Kagan, popularly known as the Chofetz Chaim, discussed the significance of the ritual in his *Mishnah Beruriah*. He did not forbid it outright, but stressed that a person cannot obtain purification from sin without repenting. The Chofetz Chaim concedes that the death of the fowl might remind a person of his or her own mortality and thereby stir the soul to repentance, but by no means did the slaughter itself eradicate one's sins. If that were the case – if it were really possible to transfer sins to a bird – than what would be the need for prayer, fasting, and repentance on Yom Kippur?

Was Kapporos adopted from Christian beliefs?

I find myself wondering if "pagan" is a code word for "Christian" here. Recall what I said earlier about the Christian belief that blood sacrifices are necessary for the forgiveness of sins. By the time we get to the Middle Ages, Jews had been living among Christians for several centuries, and were being severely pressured by them to convert – often with the claim that the blood sacrifice of Jesus was needed for atonement or else the Jews would all go to hell. Jews are *still* being pressured with this line, and I myself have frequently encountered it. So it is not beyond the realm of possibility that some people began to assimilate this view from the surrounding culture, and then looked for a ceremony that would fulfill the supposed "require-ment" in a Jewish context.

This would not be the only example of an originally non-Jewish ritual making its way into the Jewish community. The widespread custom of lighting a memorial candle on the anniversary of a death is similar to a Roman Catholic custom from medieval Germany – so much so, that the very name for it – *Yahrzeit* candle – is taken from German into Yiddish. There is no native Hebrew term for such a custom. Yet the *Yahrzeit* candle is now so deeply ingrained that most Jews, even non-religious ones, do light one in remembrance of the dead.

Because there was heavy censorship by the Church in the Middle Ages, Jewish scholars could not come right out and criticize something as a Christian superstition. In Tsarist Russia, publishers were required to submit their books to government censors for approval. Rabbi Nachman of Breslov's major work, *Likutei Moharan,* opens with the standardized statement that the "peoples" and "nations" referred to in the book were those of ancient cultures "who were idolators who worshipped the stars and constellations and were attached to all forms of abomination," and not at all like "the nations of our day who fear God," that is, the Christians.

Nevertheless, many Jews of the time regarded Christianity as a form of idolatry, as do many Orthodox rabbis today. It would be the greatest of ironies if these communities who practice *Kapporos* with chickens, and who regard themselves as the bastions of tradition, have nevertheless assimilated an alien atonement ceremony from the gentile world.

Or did it really come from paganism?

It is also possible that *Kapporos* really is based on some form of pre-Christian paganism. The *Shulchan Arukh* (Code of Jewish Law) says not to specifically seek out a white chicken (in reference to Isaiah 1:18)[27] for *Kapporos*, or pay more for it

---

[27] The Isaiah text reads: "Though your sins be as scarlet, they shall be as white as snow.' This is also the basis for wearing white clothing on Rosh Hashanah and Yom Kippur, using white Torah scroll covers, white flowers on the table, etc.

than usual, because this resembles the superstitions of the pagans *(darchei ha-Emori)*. Instead, people should use whatever chickens they already have on hand, regardless of their color.

White animals were rare in ancient times. Today's white chickens are the result of breeding programs in the meat industry, where a white bird is preferred because it does not have dark pinfeathers. But until modern times, white animals were unusual, and brought a high price. They were considered sacred by many pagan cultures and/or were often sacrificed to various gods. Google "sacred white animals" and you will still find examples of this belief today, such as the White Buffalo of the American Indians, the White Stag in Celtic traditions, or the sacred white elephants in Hinduism.

Seeking out a white animal for a sacrifice, therefore, borders on idolatry, because it is copying the worship forms of the non-Jews. Therefore the *Shulchan Arukh* says that if you already have a white chicken in your flock, it is preferable to use it for the symbolism, but don't go out specifically looking for one, and don't pay a fortune for it.

On the other hand, there is a belief that one should never use a black chicken, because black is the color of severity *(gevurah)* or strict judgment in kabbalah. Using a black bird would invoke a harshness of discipline that you do not want during the High Holy Days, when God judges the world.[28]

Among the common people, however, the color of the chicken sometimes took on a more magical purpose. Chayyim Shoys, writing in 1938, states that the ritual was seen as "a means of frightening and chasing away the evil spirits."[29] However, Shoys goes on to say, that there were two opposing opinions about using a black fowl. On the one hand, since black is the color of the devil *(ha-satahn)* in Jewish folklore, some people believed one should fight fire with fire and use a black fowl to drive the devil away. Others thought just the opposite: that white was the proper color to dispel the darkness of evil.

Using a white chicken seems to have prevailed among the more knowledgeable rabbis and mystics, and is the preferred

---

[28] http://www.chabad.org/15932" \l "v18

[29] Shoys, Chayyim, *The Jewish Festivals: From their Beginning to Our own Day,* Union of American Hebrew Congregations, 1938.

practice today. The fear of using a black chicken was so deeply engrained in some communities, that a miracle was attributed to a sage known as the White Tzaddik (saint):

Jews in Tsefat [Israel] were faced with a dilemma one year as Yom Kippur approached. The Turkish sultan [ruler of the Ottoman Empire] had prohibited the purchase of white chickens for use as *kapparot* and they were forced to buy black ones.

Just before Yom Kippur they came to the tomb of Rabbi Yosef Bena'ah, pouring out their hearts and asking forgiveness before using the black chickens for their ritual. Upon their return home they discovered that those chickens had miraculously turned white. From then on this Sage became known as the "White Tzaddik."[30]

As this story illustrates, not all rabbis opposed *Kapporos* as a superstition. The Tsfat Kabbalists, led by mystics such as Rabbi Isaac Luria (the Holy Ari) and Rabbi Isaiah Horowitz, saw a mystical significance to the ritual. They pointed to a mystical connection between *gevurah* (strict judgment) on the Kabbalistic Tree and *gever* –"rooster" – deducing that the bird being slaughtered was a way to conquer any possible harsh decree against the people. Because Rabbi Luria's form of kabbalah eventually became the standard interpretation of Jewish mysticism, his use of a chicken also became the most widely accepted form of *Kapporos.*

However, note that the chicken was not actually taking on the sins of the practitioner, as is often claimed today. It was being used to dispel or ward off the negative forces of severity or divine judgment, leaving room for God's mercy. And, as we will discuss in the next chapter, it was also eaten at the pre-Yom Kippur meal. This is more like a peace offering than a sin offering, which was never eaten by the person offering it. In some cases a sin offering was burned on the altar, and in other cases the officiating priests *(kohanim)* could eat it. The scape-

---

[30] As told by Rabbi Mendel Weinbach on the Ohr Sameach website at http://ohr.edu/3717

goat, which was offered on Yom Kippur, was never eaten at all, but was released into the wilderness (Leviticus 16:10).

Kapporos cannot really be a sacrifice, for atonement or otherwise, most rabbis have argued, because sacrifices were not permitted outside the Temple. Once the Temple was destroyed, all sacrifices were invalid. In fact, one reason *Kapporos* practitioners use a chicken is because it is an animal that was *not* offered in the Temple.[31] However, this distinction sometimes gets blurred among the common people.

Rabbi Moshe Isserlis (the major 16th century scholar known as the RaMA), whose interpretations of the *Shulchan Arukh* are authoritative for Jews of Eastern European descent, endorsed *Kapporos* as valid and proper. He thereby set the precedent for generations of Ashkenazic Jews, including those whose descendants eventually came to the United States.

Rabbi Israel Baal Shem Tov (1698-1760), founder of Hasidism, also practiced *Kapporos,* based on the teachings of the Holy Ari. The custom then passed down to his disciples who, in turn, founded various schools of Hasidic thought.[32] Most Hasidic communities are still in favor of keeping the custom as part of their traditions. Which brings us to our next topic: the revival of *Kapporos* by Chabad-Lubavitch Hasidim in modern America.

---

[31] Technically it can be any fowl except doves, which were offered in the Temple. This is also the reason why rabbinical Jews do not serve lamb on Passover anymore, lest people think they had offered the Pascal lamb sacrifice. Only the Samaritan sect retains a tradition to sacrifice sheep on Mount Gerizim for Passover. The Samaritans never accepted the centrality of the Jerusalem Temple, which is the meaning of the objection of the woman in the Gospels, who says, "Our ancestors worshipped on that mountain but now they tell us we must go to Jerusalem." (John 4:20)

[32] Hasidic groups are typically named after their towns of origin in Europe, or where their founding Rebbes came from: Lubavitchers from Lubavitch, Russia; Breslovers from Breslov (Bratzlav), Ukraine, etc. There is also a Bostoner Rebbe in America.

Chapter 3:

The Rise of Modern Kapporos Centers

In the last chapter, we examined the history of sacrifices and *Kapporos,* as well as some of the objections that have been raised by rabbis and scholars down through the centuries. We turn now to the question of *Kapporos* in modern times, and the more recent controversies surrounding it. Once again, I remind both sides to keep an open mind and try to understand the issue from both viewpoints. On the activist side, it will be difficult to read about people who practice animal sacrifices. On the Orthodox/Hasidic side, it may sometimes be challenging to read criticisms of respected leaders of your communities. For myself, I think we need to keep in mind the line from *Pirkei Avot:* "Who is wise? The person who learns from all people."

Jewish life in pre-Holocaust Europe

Jews in Eastern Europe were much closer to nature and animals than today's urban communities. In the old Hasidic stories, we read of people in small towns *(stetls)* keeping their own sheep, horses, donkeys, mules, goats, geese and chickens. We can also see this in photographs and art. For example, the folk paintings of Ilex Beller, who depicts actual scenes from his pre-Holocaust Polish village, show horses, cows, goats, cats, dogs and chickens, as well as storks, ducks, doves, finches, and other wild birds. Nature was a daily part of *stetl* life.

I was not consciously aware of this rural Jewish culture until adulthood. I had been taught that Jews were literally locked into crowded urban ghettos, forbidden to walk in the fields or forests of their gentile neighbors. This was true in some parts of Western Europe during the Middle Ages, but in Eastern Europe there were many Jews living in the country. True, they were often forbidden to own land, but that does not mean they could not work the land they rented from the local rulers. And many did.

Two hundred years ago, Charles Fenyesi had an ancestor named Daniel Fenyesi, who not only worked land in Hungary, he was the first Jew to own land in his Hungarian county even before it became legal for Jews to do so. This farm was passed down through the family right up until the Holocaust. The Fenyesi love of land is carried on today, both by family members in Israel and Charles himself, on a 7.5 acre farm in Maryland.[32]

Fenyesi tells the story of his ancestor Daniel and a young Jew named Isaac Taub. The two had met on the road – Daniel on the way to sell sheep fleece, and Issac going to his first rabbinical post. But Isaac was not sure he was cut out to be a congregational rabbi. He liked to sing and walk thought the forests and fields, and hated to be shut up in a room all day. He doubted he could adapt to the life of a Torah scholar.

Daniel told him that the Jews in his village of Derz also liked to sing and walk through the fields, and that he wanted to be a farmer. He asked the newly ordained rabbi if it would be OK for him to buy land. This may seem like a strange question for us today, but in his time, land was regarded as a foolish and risky enterprise by most Jews. Why? Because you could not pick it up and take it with you in times of persecution or expulsions. Such was the sad history of Jews in Europe.

This was Isaac's first *shaila,* a rabbinical question, and he took it very seriously. The two young men discussed how Jews in biblical times had been farmers and owned land. So, the young rabbi said, there was nothing wrong with his desire to own a farm. As they parted, Isaac gave Daniel a blessing that his enterprises should thrive. And they did.

Isaac Taub went on to become the Kalever Rebbe, one of the most beloved Hasidic teachers in 19th century Hungary. He was known for his beautiful songs, which used things in na-

---

[32] Fenyesi, Charles, "Practical Kabbalah: A Family History," included in *Ecology and the Jewish Spirit: Where Nature and the Sacred Meet,* Ellen Bernstein, ed., Jewish Lights Publishing, Woodstock, Vermont, 1997.

ture as symbols of higher realities. One of these, "The Rooster is Crowing," is still sung by both Jews (in Yiddish) and gentiles (In Hungarian) today. It describes a rooster walking through the woods at dawn, longing for the coming of the Messiah. (See end of Chapter 7 for the lyrics in English.)

In 1988, when my wife and I first moved to a small town in rural Minnesota and began to garden and keep chickens, one of my neighbors, an elderly Christian immigrant from Poland, told me that in the Old Country the Jews always had the best vegetables. At the time I was still thinking in terms of the Jews living in urban ghettos, and thought he was referring to Jews *selling* the best vegetables. After all, the old stereotype said that Jews in Europe were mostly merchants.

Then in 1997 I traveled to Uman, Ukraine, on the annual Breslov pilgrimage to Rebbe Nachman's grave. I was amazed at how rural the area was. Everything in the stories came alive for me. Here was the town where Nachman, great-grandson of the Baal Shem Tov, had walked among the woods and fields. Here was Sophia Park, with its little stone bridges that probably inspired Nachman's "Narrow Bridge" song. People were still keeping goats in their yards, with chickens, ducks, and geese running loose. It was like going back in time.

This pilgrimage has had a lasting effect on my perception of Judaism. I saw how the beauty of God's creation surrounded the Baal Shem Tov and his disciples. And I believe that such closeness to nature helped give birth to the Hasidic movement itself. Returning from Uman, I began to pay more attention to references to nature and animals in the Hasidic stories, as well as in more recent times.

Kapporos in stetl days

Although the Jews of pre-Holocaust Eastern Europe were more connected to nature than their modern descendants, they were not, by and large, vegetarians. On the other hand, they didn't eat meat three times a day, either. Animals were not mass-produced like they are now, and meat was mostly for celebrations, after the manner of Abraham, who slaughtered a calf to honor his guests. Chicken was a luxury best saved for the Sabbath and festivals. During the week, the average person ate very little meat, if at all. An old Yiddish folksong laments that the daily menu was always "Monday potatoes, Tuesday potatoes, Wednesday potatoes, Thursday potatoes..."

Jewish law mandates that on the afternoon before Yom Kippur, people must have a festive meal. One interpretation of this requirement is so that people are entering the fast with joy and hope. And, of course, it is a good idea to eat before a 26-hour total fast.[33] Traditionally, the *Kapporos* chicken was served at this meal and poor members of the community were invited to share in it. Alternatively, a *Kapporos* chicken could be given directly to a poor family for their own pre-Yom Kippur meal. It was important for every Jew – even the beggars and the homeless – to be able to feast before the fast.

Giving charity is traditional on the day before Yom Kippur, and in most synagogues this is when members turn in their annual pledges. (Because it is forbidden to handle money on the Sabbath and holy days, Jews do not pass a collection plate like other religions do.) Some congregations still follow the old custom of having a number of different collection boxes at the door, where people can donate to various causes before the holy day actually starts. The gift of a *Kapporos* chicken should be seen in this light, as part of a general practice to help to those in need. And, as the liturgy says, "Repentance, prayer, and *charity* avert the harsh decree (for our sins)."

In *stetl* days, the *Kapporos* chicken was a locally raised bird. A person would choose one from their own flock or buy it from a neighbor, then walk across the village square, have it slaughtered, and take it home to be plucked, cleaned, and prepared for dinner. Every Jewish housewife knew how to soak and salt meat to *kasher* it, and could examine the carcass herself to see if there were any problems. If she had a question, she went to the local rabbi. But for the most part, the woman of the house was trusted to know what to do.

As we noted in chapter 2, the *Shulchan Arukh* tells us not to specifically seek out a white chicken for *Kapporos*. In-

---

[33] 26 hours: the day itself is 24 hours long, but people begin fasting before sundown and do not end until after dark the following day, which adds an extra hour or more to the fast. As "26" is the numerical value of the four-letter Name of God, some people extend the number of hours to 26. Many people do this on the Sabbath also.

stead, people should use whatever chickens they already have on hand, the same as for any other meal. This clearly indicates that people actually *had* chickens, and that raising them was an common part of everyday life. *Kapporos* was not, as it has become today, something completely out of the ordinary.

Chickens in *stetl* days were hatched naturally under mother hens and allowed to run free, to scratch, peck, eat bugs and live in flocks, as a chicken was created to do. There was nothing in pre-Holocaust Europe that even vaguely resembled the year-round factory farm conditions of today. There were no electronic incubators, no "battery hen" cages, and no way to "sex" baby chicks to sort the males from the females.

Most hens only hatched one or two broods per year, so chickens were in limited supply. Without artificial incubators, chicks could not be mass-produced. The birds used for soup and *Kapporos* were usually the older culls, such as hens that no longer laid eggs or old roosters who were not breeding anymore. Even then, a farmer could not afford to kill too many birds at once. This is why chicken soup was something special for the Sabbath. In many families, it was the only time they ate chicken. And they used every part of the bird, including the feet. Nothing was wasted.

Animal right activists will argue that it was still cruelty to slaughter the chickens in the first place. This may be true – even I.M. Levinger, Ph.D., an Orthodox rabbi and veterinary author of a classic physiological study on kosher slaughtering, acknowledges, "The terms humane and slaughter represent a paradox. Slaughter cannot be humane by any method, for slaughter is cruel. And yet the slaughter of animals being a necessity, [it] must be performed as humanely as possible."[34]

Rabbi Levinger is not without sensitivity. In the introduction to his book he tells how he left the field of laboratory experimentation because, he explains, "I was concerned by each experiment I performed. I felt my work was not always necessary, and I abandoned the world of research, and changed to another field of work." His book also contains a section on Jew-

---

[34] Levinger, I.M., *Shechita in the Light of the year 2000: Critical Review of the Scientific Aspects of Methods of Slaughter and Shechita,* Maskil L'David, publisher, 1997, Jerusalem, p. 12.

ish laws concerning kindness to animals, and he notes that any use of animals that is not absolutely necessary is forbidden. Nevertheless, he upholds *shechita* and is not a vegetarian.

Whether or not meat is a "necessity" depends on when and where you live. In modern times it is possible to live a healthy life on a vegetarian diet. But this was not the case for most of human history. Before the days of refrigeration and mass transportation, before it was possible to fly in fresh vegetables from around the globe, the choices were far more limited. Had humanity tried to be vegan in ancient times, we would never have made it out of the Ice Age. The Torah permits slaughter because God knew that Jews would sometimes live in harsh climates where year-round gardening was not an option.

Certainly in Eastern Europe, in the time period we are discussing here, being a vegan would have been extremely difficult, if not impossible. Fresh greens were so rare in winter that to this day, the Lubavitcher Hasidim – who originally came from Russia – traditionally use a piece of onion or boiled potato for the *karpas* vegetable on the Seder plate, rather than the more common sprig of parsley. There simply were no fresh vegetables available in the far north in late winter.

My point in this section is that *Kapporos* in the past was done with free-range, naturally raised adult chickens, and it was done very locally. People raised their own chickens or got them from nearby neighbors, and they *kashered* the meat themselves. In that sense, they took personal responsibility for the bird they would eat. They also knew the proper way to hold a chicken, and the meat was never wasted. There was still a sense of sacredness and respect for the bird whose life was taken.

The modern revival by Rabbi Hecht and Chabad

With the rise of the modern meat industry in the 20th century, fewer and fewer Jews were buying live chickens to be slaughtered at local butcher shops and *kashering* them at home. Instead of women cleaning and inspecting the chickens themselves, professionals in the packing plants now did this, resulting in the loss of a skill that had been passed from mother to daughter for millennia. Except for a few very traditional neighborhoods, local kosher butcher shops began to disappear, and with them went the possibility of doing *Kapporos* with live chickens. Those Jews who did it at all tended to use money. It looked as if the custom was going to die out completely.

At the same time, communities of Orthodox Jews who came to America during and after the Holocaust (1940s and 50s) were establishing themselves with new congregations, religious schools, and successful private businesses. Unlike previous waves of Jewish immigrants, who wanted to assimilate into American society, the Hasidim saw themselves as the last remnants of a culture destroyed by the Nazis. They set about to preserve that culture and rebuild it in America, as well as in other cities around the world where they had settled. Any change of custom, they felt, would be a betrayal of the memory of those who had perished. Everything, from dress to recipes to styles of learning, was seen as the last remnant of a lost civilization.

Enter the Hecht family of Chabad-Lubavitch. While other groups of Orthodox Jews besides Chabad also do *Kapporos,* we shall focus on Chabad for three main reasons:

1. It is primarily the Hecht family that is responsible for establishing the modern mass-*Kapporos* centers in New York and elsewhere, and for publicizing the ritual.

2. Rabbi Shea Hecht has been the most outspoken supporter with the most media coverage, thereby becoming the nemesis of Karen Davis, the most outspoken animal rights opponent.

3. Rabbi Hecht is chairman of the board of the National Committee for the Furtherance of Jewish Education (a major Chabad organization), and has a great deal of influence in Chabad and the Jewish community at large. What he teaches about *Kapporos* carries authority in the public eye and has far-reaching effects.

As I said at the beginning of this book, I am assuming good faith on both sides of this issue. However, there is one thing we should clear up here: namely, the question of money. Karen Davis has accused Rabbi Hecht and others of using *Kapporos* to make a lot of money for themselves and/or their organizations. In one interview Davis was outraged that some unnamed *Kapporos* center (not necessarily Hecht's) was charging $18 for the chickens. She accused the rabbis of buying cheap and selling at a high price. Davis was apparently unaware that Jews almost always give charity in multiples of 18 (representing *chai,* "life," in Hebrew),[35] so even those who use money instead of chickens would naturally give that same amount, and not see it as anything excessive. This is a case of an outsider not knowing Jewish culture.

At the same time, Davis' own organization, United Poultry Concerns, spent over $23,000 on the anti-*Kapporos* campaign in 2014, according to her own financial report,[36] so obviously UPC raises a lot of money as well. Much of it is probably coming in because of her protests and articles opposing *Kapporos,* which means that she profits from the issue, too. So let's just agree that fundraising is not, in and of itself, a sin on either side. All organizations need money to operate, whether for or against the ceremony. Enough said.

Rabbi Hecht's father, the late Rabbi Jacob J. Hecht, missed being able to do *Kapporos* with chickens, so in the 1970s he began to truck some chickens into his Brooklyn neighborhood. At first this was done on a small scale, but over the years it grew into something much bigger, attracting a lot of media attention in recent years.

Chabad Hasidim regard publicity in general as a good thing; in fact, they actively seek it. Chabad is rather unusual among Hasidic groups, in that they reach out to non-Orthodox Jews through public performance of various Jewish rituals in the streets. Most obvious have been their "Mitzvah Mobiles,"

---

[35] In Jewish numerology, each Hebrew letter has a numerical value. 18 is the value of the word *chai* meaning "life." (*chet*=8 and *yod* =10). It is an old custom among Jews to give charity in multiples of *chai.* Even fundraiser letters commonly use this figure for suggested donations. Instead of the usual check-off amounts for $25, $50, etc., there will be choices of $18, $36, etc.

[36] *Poultry Press,* United Poultry Concerns, Winter 2014 issue, p. 12.

consisting of trucks or vans that drive around town and encourage people to do mitzvahs[37], according to whatever holy day is at hand. There have been portable *sukkah* booths on trailers, with Hasidim encouraging Jews to stop and wave the biblical Four Species (palm, myrtle, willow and esrog) during the festival of Sukkot; women handing out Sabbath candles; men encouraging other Jewish men to put on *tefillin*; free Purim kits for observing that holiday; and huge outdoor Hanukkah menorahs lit in public places. These outreach activities have done a great deal of good toward bringing wayward Jews back to Judaism, and for that I do give Chabad credit where credit is due.

Given this tendency toward street activities, it was perhaps inevitable that Chabad would hold big *Kapporos* gatherings where people could buy a chicken and do the ritual on the spot. In this case, however, the publicity backfired. People in the general public, most of whom had never heard of *Kapporos,* were horrified that makeshift slaughterhouses were springing up in their neighborhoods. As we learned in chapter 1, there were also protesters who began to picket the centers. Judging from the articles available online, there has been far more negative publicity than positive. (We shall deal with the question of public relations in Chapter 6.) In addition, there are a lot of practical problems that have come up as the volume of *Kapporos* chickens greatly increased in recent years.

Lack of familiarity with chickens leads to cruelty

The Hasidic communities of today no longer have the personal connections to animals and nature as described in the old stories. In many cases, they don't even have the stories. Or if they do, then they have lost the understanding of what the stories mean in daily life.

Although the Torah, Talmud, and later texts are filled with positive references to nature and animals, these sources are seldom studied in any depth, because there is no real contact

---

[37] Mitzvah: Often translated "good deed," a mitzvah is more correctly defined as the fulfillment of a Torah commandment. Colloquially, it can refer to any Jewish practice. The Hebrew plural is *mitzvot.* However, since the word has entered the English language, I have chosen to use the Anglicized "mitzvahs" and not italicize it.

with animals or nature to ground the texts in everyday life. Without such experiences, the texts have become meaningless. In many of our yeshivas, even the teachers often lack these firsthand experiences with nature. So they focus on stuff that is familiar to them, namely, the rules of *kashrut* and using animals as food. Orthodox Jews tend not to keep pets, and very little effort is made to educate their children about animals, ecology, or nature in general.[38]

The result is that, for many people, the only time they have any kind of interaction with a live chicken is at *Kapporos*. More than once I have been told that holding such a chicken was the first time they had ever touched a live animal. And these are not the healthy, mature, free-range chickens in the flocks of their ancestors. The chickens used today come from commercial factory farms. They are often so young that they peep like baby chicks, and are not even fully feathered out. They have been crammed into small crates, stacked onto open trucks, driven for many miles, then stacked again in warehouses for days without food or water. By the time people in the neighborhood see them, these chickens are so badly traumatized that many of the birds are not even moving.

This lack of movement is mistaken for calm, because people in the city, who are not familiar with chickens, simply do not know any better. Rabbi Hecht, in demonstrating his method of holding the chicken by the wings, claims that it calms the bird. But in fact, the bird is going into the "play dead" mode that many prey animals use when grabbed by a predator. I have observed the same behavior with wild birds that I rescued from my cats. As soon as the cat lets go, the bird "springs to life" and flies away. The same ruse is recommended if you are ever attacked by a bear. Play dead, and the bear will hopefully lose interest in you. But in no way will you be calm or relaxed while lying there on the ground. You will be terrified!

The same kind of misunderstanding goes for lack of appetite. *Kapporos* practitioners have told me that they tried to feed their chickens, but they were not hungry. More likely, the

---

[38] In recent years the Orthodox Jewish community has shifted to the far right politically, and many have bought the propaganda that climate change and other environmental issues are just something "made up by Al Gore." For an in-depth analysis of this issue, read *Who Stole My Religion?* by Richard H. Schwartz.

birds were in such a state of shock that they had no appetite. This same reaction can be seen in traumatized humans after a severe accident or other tragedy. When there is pain or trauma, shock sets in and the appetite normally shuts down. And shock in chickens, as in humans, can be fatal.

In addition, there is the strong possibility that the food people offered the chickens was not recognized as food. In a normal chicken flock, the mother hens teach the chicks what to eat and how to drink. But factory farm chickens are raised on ground-up powdery mash and do not get to go out and search for a variety of foods. Chicks will instinctively peck at things, but *what* to eat is a learned behavior. This is similar to how human babies will put everything and anything in their mouths, and must be taught what is safe to eat.

I have taken in rescue chickens that literally did not recognize worms or seeds or fruit as food, even though these are things that my mother-hen-raised birds will gobble up in a New York minute. Even bread – a likely food that urban people might try to feed them – was left untouched. Eventually, as the rescue chickens mingled with my flock, they learned what to eat by watching other chickens. But in the beginning, they only ate commercial feed because that was what they were used to.

The breeds of chickens used nowadays also differ considerably from the past. A hundred years ago, chickens came from traditional, hardy, farmyard breeds like Barred Rocks and Rhode Island Reds. These breeds grow at a natural rate and develop strong bones and healthy muscles, along with smooth, attractive feathers. They look like the illustrations of chickens we see in children's picture books.

But today's "broiler birds" have been artificially selected and bred to put on lots of weight as fast as possible and to be constantly hungry so they will eat continuously. The results are chickens with weak muscles that easily tear and underdeveloped bones that easily break.[39] It is not uncommon for birds

---

[39] See "the Truth About Chicken," a campaign launched by the ASPCA in 2015 at truthaboutchicken.org concerning how modern methods are not only cruel to the chickens, they produce meat full of antibiotics and diseases that are not healthy for humans to eat. Also in 2015, PBS's *Frontline* program aired "The Trouble with Chicken," an investigation into how dangerous pathogens like salmonella are evading

raised commercially to be so weak that they cannot even walk to the feeder. Nor can they properly care for their feathers, because the tips of their beaks have been cut off to prevent cannibalism in over-crowded barns, and there is no place to take a dust bath to clean themselves like in a free-run flock. So they arrive at the *Kapporos* sites looking filthy and bedraggled, often covered with their own feces.

The terrible conditions on factory farms raise questions of animal cruelty that we shall deal with later. For now, we are concerned with the fact that many urban Jews see these conditions as normal. They do not understand that the constant peeping one hears at *Kapporos* centers is *not* normal and is not the sound of a happy chicken. It is the terrified cry of extreme distress. The only time I ever hear that call in my own flock is when a chick has become separated from its mother. Once I rescue the chick and reunite it with its family, the shrill peeping stops immediately, replaced by silence or a very low type of contented peep that sounds completely different. But if the only chicken sound you have ever heard is the distress call, it's easy to be misled into thinking "they always do that."

Animal rights activists see the apparent indifference to suffering at the *Kapporos* centers and wrongly assume that the Hasidim actually *want* the chickens to suffer. Activist Karen Davis, leader of the Alliance to End Chickens as Kapporos, has come right out on more than one occasion and stated:

> "[The chickens] are treated like what they are intended to be in the ritual, punished objects. The only role of the chicken in the ritual is to be a symbolic recipient of the sins or wrongdoings and the punishment of the practitioner, to be mistreated, to be punished."[40]

---

food inspection and entering our food supply. Although the salting process in *kashering* meat reduces this risk somewhat, it is still a serious health concern.

[40] "Gahari, Dave, "Jewish Animal Sacrifice in America's Streets Protected by Government," October 2, 2014 at http://americanfreepress.net/?p=19941 (Warning: this is an antisemitic website. Davis has since told me she was unaware of this at the time of the interview and had she known that, she would have refused. I believe her. However, that does not negate her statement, which she has also made elsewhere.)

This is Davis' non-Jewish take on what she thinks is happening. Recall what I said about Christian concepts of suffering and sacrifice in Chapter 2. Davis is confusing *Kapporos* with Jesus suffering on the Cross, and elsewhere has actually made that exact analogy. But Judaism is not Christianity, and her interpretation is not what I hear from actual Hasidim.

Nobody has ever told me that they are "punishing" the chickens for their sins, nor does the ritual require the birds to be mistreated. True, there is often callousness toward the chickens out of ignorance, but this is a far cry from purposely inflicting pain on a living creature. Hasidim are not sadists; they do not purposely abuse animals. On the other hand, they are often ignorant about the right way to handle the chickens. And in their ignorance, they do sometimes mistreat them or justify why what they are doing is not cruel.

Once again: If you do not understand even the basics of chicken behaviors, it is easy to misinterpret what is happening as normal. Chickens in free-range flocks have a complex social structure and over 40 different calls. They are also capable of passing down learned information from one generation to the next. That, in anthropological terms, is the beginning of a rudimentary culture. No, chickens do not write symphonies or paint masterpieces as "culture" is normally defined, but neither are they as stupid as many people assume. Unfortunately, the factory farm chickens are never given the opportunity to develop these normal, healthy flock behaviors. So they grow up unsocialized and stunted. They are similar to cases of so-called "feral" children who have been severely isolated and/or abused and never learned basic language or social skills.[41]

Plus there is the issue, described above, of how modern factory farm chickens are not as healthy or strong as free-range chickens in the past. Roughly handling a chicken nowadays is far more likely to tear muscles or break bones. In short, what our ancestors did safely may no longer apply. Unfortunately, many people distrust this information because they see it as

---

[41] For example, the story of "Genie," a young girl who was kept a prisoner in a bare room by her abusive parents for years, completely isolated from all human contact or any intellectual stimulation (no books, TV, etc.) Although she eventually learned a few words under therapy, she never mastered using language
See http://abcnews.go.com/Health/story?id=4804490

coming from "fanatics" who are attacking Judaism, rather than from people who care about animal suffering.

How did we come to this state of affairs? How did today's urban Jews get to be so uncaring about seeing animals suffer right before their eyes? We got there – along with the rest of society – by gradually adapting to worse and worse farming conditions over a period of decades, rationalizing that the adjustment was not all that bad, until the conditions under which we now raise animals have become horrendous.

I once read somewhere that if you were to take a frog, which is a cold-blooded animal, and put it in cool water, then slowly raise the temperature, the frog will keep adjusting its body temperature until it is literally boiled alive. (Not that I would ever really do this, heaven forbid.) We are like that frog; little by little, bit-by-bit, we have ignored teachings about *tzaar baalei chaim* (cruelty to animals) in Jewish law, and kept adjusting to the modern meat industry. The result is, that chickens are now treated in ways that would have absolutely horrified the rabbis of old.

Practitioners of *Kapporos* will point out that the way they treat the chickens is no different than the way meat is normally raised and slaughtered. Sadly, they are correct, which is why many of the activists are also vegetarians or vegans. But one does not have to go that far in order to begin questioning whether there is any merit in doing *Kapporos* under modern conditions. In fact, this is precisely the reason that many rabbis –even some very Orthodox ones – are now telling their followers to use money instead. (See Chapter 6 for examples.)

Controversies within the Orthodox community

Up to this point, we have mostly discussed the objections of outsiders to the ritual. But there are many Orthodox and Hasidic Jews who do not use chickens as *Kapporos,* based on the principle that you cannot commit a sin to do a mitzvah. They argue that the cruelty involved in transporting and storing the chickens under modern conditions cancels out any spiritual value of the ceremony. Most of these people are not vegetarians, nor do they feel that slaughter itself is wrong. But they do make a distinction between what is necessary and what is not. Since there is an acceptable substitute for the fowl, they prefer to use that instead.

There is merit in this stance that goes beyond the issue of animal cruelty. According to the first Lubavitcher Rebbe, Rabbi Schneur-Zalman of Liady (known as the Alter Rebbe), giving charity is an essential part of the ritual. He said[42] that if one prefers to keep the chicken and does not give it to a poor person, then one is supposed to give him or her its value in money. This is called *pidyon kapporos,* "redeeming" the chicken and is in addition to any money paid for the chicken itself. This would also apply if for some reason the chicken was not kosher and could not be eaten. Then you should also give charity, in addition to having killed the chicken. The bottom line being, that the poor are supposed to directly benefit from *Kapporos*, either with actual chickens or with money.

However, there have been cases where huge numbers of *Kapporos* chickens ended up in the garbage at *Kapporos* centers, either because they were declared not kosher after slaughtering, or because there were no proper facilities to process them.[43] Recall what I said about how people used to take home their own chickens, to clean and *kasher* them personally. Under such conditions, there was probably very little waste.

But nowadays, when people are no longer doing this for themselves, there is the very real problem of how to handle so many chicken carcasses right before Yom Kippur. Makeshift *Kapporos* centers are not meat processing plants; they do not have on-site refrigeration, nor do they have other facilities for cleaning and sanitation. People assume that their chickens are going to food shelves or religious institutions, and many do. But in other cases they may simply end up in the city dump.

---

[42] Shulchan Aruch Orach Chaim Siman 605

[43] For example, in 2012 the Los Angeles sanitation department reported 19,685 pounds of dead chickens were collected at area *Kapporos* sites. Given that the chickens being used at the time were older laying hens that weighed about 4 pounds each, this would be a waste of at least 5000 birds.
http://www.jewishjournal.com/los_angeles/article/atonement_chickens_swung_and_t ossed)

In 2012, the *Los Angeles Jewish Journal* reported that $50,000-$100,000 worth of chicken meat was found in dumpsters around the city. In Israel, Jerusalem authorities centralized *Kapparot* into four supervised locations and closed down others after complaints from residents. And in Tel Aviv, residents petitioned the mayor to stop the ceremonies altogether after dead chickens were found in trashcans.

In addition to obvious waste of food, this creates a major ritual problem. If a person thinks their chicken is going to the poor, but in fact it ends up in the garbage, then they will not know they are supposed to do *pidyon kapporos* for a chicken that did not go to charity. Religious opponents of the Hecht family's *Kapporos* centers have raised this very objection. This criticism is coming, not from animal rights activists, but from within Hasidic circles themselves. Chabad is not monolithic; since the death of their seventh Rebbe, Menachem M. Schneerson, in 1994, there have been some splits within the movement. So even inside Chabad there is controversy over whether Rabbi Hecht is doing it properly. And again, there are many Orthodox Jews, including many Chabadniks, who avoid the controversy altogether by giving money directly to charity.

Is kapporos really a sacrifice?

There is also a diversity of opinions about what this ritual actually means. As we noted in Chapter 2, there has been controversy over *Kapporos* ever since the first written references to it appeared – and probably long before that. For some people, it is a magical act to ward off evil. For others, the central point is giving charity. For still others, it borders on actually being an atonement sacrifice.

In recent years, there have been direct comparisons with the biblical scapegoat, which was seen as taking away the people's sins. However, the comparison is not exact, nor is it theologically accurate. For one thing, there was only a single scapegoat for the entire Jewish people collectively. By this analogy, there should be only one *Kapporos* chicken each year. And the scapegoat was not slaughtered; it was sent away to the wilderness (Leviticus 16:10). So, if *Kapporos* really were to be an an equivalent to the scapegoat, then a priest *(kohane)* should put everybody's sins onto a single chicken, say the prayer, then turn the bird loose alive.[44] Obviously, this is not what happens.

Another reason it cannot be a sin offering is because an ordinary person can eat it. Sin offerings were either burned on the altar or eaten by the Temple priests. The only sacrifices that were eaten by the people who brought them were the peace offerings *(shlamim)*, which were used to show gratitude to God or to celebrate a special event. A portion of the offering was burned on the altar, another portion was given to the priests, and the rest was eaten by the worshiper and his family, as described in the story of Hannah in First Kings, chapter 1. Since the *Kapporos* chicken was traditionally eaten at a family feast, it would more logically fall into this category.

But the strongest argument against *Kapporos* being a sin offering is this: There cannot be any real sacrifices outside the Temple, period. Since there is at present no Temple in Jerusalem, *any* form of animal sacrifice is not valid. This does not mean you cannot slaughter and eat a chicken, but it does mean that there is no way it can actually take away your sins.

We should also note that Maimonides (1134–1204) was of the opinion that the biblical scapegoat did not really take away one's sins either, but was intended enable the penitent to discard his own sins: "These ceremonies are of a symbolic character and serve to impress man with a certain idea and to lead him to repent, as if to say, 'We have freed ourselves of our previous deeds, cast them behind our backs and removed them from us as far as possible." *(*Maimonides' *Guide, 3:46)*

Rabbi Hecht on using chickens

If the chicken cannot take away your sins, then what is the purpose in killing it? One common interpretation is that it reminds us of our own mortality. This is the stance that is taken by

---

[44] Some later commentaries (dating from the Second Temple period) say that the scapegoat was thrown over a cliff outside Jerusalem to prevent it from returning to town. In dispute is the meaning of "for Azazel" which some see as the name of a location, and others as meaning "to carry away sins." Yet a third opinion sees "Azazel" as the name of an evil force that would devour the goat. See http://en.wikipedia.org/wiki/Azazel

Rabbi Hecht. When asked by National Public Radio why he does not use money instead, he answered that waving something, be it money or a chicken, is not the main part of the ritual. For him, it is the moment of slaughter:

> "The main part of the service," he says, "is handing the chicken to the slaughterer and watching the chicken being slaughtered. Because that is where you have an emotional moment, where you say, Oops, you know what? That could have been me."[45]

The use of "emotional moment" was a poor choice of words, because it was picked up by Davis and other opponents, who interpreted it as Hecht *enjoying* the death of the chicken. The comment went viral in animal rights groups on the Internet, and is probably the most widely quoted Hecht reference to *Kapporos* among the protesters. However, "enjoyment" is not the emotion that the ritual is supposed to evoke, nor is it what the rabbi meant. Rather, it should remind us of our own sins, and bring about a fear of death that moves us to repent and change our ways. Rabbi Hecht feels that waving money instead of a chicken does not have the same impact.

Maybe not. But frankly, this statement disturbs me deeply, for the following reason: What kind of message are we sending to our children about Judaism? And yes, there are children present at *Kapporos* ceremonies.[46] Are we telling them, "If you don't behave, you could end up dead like that chicken"? Are we telling them that Judaism is a religion of fear, and that they should live in terror of God slaughtering them like a helpless bird if they step out of line? Do we want them to harden their hearts against the suffering of animals?

It is well known than abuse of animals can lead to abuse of people. This was probably not the case when raising animals

---

[45] National Public Radio, Weekend Edition, September 26, 2009.

[46] Whether or not the children witness the actual slaughter varies from group to group and even from family to family. Some groups have a "children's day" where they wave the chickens and say the prayer but do not slaughter until later, when the children are not present. Several people have told me that they take their chickens home for the family to do the blessings, then return them to be slaughtered. But in other cases, the children do see the actual killing.

for food was part of village life, and slaughtering a chicken was nothing out of the ordinary. But nowadays, it is being done completely out of context, as a strange, scary, bloody ceremony meant to frighten us into obedience. And what kind of message does that send to our children? Certainly not a message about the love of a mother hen for her chicks – an image we sometimes use of God, who shelters us "under the wings of the Shechinah" like a mother bird.

Bella Chagall, wife of artist Marc Chagall, tells the how it impacted her during own childhood in Vitebsk, Russia. After he father's panicked rooster was chased around the courtyard and slaughtered, the time came for hers:

> "Mother's and my own white chicken hid in a hole in their fear. One could only hear them clucking low and crying.
>
> "The cook caught both chickens at the same time and put them at the shochet's feet. Blood poured over the whole balcony. When I came to myself, all the cocks and hens lay on the ground. From their necks ran threads of blood. Blood had spattered their white feathers. They were left to cool off in the dark night.
>
> "I remember how my little chicken quivered in my hands when I held it upraised for the rite. I too was quivering. My finger recoiled at once when I touched the chicken's warm belly. The chicken uttered a shriek and tried to fly over my head, like a little white angel.
>
> "I raised my eyes from the prayerbook. I wanted to look at the chicken. It cried and clucked as though begging for mercy of me. I did not hear the passages I was to repeat."[47]

Was little Bella moved to repentance? Or was she traumatized by seeing the death of one of God's creatures – an innocent bird that fluttered like a little white angel?

---

[47] Chagall, Bella, "Day of Atonement in Vitebsk, Russia," from her book *Burning Lights*, cited in *The Yom Kippur Anthology*, edited by Phillip Goodman, Jewish Publication Society, 1971, pp. 179-180

Chapter 4:

Kapporos and Jewish Mysticism

In the previous chapters, I discussed *Kapporos* from the standpoint of history and Jewish culture. In this chapter, I will present the mystical and spiritual teachings behind the practice. This section is the heart of the book, because it lays the foundation for what I believe to be the best argument for *not* using a chicken in the ritual. But in order to understand how this can be so, it will be necessary to enter into a worldview that may seem strange to modern readers.

Much of this chapter will be familiar to Hasidim and kabbalists, but for vegans and animal rights activists, it could be rough going. This is not a vegetarian philosophy. But it can lead in that direction (as it has for me), so please withhold judgment until the end of the chapter.

For over four decades, I have been telling animal rights and vegetarian activists that in order to have meaningful dialogues with Hasidic Jews about diet and religion, it is necessary to understand a teaching known as "raising holy sparks." In fact, I was primarily responsible for the inclusion of this doctrine in the Q and A section of the current edition of Richard H. Schwartz's now-classic book, *Judaism and Vegetarianism*. Later, Schwartz also published an interview with me called "Raising Holy Sparks: Hasidic Thought and Vegetarianism," included in his 2010 work, *Who Stole My Religion?*[48] Yet in

---

[48] A new edition of *Who Stole My Religion?* is in the pipeline from Ktav Publishing. Due to a request by that publisher to shorten the book, it will no longer include this essay. However, the entire interview can be still downloaded at JewishThoreau.com.

spite of this effort to educate the activist community, most have written it off as superstition or worse.

This, in my opinion, is a big mistake. As any anthropologist will tell you, in order to have meaningful conversations with another culture, it is important to be able to understand *and respect* that culture's worldview. Respect does not mean you must agree. But it does mean you must be willing to go beyond derision and ridicule to *really hear* what is being said. Without such respect, you end up shouting across an empty canyon and hearing nothing but the echoes of your own voice. And this goes for both sides of the dialogue; Orthodox and Hasidic Jews need to be willing to listen, too. That said, let us work to build some real bridges of understanding.

Kapporos chickens don't sing

I will begin by addressing one particular quotation that got wide publicity in a number of articles in September 2013. According to Rina Deych, a Jewish activist in Brooklyn who has been protesting the ceremony for years:

> Every year I'd see little kids tell their parents, "The bird is crying!" and the parents would say, "No, it's singing. It's happy to help us." I'd come over and tell them the kid is right.[49]

Having viewed numerous videos of *Kapporos* ceremonies on YouTube recently, I would agree that the chickens are definitely not singing. Nor are they very happy. The call heard most often on the soundtracks is the incessant, shrill, high-pitched peeping of terrified, distressed half-grown chicks.

In many *Kapporos* centers, the birds being used are not yet mature enough to crow or cluck. Very often, they are factory-farmed, eight-week-old broiler birds, not even fully feathered out, peeping in miserable baby voices. Most definitely, the children are right. The *Kapporos* chickens are crying.

---

[49] See "Crazy Chicken Lady and the 20-year fight against the chicken ritual" at http://www.haaretz.com/misc/iphone-article/1.546684

The only time I ever hear that distress call among my own free-range flock is if a chick is in trouble, perhaps separated from its mother or lost outside the chicken wire fence. Normally, chickens do not constantly peep or shriek in those shrill, high-pitched voices unless something is seriously wrong.

Chicks hatching under a mother hen will bond with her and their nestmates while still in the egg. The hen clucks softly to her eggs, and the chicks begin peeping softly to each other from inside their eggs – a very different sound than the distress call. By the time the hatch is over, they are already a bonded family unit. Incubator chicks can't bond with a machine, but they probably do bond with each other. Separation from the flock is very traumatic. Hence the terrified peeping.

As I explained in previous chapters, most urban Jews do not have any contact with live chickens outside of this ritual. If the distress call is the only chicken sound they ever hear, then it is understandable that they would think this call is normal. However, ignorance is no excuse. It is important to educate people that these chickens are not singing in joy.

They are also not "dumb clucks." An online heckler once asked me, "Do you really think chickens are smart enough to know what is happening to them?" Yes, I do. Modern research shows that chickens have an intelligence level at least as high as that of a three or four year old child. Think about that next time you see a pre-schooler or bounce your own child on your knee. That child is certainly aware enough to suffer pain, hunger, and fear of death. That child would be in agony if you crammed him or her into a tiny cage all day. And so it is with a chicken. Not that "intelligence" per se should be a criterion for how we treat animals. But you get my point.

"Raising sparks" in a kabbalistic universe

To understand why the parents in the Rina Deych quote would say the chicken is "happy to help us," we must go to kabbalah and a doctrine called "raising holy sparks." Briefly summarized, it goes like this: During the Creation of the universe — even before Eden, at the time of "In the Beginning"— the first set of Holy Vessels *(Sephirot)* that were intended to contain the Divine Light were shattered because they were cre-

59

ated to receive the Light, but not to pass it on. So they became overfilled and burst, so to speak.

This is, of course, all symbolism. A "vessel" in kabbalah refers to something that is able to receive and contain, not literal jars or pots. The same goes for "holy sparks" *(netzotzot)* — these are a type of spiritual energy. However, it has been noted that the "shattering of the vessels" *(shevirat ha-kelim)* bears an uncanny resemblance to the scientific theory of "broken symmetry," where a lack of balance in the universe allows for energy – in this case, the physical kind – to flow from one state to another. According to modern astrophysics, this "broken symmetry" occurred at the very beginning of the universe, as part of the Big Bang process.

A perfectly balanced universe would be static, like the first kabbalistic Vessels that could receive the Light but not pass it on. All of our biological processes, as well as many inorganic ones, require the constant flow of energy from one place to another. Seen in this light, the "shattering of the vessels" was necessary for the universe as we know it to exist.

There is a very old Jewish teaching *(midrash)* that says God created and destroyed many worlds before this one. Commenting on Genesis 1, the *Midrash Rabbah* says:

> "And there was evening…" Rabbi Judah ben Simon said: "It is not written 'Let there *be* evening' but rather, 'and there *was* evening.' Therefore we know that a time-order existed before this current one."
> Rabbi Abbahu said: "This proves that the Holy One, blessed be He, went on creating worlds and destroying them until He created this one and declared, "This one pleases Me; those [others] did not please Me."
> (Genesis Rabbah 1:7)

Tradition says that God created a thousand worlds before making this one. It was as if God were trying out various models to see which one would work best for His purpose. Given that there is so much suffering in today's world, how can it be that this is the one that finally pleased God? Surely He could have made a world that was perfect! But seen in the light of "broken symmetry," the lack of perfect harmony is the only way we could have a world where energy can flow and life as we know it can exist. "Let there be Light" was the Big Bang, and everything flowed forward from there.

However, according to kabbalah, when the vessels shattered, some of these sparks of holiness fell to lower levels than they were supposed to be, ultimately becoming entrapped in material things. So God created humans to help "raise" these sparks back to their proper places in the universe, through the mitzvahs. When the mitzvahs are done with the proper intention *(kavannah),* these acts can "elevate" the sparks within the material world back into their proper place in creation. This, in turn, is part of the kabbalistic process of *tikkun olam,* repairing the universe, as taught by Rabbi Isaac Luria in the 16th century, and later by the Baal Shem Tov. This process culminates in the coming of *Moschiach* (Messiah), and the restoration of spiritual harmony among all of God's creation.[50]

Animals as beings with consciousness

Both kabbalists and Hasidim see eating food as part of this process, because they believe that the sparks within the foods are thus elevated into their proper levels of holiness, provided that the blessings *(brachot)* are said and the food is eaten with the proper consciousness.

They also believe that animals want to be eaten for this purpose, the same as a human might be willing to give up his or her life for a holy cause. I have many times been told that the chickens are hoping to be eaten by Jews at a Sabbath or other sacred meal, and thus have their own spirits elevated through this service to God. I have also seen this explanation given in the "comments" sections of online discussions in answer to why the person commenting still eats meat. Clearly this belief is an important part of the *Kapporos* practitioners' worldview and a major reason why they use a chicken in the first place.

And yet this teaching is rarely, if ever, discussed among those activists who are trying to end chickens as *Kapporos.* Or,

---

[50] This does *not* mean returning to the static state *before* Creation, but rather, returning to the peaceable kingdom of Eden. "Broken symmetry" would still exist and energy would still flow, but all the "sparks" would now be in their proper places.

if it is discussed at all, it is only to put it down as, in the words of one activist to me, "a solipsistic conceit" to believe that humans have this kind of central role in the world. This judgmental attitude only hinders the dialogue.

In a way, this belief is not unlike the philosophy of the North American Indians, who believe than animals willingly give their lives so that the people may live. It's an idea that sounds foreign to modern ears, but is quite common among the tribal peoples of the world. It implies a reciprocal sacred relationship between animals and humans in the natural order of creation. The idea that animals might consciously allow themselves to be eaten in order to serve a higher purpose is very widespread around the world.

Buddhists tell the story of a rabbit who offered his body to a starving man as food – and was rewarded by becoming Moon Rabbit, the "rabbit in the moon." Folktale? Maybe. But Moon Rabbit is widely believed to have been an earlier incarnation of the soul that would become the Buddha. His story is told to Buddhist children as the epitome of self-sacrifice.

American Indians also have similar tales, such as the story of Jumping Mouse, who selflessly gave up parts of himself to heal others, and was reborn as an eagle. We should also remember the widespread custom among Native hunters of thanking the animal for giving its life so the people may live. This idea is also portrayed in the science fiction movie, *Avatar,* where an alien race called the Na'vi[51] lives in total harmony with their planet, as part of a vast web of life. Nevertheless, the Na'vi hunt to survive. The hunter says to the dying animal, "Your spirit goes with *Eywa* (their deity), your body stays behind, to become part of the people."

Ironically, this movie is very popular among the same "deep ecology" folks who tend to put down Jewish mystics for believing in essentially the same thing, namely, that all energy comes from God and will eventually return there. Tribal cultures are seen as spiritual and in tune with nature; but in the case of the Jews, a form of prejudice is at work, blocking the ability

---

[51] In Hebrew, "*navi*" means "prophet," from the verb "to flow" or "channel." I have no idea if film director James Cameron consciously made this connection, or if it is merely coincidence.

to see Jews as anything beyond "letter of the law." Antisemitism, like racism, is deeply embedded in Western culture.

So, as we talk about the Hasidic belief in "raising holy sparks," please strive to see it in the light of these stories from other, better-known (and often better respected) cultures besides Hasidic Judaism. If you can honor the teachings of Buddhism and Native Americans, or a film by James Cameron, then at least try to understand similar ideas within Judaism.

In kabbalah and Hasidism, the animals get to participate in the cosmic process of *tikkun olam,* repairing the universe, and their spirits are elevated in this process. There is a reincarnation aspect to this teaching as well. Sometimes a human soul is reincarnated as an animal, but retains its human consciousness, in order to atone for a specific sin. In *Shivchei Ha-Ari* (a collection of stories about Rabbi Isaac Luria, a 16th-century mystic known as the Holy Ari), there are several tales about the Ari communicating with human souls in animal bodies. Similar stories are also recorded about the early Hasidic masters. In many of these cases, the soul in the animal asks the Rebbe to use its meat for a specific mitzvah, in order to offset the sin and set the soul free to reincarnate as a human being once again. This, too, is part of the process of "raising holy sparks."

Today, however, Chabad Hasidim primarily view this process as a sort of food chain, where plants absorb the minerals, animals eat the plants, and humans eat the animals. For many, it remains on a physical level. In a recent conversation with a Chabad Hasid who is also a physician, he explained to me that meat does not give you energy – carbohydrates do that. Meat gives you protein to form strong muscles and a healthy body with which to do mitzvahs and serve God. Quite true biologically. But when I began to talk about the spiritual aspects of *tikkun olam* and elevating the sparks within the animals, he suddenly had something else to do and bid me goodbye.

Although this man comes from a tradition that says animals want to be eaten in order to help us do mitzvahs, he apparently could not take this "wanting" literally. He did not see animals as having any sort of awareness beyond mere instincts. Nor did he see the contradiction in his beliefs: If animals really do "want to help us," then doesn't this imply they are in some way consciously choosing? If this is so, then animals must have some type of awareness that goes beyond instinct.

While the "food chain" model is true on the biological level, it is also true that it would be impossible for humans to eat every animal on the planet in order to elevate all their sparks. Nor does this model offer any *other* ways that an animal might contribute toward planetary healing and thereby become elevated spiritually. What about a rescue dog who saves human lives, or a service dog who safely leads her blind companion for many years? Couldn't these dogs receive some sort of merit for this service to humanity? Surely God, in His infinite mercy, must have provided for the spiritual advancement and *tikkun* of all His creatures, even those we do not eat. Which brings us to the next section.

Do animals have souls?

This question is the number one, all-time favorite on my blog, and continues to get more daily "hits" than anything else I have written there. So – do Jews believe that animals have souls? People want a quick yes-or-no answer, but the problem is, the Hebrew language has five different words that get translated as "soul" (*nefesh, ruach, neshamah, chayah* and *yechidah*) and they mean different things in Jewish mysticism. So before I can answer the question, I need to define the five levels of the soul. Sorting this out is not always easy, because different commentators have interpreted these terms in different ways throughout the centuries, and they don't always agree. Here are the basic definitions, as I understand them:

1. Nefesh (NEH-fesh) the physical life force of the body. All animals certainly have this, or they would not be alive. For that matter, so do plants have *nefesh*. Rebbe Nachman of Breslov encouraged his followers to pray outdoors in a field or forest, because, he said, all the trees and grasses will join in your prayers. He meant this literally.

In her book, *Partnering with Nature,* Catriona MacGregor describes how, upon coming home from grocery shopping one evening, she saw a mysterious glowing light in a nearby vacant lot. Upon investigating, she discovered that it seemed to be coming from a big old tree in the center of the lot. She looked around for another source of the light, but found none:

> Instead, the tree illuminated the lot and surrounding buildings as brightly as if the moon had come to rest gently upon the soft grass... My cares fell away as a deep peace enveloped me. Looking back upon that experience now, what I recall most was the sense of pure beauty and joy. With that glimpse of an infinitely wise and compassionate universe, I knew that the light was the fire of the tree's spirit – the tree's very soul. There are no words to describe that which is known as intimately as a lover yet remains unfathomable.[52]

The next day, the beautiful tree was cut down. "My sadness was immeasurable," she writes, "Yet I also recognized the miracle that had occurred. The tree, knowing of its impending demise, shone forth its inner light, sharing its everlasting soul with the rest of the worlds as if to say: Behold, I am more than bark and limbs and leaves and roots..."[53]

Nefesh is also the word used by King David for "soul" in Psalm 25:20: "O guard my soul and rescue me." Some modern versions of the Bible translate this as "guard my life." In Jewish thought, to "guard your soul" means to take care of your health and safety. We are also commanded to take care of our animals in the same way, giving them proper food, water and shelter: "A good man takes care of his animals, but wicked men are cruel to theirs." (Proverbs 12:10)

So before we go any further, let's be very clear that whether or not animals have souls in the theological sense is irrelevant in terms of our responsibility to care for them. One cannot argue that animals are "things" and then go abuse them, heaven forbid. In fact, even inanimate things have a *netzotz* – a divine spark of holiness – within them.

---

[52] MacGregor, Catriona, *Partnering with Nature: The Wild Path to Reconnecting with the Earth,* Beyond Words Publishing, Simon and Schuster, Inc, 2010. p 8.

[53] *Ibid.,* MacGregor, p. 9.

2. Ruach (ROO-akh) literally means "wind" or "spirit" and is the emotional level of the soul. In Hebrew/Yiddish idiom, to do something "with *ruach*" means to do it with feeling – such as singing a song or playing an instrument with "soul." Biologically, I would associate *ruach* with the limbic system, the "mammalian" part of the brain that controls emotions.

Maimonides, an important 12th-century Jewish philosopher, clearly states in his *Guide for the Perplexed* that when it comes to the love between a mother animal and a mother human, there is no difference, because love comes from the emotional level.[54] Both humans and animals have emotions. This is the reason the Torah forbids slaughtering a baby animal on the same day as its mother (Leviticus 22:28) because the mother might see this and feel emotional pain. By extension, Jewish law forbids slaughtering any animal in front of another.[55]

Maimonides also argues that the commandment to send away a mother bird before you take eggs or young from a nest (Deuteronomy 22:6-7) is meant to teach us compassion for the feelings of the mother bird. I have chickens and, believe me, the hens do indeed get upset if you reach under their wings to take away their eggs. So clearly, from a Jewish perspective, birds and mammals have *ruach*. Whether or not insects, fish, reptiles, etc. have this level is up for debate. Certainly they experience fear; otherwise, they would not run or swim away. But does a snake feel love?

Rabbi Schneur Zalman of Liady (the first Lubavitcher Rebbe, 18th century) wrote in his master work, the *Tanya,* that humans actually have two souls: an "animal" soul that they are naturally born with (which seems to correspond to the *nefesh-ruach* levels described above) and a "divine soul" which is "a part of God above" and must be developed and consciously focused on spiritual things.

These two souls have been compared to a rider and a horse; when they work together, all is well, but if the horse throws the rider, the lower body desires take over and a person acts only on animal instincts. From Rabbi Schneur Zalman's

---

[54] Maimonides, *Guide for the Perplexed*, section XLV

[55] *Shulchan Arukh*, Yoreh Deah 34:14

perspective, only humans have the higher soul level. This is usually interpreted to mean that animals do not have immortal souls. However, his opinion is not necessarily the last word on the subject, as we shall see.

3. Neshamah (neh-SHAH-mah) is the word most commonly used in colloquial speech for "soul" in the usual sense, that is, an immortal soul that survives death. But it is also the word used in Psalm 150 for "let everything that has a soul praise God." Some translations render this as "everything that has breath," because *neshamah* is etymologically related to the word *neshimah,* meaning "breath."

Now, if everything that has breath is to praise God, wouldn't that suggest that animals, too, have a *neshamah?* In Psalm 148, everything in the universe is praising God, even inanimate objects such as the sun, moon and stars. The same is true in the ancient text, *Perek Shirah,* "The Song of Creation."

So "praising God" can't really be used as a criterion for whether or not something has an immortal soul. However, we should note that there are many anecdotal stories of people encountering "ghosts" or spirits of animals. So it does appear quite possible that something in an animal survives death. That "something" might not be a *neshamah* in the human sense, but it could be some other form of existence. Rabbi Saadia Gaon, who lived in the 11th-century, stated in regards to slaughtering:

> The Creator has decreed death over all the living creatures. He has determined for each human being the measure of the duration of his life. But God has set the limit of the animals [we eat] at the time they are slaughtered, so that the slaughtering takes the place of natural death. Should the slaughter involve pain over and above this, God would certainly compensate the animal in accordance with the excess of pain. (*Emunos v'De'os* 3:10)

Note that this well-known and respected rabbi, who was regarded as the greatest Torah scholar of his generation, claimed that an animal *will be compensated after death* for excess pain during slaughter. Since Saadia Gaon did not believe in reincarnation, he must be implying that animals have a form of after-life. How else could they be compensated post-mortem?

Chabad Rabbi Nissim Mindel, in his book, *My Prayer,* goes into considerable discussion of "holy sparks" in his intro-duction to the Grace After Meals. Regarding the responsibility to use the energy from food in a responsible manner, he states:

> When a Jew has a kosher chicken dinner in the proper manner, he has enabled the chicken to serve God through him; not only the chicken, but also the chicken feed upon which the chicken was reared. But if he uses the energy from his chicken dinner to cheat or steal, the chicken can justly demand, "By what right have you taken my life, and involved me in crime, which I could never have committed otherwise?"[56]

If a chicken can demand justice after death, then it must have an afterlife. In a similar vein, the first Lelever Rebbe once scolded a man for whipping his horse, saying, "After your demise, this horse will place your soul on trial before the Heavenly Court. Do you want to have to engage in a lawsuit with a horse?"

These and similar stories indicate that there is room in Judaism for a belief that animals have some form of life after death. Granted, these stories are not very well known among Jews today, and your average rabbi is likely to say that animals have no afterlife. However, this does not negate the fact that such teachings exist in earlier Jewish writings.

In kabbalah, *neshamah* is also associated with the higher levels of the mind and, interestingly, some Jewish philosophers felt that we are not automatically born with a *neshamah,* that we must develop it. This is supported by modern brain research. The more we use our brains, the more synapses we develop among the neurons, and the more intelligent we can become. Conversely, a brain that is not stimulated will lose synapses and, in some cases, fail to learn even basic language and reason-ing skills. "Use it or lose it" apparently applies in both biology and theology.

---

[56] Mindel, Nissim, *My Prayer, Kehot Publication Society,* 770 Eastern Parkway, Brooklyn, NY. 1972 edition. p. 280

Jewish philosophy has long regarded knowledge as the only thing we take with us to the Next World, which may be why developing the intellectual *neshamah* is associated with immortality. But does this mean we are developing a "soul," or simply improving the physical brain? Hard to say. The fact is, we can't really prove there is an immortal human soul, anymore than we can prove – or disprove – the existence of an immortal soul in animals. These are things we take on faith.

What we can say is that humans do possess a level of intelligence that is greater than even the higher primates, and that we humans can develop a conscious sense of moral right and wrong that animals lack. A lion may kill prey or fight with other lions, but he does not murder, because it is in his nature to be a predator. When a lion kills, he is merely being a lion. Most Jewish thinkers also maintain that humans are the only beings who can consciously choose to know their Creator.

Neshamah is generally connected not only with intellectual pursuits, but also with moral responsibility. In Yiddish, to have a "Jewish soul" *(yiddische neshamah)* means to have a sense of proper humanity and compassion. In other words, to be a *mensch* – an upright person of true integrity and honor – the highest compliment one can give in the Yiddish language.

4. Chayah (KHAI-yah) literally means "living." It is used in the Torah in Genesis 2:7, where God breathed the breath of life into Adam and then Adam "became a living soul *(nefesh chayah)."* Note that this term combines *nefesh,* the life force of the body, with *chayah,* "living." But isn't a body with *nefesh* already living? In the biological sense, yes. So *chayah* must add another dimension to human existence.

In kabbalah, *chayah* refers to a higher spiritual level, something like a collective consciousness, where all members of humanity are connected together. The word *adam* literally means "human being" – *homo sapiens* – in Hebrew, and only later in the story does it become the name of a specific man. At the point where *nefesh chayah* is breathed in, Adam is the archetype of the species. Adam Kadmon – the Primal Adam – is often pictured as a hermaphroditic cosmic being who contains all the souls of all the humans who ever were or will be born. He/she is the *chayah* level of the human species.

69

Do other species also have a *chayah* level? If we define it as the species archetype, then every pair of animals in the Garden of Eden would be that species' *chayah*. However, there is still a difference between the creation of humans and other species. Everything else in the Eden story is created by God simply speaking it into existence: "Let there be light – and there was light." Even in the case where the term *nefesh chayah* is used for animals, it is issued as a direct command: "Let the waters bring forth swarms of *living creatures."* (Genesis 1:20) Only in the case of humans does God first create a physical body, and then "breath the breath of life" into it directly.

Again I stress: This does not mean that other creatures don't have life. And we have already demonstrated that many creatures have feelings. But Judaism does take Adam's *nefesh chayah* to mean that there is something different about humans as compared to the rest of creation.

Rabbi Nathan Slifkin, known as the "zoo rabbi" and author of *Man and Beast: Our Relationship with Animals in Jewish Law and Thought,* clearly states that humans are the only beings that have a "divine soul" in this sense. But on the other hand, he also devotes many pages to our responsibility toward animals as stewards of the earth. "We need to be kind to animals," he says, "because *we* are humans, not because *they* are."[57] He does not see animals and humans as equal, but on the other hand, it is precisely *because* we are on a higher level that we have a greater responsibility to be kind to them. (This is in strong contrast to the common non-Jewish attitude that being "superior" means to "dominate" and be cruel to animals.)

On the scientific level, for those attempting to reconcile evolution with theology, it could be argued that the "breathing in" of Adam's *nefesh chayah* represents the point at which *homo sapiens* emerges from the level of pre-human primates to become modern man. There are some rabbinical commentaries that define the "us" in "let us make human beings" as the rest of creation participating in the formation of Adam's body. This fits nicely with the scientific idea of human evolution from lower life forms. Perhaps the "breathing in" was God causing whatever mutation changed us from ape to human. Here is not

---

[57] Slifkin, Nathan, *Man and Beast,* ZooTorah, 2006. p. 158.

the place to go into detail about this theory, but it is an interesting idea for those who want to pursue it.[58]

5. Yechidah (yeh-KHEE-dah) means "unity" and comes from the same Hebrew root as *echad,* "one" as in "God is One." *Yechidah* does not appear in the Bible as such, but is a kabbalistic term developed in later Jewish mysticism. *Yechidah* is the level of the soul where we can "touch God."

Judaism does not teach that we can become God or merge entirely with God as some mystical systems do (although some Hasidic thinkers came pretty close to that.) We Jews are not pantheists. But there is a level where we can experience oneness with God's Creation and, through this experience, get a "taste" of the oneness of God. People all over the world have reported this type of experience.

Do animals also experience oneness with God? It is impossible to say, because they cannot tell us. Some Jewish thinkers (as well as others) maintain that animals – and, in fact, all created beings except humans – automatically do the will of God because they were created that way, with no free will to do otherwise. In that sense, animals may be more in tune with God than we are. At the same time, they do not seem to have the same level of creativity that comes with our free will.

It is also worth noting that the Jewish metaphor for Heaven is the Garden of Eden. The *Yizkor* (memorial service) expresses the hope that the soul of the deceased will "be under the wings of the *Shechinah* (nurturing aspect of God) and "dwell among the shining beings in the Garden of Eden." Jewish thinkers differ on where this "Eden" is. For some, it will be a restoration of Eden on earth when Moschiach comes, with a physical resurrection of the dead. For others, it refers to a spiritual Garden of Eden on another level of consciousness. Either way, the Torah tells us that Eden has animals in it.

* * *

---

[58] A good place to start is with *The Challenge of Creation: Judaism's encounter with science, cosmology, and evolution* by Rabbi Nathan Slifkin, (ZooTorah 2006). For those with a mind open to both modern science and Orthodox Jewish texts, it is the best book on the subject to date.

In summary: Whether or not you believe animals have souls depends on how you define "soul," and Judaism does not speak with one voice on the subject. The more rationalist branches tend to say no, the mystics lean closer to yes. Each side quotes its own favorite sources to defend their position. But one thing is certain: Judaism clearly says that animals are living beings with feelings, that they were created by God, and that we are commanded to care for them properly. (That's three things, actually, but you know what I mean.)

Are we raising sparks – or dragging them down?

We come now to what I believe is the heart of this chapter: Are we repairing the world, or are we tearing it down?

It happened one day in Sfat, Israel, that Rabbi Isaac Luria, the great kabbalist known as the Holy Ari *(Ari-Hakodesh),* ordered one of his students to leave him immediately. The student felt terrible. What sin had he committed to deserve this? All that day he wept and prayed to God that his sins should not keep him banished from his Rebbe's presence.

The next morning he came to the Holy Ari and begged to be told what wrong he had done. The Ari said, "It is because of your chickens. Three days now they have been without food. They cried out to God and because of this, you have been under a ban *(karet)* from Heaven. Now, if you promise to feed your chickens even before your morning prayers, I will lift the ban on you." The student promised to do so, and the ban was lifted. (From *Shivchei Ha-Ari*)

From this we learn how much our Creator, who "has compassion for all the creatures," cares about the suffering of chickens. The student's sin was *tza'ar ba'alei chayyim,* cruelty to animals. The cries of those starving chickens were canceling out his Torah learning and banning his prayers from reaching Heaven. And because of this, he was also excommunicated from his Rebbe's presence until those chickens were cared for.

This brings us to the "down side" of the "holy sparks" teaching: Just as it is possible to elevate energy through using the material world to serve God, so is it also possible to drag down the sparks into lower levels. A person who is not worthy, or who does not eat with the proper spiritual intentions, can impede the whole *tikkun* process.

And that's what I believe happens when a glutton gobbles a fast-food hamburger on the fly, and then curses other drivers on his way to work. Even if the beef in his burger is technically kosher, he does nothing to elevate the sparks. Instead, he drags them down to a grosser material level with his road rage. This is why the Talmudic sages taught, "One who is ignorant of Torah is forbidden from eating meat" (Pesachim 49b). It wasn't only about knowing the Torah texts; it also involved understanding the spiritual processes involved. How many of us in this day and age are holy enough to eat meat with the right consciousness to raise the sparks?

When I brought up this point to a Chabad rabbi recently, he replied that one does not need to be have *kavannah* in order to raise sparks. If you are a Jew, and if the meat is kosher, and if you say the proper blessings before and after eating, then the sparks are *automatically* raised, no matter who you are or what your inner consciousness – or lack thereof – might be. This turns the whole thing into a mechanical process that, in my opinion, goes against what the teaching originally was.

This rabbi was confusing *yotzeh* (the minimum requirement to fulfill Jewish law) with *tikkun,* the process of redeeming sparks and repairing the universe. The guy gobbling his kosher burger is *yotzeh* on keeping kosher. But to me it is doubtful that he has accomplished any kind of *tikkun.*

This attitude about *kavannah* appears to be a major difference between Chabad and Breslov. Rabbi Nosson Sternhartz, disciple of Rebbe Nachman of Breslov, wrote in his commentary on the *Code of Jewish Law:*

> The main purpose of *shechita* is to elevate the souls that have been reincarnated in the form of animals or birds. These souls were reincarnated in these lower forms because of the severity of their transgressions… The *shochet* must be extremely pious and God-fearing. He must recite the blessing prior to slaughter with deep concentration and exercise the greatest care concerning

every detail of the laws involved. Thus, he will redeem the soul and elevate it to the human level.[59]

The Baal Shem Tov, great-grandfather of Rebbe Nachman of Breslov, warned us to be very careful in how we use and
treat all of our possessions, not just the foods we eat:

> All things of this world that belong to man desire with
> all their might to draw near him in order that the
> Sparks of Holiness that are in them should be raised by
> him back to God... Man eats them, man drinks them,
> man uses them; these are the Sparks that dwell in the
> things. Therefore, one should have mercy on his tools
> and all his possessions for the sake of the Sparks that
> are in them; one should have mercy on the Holy
> Sparks.

"Having mercy" in this context means treating things with care
and respect. Use your hammer, but do not abuse it. Never destroy things needlessly, and use them only for the good of all.

However, "mercy" does *not* mean we should never kill
anything, and the Baal Shem Tov himself ate meat. In fact, it
could be argued that there are times when killing an animal is in
itself a form of mercy, as in stories where the animal comes to a
Rebbe and ask to be used for a specific mitzvah.

For example, we have the story of Rabbi Yehuda Hirsch
of Strettana, a 19th-century Hasidic Rebbe, who had once been
a slaughterer. So pure and holy was he that flocks of wild
doves came of their own accord to lie down under his knife, because they trusted him to have the proper spiritual focus to free
their souls. To those doves, death was a mercy. And certainly
animals eaten by the Baal Shem Tov and his disciples at the
Sabbath table would have been raised to a very high level.

Nevertheless, the Baal Shem Tov was also sensitive to
animals as living beings. Consciousness certainly played a role
in the way he saw things. He taught:

---

[59] *Likutei Halachot*, shechitah 2:10 and 4:3.

74

> A worm serves the Creator with all of his intelligence
> and ability… A person should consider himself and the
> worm and all creatures as comrades in the universe, for
> we are all created beings whose abilities are God-
> given. (Tzava'as HaRivash 12)

The guy gobbling his burger during a road rage tantrum is *not*
treating the meat with due respect. Neither are modern *Kapporos* centers "having mercy" on the chickens they sell and use for
the ceremony. Nor are they considering them "comrades in the
universe." People stand around dangling their chickens by the
wings as if they are nothing but inanimate objects.

I have been laughed at and ridiculed by fellow Hasidim
for saying that my chickens are friends and that they have feelings. The Baal Shem Tov understood this, but his modern followers do not. Many Hasidim have probably never even heard
of the above quotes from their founder. Their lack of sensitivity
to animals proves this; otherwise why would they go against his
teaching about treating animals as comrades in the universe?

These modern-day Hasidim should perhaps consider the
story of the butterflies at Ground Zero. In her book, *Messages:
Signs, Visits, and Premonitions from Loved Ones Lost on 9/11,*
author Bonnie McEneaney tells about how her friends, Don and
Katie Lee, saw huge flocks of butterflies over the pile of rubble
that had been the World Trade Center and fluttering down towards the Hudson River:

> "It was unbelievable, "Don said. "There were hun-
> dreds, maybe thousands of butterflies. They filled the
> sky. They were the most beautiful colors."
> Katie said. "You know what we thought?" She
> whispered. "That they were the people; they were the
> souls, and they were trying to help us cope with the
> pain and anguish we felt by appearing as beautiful,
> floating, free creatures of the world still here with us.[60]

---

[60] McEneaney, Bonnie, *Messages: Signs, Visits, and Premonitions from Loved Ones
Lost on 9/11,* Harper Collins, New York, 2010. p. 155.

Nor were Don and Katie the only ones to see these amazing flocks of butterflies that, for some unknown reason, spent a day around the piles of debris. Rescue workers saw them, too. McEneaney continues:

> Workers on their hands and knees sifting and raking through the piles stopped what they were doing to stare. To many of the workers, the butterflies looked almost as if they were emerging from the site. What were they doing in the smoke? Why would butterflies choose to be at Ground Zero? Nobody had any answers. I was told that many of the workers almost immediately began referring to them as 'the souls.' When I did a little bit of research, I discovered that butterflies hold a special place in the spiritual beliefs of many cultures. In Ireland, they are, indeed, thought of as souls.[61]

Whether or not the butterflies were literally "souls" is up for debate. Some observers described a mixed flock of multi-colored butterflies; others identified them as Monarchs, which normally migrate south in huge flocks during the fall. That would be a rationalist's explanation for this phenomenon. But the question still remains: Why did they show up deep in the heart of a city, at exactly the right time when people needed a sign of hope? Personally, I believe God sent the butterflies there – and, like the worm in the Baal Shem Tov quote above, they, too, were serving their Creator to the best of their ability.

McEneaney tells other stories about birds and animals who, for whatever reason, acted in ways that brought emotional healing to humans. Many family members of victims reported seeing white doves at auspicious moments, sitting on the rooftop, or on top of a car, or in the yard. Granted, these birds were more likely pigeons than doves in New York City, but still, how many pure white pigeons are there in any given area? And why would "white doves of peace" appear so often, alone or in pairs, at particularly meaningful moments?

---

[61] *Ibid.,* McEneaney, p. 156.

Prayers that do not rise

The Baal Shem Tov once refused to enter a synagogue because it was so full of prayers that there was no room for him to go inside. His followers were puzzled by this. Full of prayers? What was wrong with that? Isn't a house of worship *supposed* to be full of prayers? But he answered, "Those prayers are all dead prayers. They have no strength to fly to heaven. They are crushed, they lie one on top of the other; the house is filled with them."[62] And so he could not enter.

We must ask ourselves: Would the Baal Shem Tov be able to enter today's *Kapporos* centers? Or would his path be blocked by piles of dead prayers that do not rise upward to heaven? Is the cruelty in today's *Kapporos* centers canceling out our prayers on Yom Kippur, like the cries of the hungry chickens in the story about the Ari? Is all this suffering adding to the burden of sin in the world on the very day when we are praying to God for mercy and forgiveness? This is not an idle question. It is central to the issue.

"Raising sparks" is the Hasidic ideal, but today's attitudes often fall far short. Would chickens ever willingly come to be slaughtered at today's *Kapporos* centers, the way the doves came to Rabbi Yehuda Hirsch? I think not. For that matter, would this holy rabbi even be willing to participate?

Since it is axiomatic that one cannot commit a sin to do a mitzvah, we must ask ourselves if the suffering of the chickens under modern conditions fails to raise the sparks and might even be dragging them – and us – down instead. We must ask ourselves: Is the callousness often witnessed at these ceremonies really the way a true Hasid should behave, or is it a sinful attitude assimilated from the surrounding gentile culture? (We shall return to this question of assimilation in Chapter 5.)

"Holy sparks" and vegetarianism

With such a heavy emphasis on raising sparks by eating meat, the reader is probably wondering how I can reconcile this

---

[62] Meyer Levin, as told in his *Classic Hasidic Tales,* p. 132

with my own vegetarianism. Let me begin by saying that I take the "holy sparks" teaching very seriously, which is why I have devoted considerable energy to the question of whether or not it is being done properly. In fact, this is the *primary* reason I am a vegetarian. I share this story here to illustrate that *it is possible* to reconcile these two seemingly opposing worldviews.

It is axiomatic in Hasidic thought that each human soul comes into this world to redeem very specific sparks and not others. According to an early disciple of the Baal Shem Tov, the main reason that Jews were scattered among the gentile nations was to redeem the lost sparks that are exiled there:

> Rabbi Yaakov Yosef of Polnoye said, "We needed the exile among all the seventy nations, where the holy sparks fell, and each individual of the people must be exiled there, in that place which contains the root from his [or her] soul, to separate and uplift them [back to God]." (*Ketonet Passim,* 1866)

According to Reb Pinchas of Koretz, another early Hasidic master, some people are born into this world only to perform one specific mitzvah in their entire lives, to redeem that unique spark that was specifically assigned to them. This fits with many of the older stories about animals and raising sparks, where there was always a very personalized aspect to it. A specific animal comes to a specific sage at a specific time and requests to be slaughtered and used for a specific mitzvah.

Today, however, this kind of personalized relationship no longer exists. Most of us don't take our own cow or chicken to the *shochet* — a lot of Jews have never even seen a live cow, and few of us ever meet the *shochet*. We know meat only as a packaged product wrapped in cellophane and Styrofoam. Nor is there much interaction between the *shochet* and the animal as in the story of Yehuda Hirsch and the doves. Everything is done at such high speed that the animals are nothing more than objects whizzing by on an assembly line. And the animals themselves have no choice in the matter.

I first realized this back in the 1980s, when I visited a kosher slaughterhouse. Up until that time, I was still thinking in terms of old Hasidic stories that took place in little 18th-century

Polish villages. I simply did not realize how much the assembly-line mentality had affected the whole process.

In past generations, an individual blessing was said with *kavannah* before slaughtering each animal, and they were slaughtered only for special occasions. But in today's high-speed industry, most *shochtim* can only make a single blessing for the whole day's quota of animals because everything moves at such breakneck speed. In chicken processing plants, for example, dozens of chickens are slaughtered *every minute*. So how can there possibly be proper *kavannah* for the elevation of the soul of each individual bird?

During *Kapporos* there is an individual blessing said on each bird by the practitioners, so from that standpoint it is better than a meat packing plant. Still, there is the question of mass production and cruelty before the ritual. I highly doubt that chickens would ever voluntarily come to be slaughtered at a modern *Kapporos* center the way the doves came to Yehuda Hirsch. The personal interaction no longer exists. The *Kapporos* chickens are randomly pulled from a stack of cages and handed to the practitioner like so much merchandise.

All of this caused me to struggle with the question of "raising sparks" for many years. I went back and forth between eating mostly vegetarian at home and eating meat when in the Hasidic community. On the one hand, I wanted to fulfill the mitzvahs connected with meat, but on the other hand, the more I learned about the modern meat industry, the more I was losing my taste for meat. This was due to both horror at how animals are treated, and an increasing sensitivity to negative "energy" in the meat. Could it be that I had already redeemed the sparks I was born to save, and that was why I no longer craved meat?

If you look at the way that people evolve into vegetarians, it often follows the categories of animals as defined by the laws of *kashrut*. First they give up seafood, pork, and exotic species that were never kosher in any case. Next, they give up red meat, which has very strict rules about which parts of the animal may or may not be eaten, such as discarding the kidney fat, not eating the sciatic nerve, etc. Next comes poultry, which is still meat, but not so strict; you can pretty much eat the whole bird, including the fat. After this they give up fish, which have rules about which species are permitted, but no specific requirements for slaughtering them.

At this point, the person is an ovo-lacto vegetarian who still eats eggs and dairy. Some people go further, giving up eggs because they are potentially a baby chicken. Vegans go the furthest, giving up milk as well, and eating only plant-based diets. People naturally follow this order even if they haven't the slightest awareness of the kosher laws.

This suggests to me that keeping kosher is not about "health rules" as the secularists claim. It's about the spiritual energy in the foods. The heaviest energy — which is forbidden for Jews to eat at all — is found in insects, reptiles, pork and shellfish. The lightest is in plant foods, with a spectrum in between. The natural order goes like this: Forbidden species, red meat species, poultry, fish, eggs, dairy, plants.

"Ethical vegans" would say that this is a process of evolving into a higher level of morality through coming to realize that it is wrong to kill animals. To them, meat-eaters are murderous barbarians, while vegans are more highly evolved and civilized. From a mystical standpoint, however, I think something else is happening. If we are assigned specific sparks to redeem in meat, and if we do indeed redeem them, then it would make sense to lose our taste for meat once our sparks have been found and elevated. There would be no need to eat it anymore. Continuing to eat meat would then become mere gluttony.

As I continued to struggle with the question, friends in the Hasidic community were not very sympathetic to my dilemma. They pointed out that the Sages, *Zaddikim* and Rebbes ate meat, so surely it must be God's will. Moses ate meat, the Holy Ari ate meat, the Baal Shem Tov ate meat… Did I think I was better than the saints of old? On the other hand, secular vegetarians were unable to understand my need to put God's will above following my own heart. They had no respect for Hasidism or any of its teachings, and often no respect for me. Neither side could give me an answer that satisfied my soul.

It took a long time for me to reconcile the two worldviews and become a committed vegetarian — but eventually I did succeed. Through my own soul-searching, I came to the conclusion that although the doctrine of "raising holy sparks" was true, and although the Rebbes of old really did it well, the modern industrial conditions have stripped away all the holiness. I came to believe that eating meat is no longer a holy act; instead, it is dragging us down. The whole process is filled with *klippot*, the negative "shells" of energy left behind when holiness is gone. Nowadays when we eat meat, we absorb this negativity, which leads to more callousness and cruelty.

Rabbi Chaim Kramer, a respected contemporary Breslov scholar who is not a vegetarian, nevertheless notes in his commentary to Rebbe Nachman's *Likutei Moharan* (section 37:6): "When a person eats the meat of an animal which lacks proper *shechita*, he also ingests the aspects of animal matter, darkness, foolishness, judgments, forgetfulness, and death." This is because the *shochet*, by not *shechting* properly, has failed to elevate the fallen sparks. So eating the meat drags the person down spiritually, instead lifting the animal's essence upward. As I already pointed out, the very nature of modern meat processing makes it very difficult, if not impossible, for a *shochet* to have the proper *kavannah* for each animal.

This is the main reason why I do not eat meat anymore. However, I do still eat eggs and dairy products. I do not feel called to be a vegan. Perhaps there are still sparks in eggs and milk that I must find and elevate. However, I take responsibility for what I eat. In fact, I keep chickens precisely so I can be sure my eggs come from a humane source.

This explanation may not satisfy everyone, nor do I put it forth as some kind of dogma. The story is my own personal journey, and I share it merely to illustrate one way in which this process might work with an individual. On the other hand, it is possible to decide to use money for *Kapporos* instead of chickens without becoming a vegetarian. Each mitzvah or *minhag* has its own intrinsic value; one need not do things "all or nothing." While it is true that many anti-*Kapporos* activists have a not-so-hidden agenda to make everyone into vegans, it is also true that this is not the only way to view these issues.

However, I do hope you will seriously consider the things I have said in this chapter. If you are a Hasid or a kabbalist, then you should be taking the Holy Ari's teachings about "raising sparks" very, very seriously. And even if you are not a mystic, consider this: If we can treat our books with care and respect, never even putting them on the floor,[63] then surely we can learn to handle live animals with equal gentleness and care. If you feel you must do *Kapporos* with a chicken, then at least recognize that the bird in your hands is a living creature, not a mere thing. Don't dangle it at your side like a lifeless shopping bag. Connect with its "spark" as part of God's universe. And if you cannot do this with empathy and true *kavannah*, then you would be much better off using money instead.

It is important to honestly ask ourselves whether we are really raising sparks, or merely satisfying our own desires. It is vitally important to *really* hear the cries of those chickens suffering in the here and how, and not overwrite them with children's stories. In the next chapter we will explore the question of animal suffering, and whether or not we have unconsciously assimilated some very alien, non-Jewish ideas on this topic.

And to my animal activist friends: Next time someone tells you that the chickens are "happy to help us," I hope you will be able to begin a meaningful dialogue with both knowledge and respect. All too often, when I have tried to explain the importance of "raising holy sparks" to those in the activist community, I have met with nothing but sarcastic put-downs. As I have said many times throughout this book, hurling insults only creates more hostility. Although it may seem egotistical or "specie-ist" for Jews to believe that our daily actions are elevating sparks and repairing the universe, nevertheless, this is the argument that *works* in the Hasidic community. It is the argument that I have found to be *the most successful* in convincing my fellow Jews not to use chickens. Far more successful, in fact, than claiming meat is murder.

---

[63] Jews never put holy books on the floor, out of respect for the wisdom they contain. There is even a hierarchy of how books may be stacked: Always title side up, with secular books on the bottom and sacred texts on top. If you drop a holy book, you kiss it when you pick it up, to show you meant no disrespect. And if, heaven forbid, somebody drops a Torah scroll, all those who see it fall must fast. This may seem silly to some, but it does teach us not to destroy things or throw them around carelessly – a behavior that I see all to often in the secular world. The first time I saw fellow college students slam their books on the floor, I was horrified.

Chapter 5:

The Question of Suffering and Cruelty

The opening paragraph in the section on "Cruelty to Animals" in the *Kitzur Shulchan Arukh* (Code of Jewish Law), section 191:1, makes three distinct points about the treatment of animals. The first part reads: "It is forbidden, according to the laws of the Torah, to inflict pain upon any living creature. On the contrary, it is our duty to relieve the pain of any creature, even if it is ownerless or belongs to a non-Jew."

This seems pretty self-explanatory, and is the part most frequently quoted by animal rights activists. However, they often take it out of context as the *only* rule on the subject, and then extend it to apply to *anything* that might cause suffering, including slaughter or using animals for work. This extreme stance goes against the Torah itself, which does permit us to eat and use animals under certain circumstances.

The key word here is "inflict." To inflict suffering is to *purposely* do something that causes pain unnecessarily, such as beating a horse, pulling a cat's tail, or, throwing hot water on a dog, heaven forbid. It would also include overloading a donkey or forcing a horse to pull a load that is too heavy for him. It most certainly includes the abominable behaviors of some children at *Kapporos* centers, who poke sticks at the chickens through the cages or laugh at their suffering if they try to get away. Parents are responsible to teach their children that this is *tza'ar ba'alei chayyim*, cruelty to animals, and is forbidden.

And yes, the duty to relieve animal suffering is also included here. It is a big mitzvah to help a stray animal by feeding it, adopting it, or, at the very least, taking it to an animal shelter. If the owner can be found, then it must be returned.

Rabbi Israel Salanter, one of the most distinguished Orthodox rabbis of the 19th century, failed to arrive one Yom Kippur eve for the Kol Nidre prayer. His congregation was very worried, because he was always on time. It was inconceivable that he would skip services on this most holy day. So they sent out a search party to look for him. Eventually they found him in a Christian neighbor's barn. On his way to the synagogue, their saintly rabbi had found one of his neighbor's calves, lost and tangled up in the bushes. Seeing that the animal was suffering, he freed it and then led it home. This act of mercy represented the rabbi's prayers on that Yom Kippur evening.[64]

So it is true that we must be kind to animals and help them when we can. But this does *not* mean we are required to practice *ahimsa,* the Eastern philosophy that says never to kill anything ever. The second part of our text goes on to say: "However, if they [the animals] cause trouble, or if they are needed for medicinal purposes, or for any other human need, it is even permissible to kill them and we disregard their pain. For the Torah has permitted people to slaughter them."

This is the section most often quoted by the opponents of animal activism. They point out that any use that might benefit humankind trumps any suffering the animals might experience. Very often these people *also* go to extremes, using "any other human need" to justify everything and anything. This is not necessarily true; there are limits as to how we can treat animals. Not every use can be justified. It must be a genuine human need, not mere selfishness or vanity.

For example, based on the prohibition of *tza'ar ba'alei chayyim,* Rabbi Chaim David Halevy, Sephardic Chief Rabbi of Tel Aviv, issued a *p'sak* (rabbinic ruling) in March 1992, mandating that Jews should not wear fur. Rabbi Halevy asked: "Why should people be allowed to kill animals if it is not neces-

---

[64] This is not to say that one can normally skip prayers anytime one pleases, as this story has sometimes been misinterpreted to mean. Since the evening prayers can be recited anytime during the night, an ordinary person would simply say them later and his or her absence would probably go unnoticed. However, Rabbi Salanter was the leader of the community, so everyone was aware of his absence. He therefore chose to use the event as a public lesson in kindness to animals.

sary, simply because they desire the pleasure of having the beauty and warmth of fur coats? Is it not possible to achieve the same degree of warmth without fur?"

So not every "human need" is legitimate under Jewish law. And even legitimate needs can change over time. Fur was once necessary to keep warm in cold climates. Today, with so many warm synthetic fabrics, it has become a luxury only. Farmers, outdoorsmen, mountain climbers, and others who work outside in cold weather don't wear fur anymore.

Regarding the Hasidic fur hats called *streimels,* the Bobover Rebbe has told his followers to wear artificial fur, because real fur is too costly. In early Hasidic communities in Eastern Europe, the *streimel* was not worn by everyone, but was more like a crown for the Rebbe as leader. But in America, where things are more democratized, it has become the custom for all married men to wear one. The *streimel* is usually presented to the groom as part of the bride's dowry. With real fur running into thousands of dollars sometimes, families were going into debt rather than be embarrassed in public by not following the custom. Hence the Bobover's ruling to use artificial fur in order to cut down on the wedding costs for everyone.

Chabad Hasidim no longer wear *streimels* at all, because the last Lubavitcher Rebbe did not wear one. His reasoning was not about fur per se. Rather, he felt he could never really "take the streimel" – a symbol of authority – of the Rebbe who came before him (Rabbi Joseph I. Schneerson), whom he continued to call his teacher even after his death. So he opted for a plain black fedora with the brim turned down slightly in front, and his Hasidim have followed suit.

Neither of these changes were about "animal rights." Nevertheless, they do represent shifts in customs due to changing circumstances. In both cases, what once was considered necessary is no longer so.

One can make similar arguments for many other uses of animal products. Goose down, for example, is usually plucked from the breasts of live geese, which does hurt the birds. Once necessary for warmth, goose-down quilts, like fur coats, can now be replaced by equally warm synthetics. Chicken fat, once a necessity in kosher cuisine as a substitute for butter in meat dishes,[65] can now be replaced with vegetable oils. Vegetarians, including a number of prominent rabbis, argue that with our modern understanding of balanced nutrition and the availability of fresh produce year round, eating meat is no longer necessary, either. It's an opinion that should be seriously considered.[66]

Nevertheless, it is clear that we are permitted to slaughter for food, and to kill animals that pose a danger to the community, such as poisonous snakes or rabid dogs. This does *not* mean we should kill every snake we see. Many snakes are harmless or even beneficial, because they eat rodents and other pests. But *if they cause trouble* and there is no way to safely remove them, then it is permissible to kill them. A friend of mine in Texas has no qualms about shooting rattlers if they get into her barn or garden, even though she is very fond of nature and animals. It is *because* she loves her animals that she protects them from poisonous snakes.

Usually the debate stops here, with the animal rights people quoting the first part about not causing suffering, and their opponents countering with why it is permitted for human needs. But there is a *third* section that neither side ever quotes in this debate. To me, it is the most instructive of all: "Therefore, it is permitted to pluck feathers from a living goose with which to write, if no other pen is available. *However, people abstain from doing it, because it is cruelty.*" (Emphasis mine.)

This third part is the balance between the first two. Yes, we should avoid causing suffering to animals. And yes, there are times when causing pain is permitted for the greater good. However, there are *also* times when, even if something is permitted, and even if we need it ("no other pen is available"), we should still abstain from doing it because it is cruelty.

I find this to be a more persuasive argument among Orthodox Jews than debating whether or not it is ethical to eat meat. No rabbi, not even the most liberal of liberals, is going to outrightly forbid slaughter or meat-eating, because the Torah

---

[65] Meat and dairy products are never served at the same kosher meal. Jews in the ancient Middle East used olive oil for basting and frying, but as they moved farther north where this was no longer available, chicken and goose fat became the usual cooking oils. In Israel today many people have gone back to using olive oil.

[66] See Bibliography for further reading.

permits it, and it is axiomatic that you cannot "forbid the permitted." However, every person is free to choose for him or herself whether or not to eat meat or, in the case of our thesis in this book, whether to use chickens in the *Kapporos* ceremony.

I often focus on the idea of voluntarily choosing not to use a chicken – even though it is permitted by Jewish law – as a *khumra,* an extra strictness that one takes upon oneself. Within the Orthodox world, taking on *khumras* as a personal discipline is an acceptable – even admirable! – behavior that allows a person to make a humane choice without demanding that we "forbid the permitted" or negate the teachings of the Torah.

One of my personal *khumras* is that I only eat eggs from my own free-run chickens or from flocks that I know are raised humanely. All eggs from kosher species of birds are kosher (unless they have blood spots in them), including those from commercial farms. But I go further: I insist that the hens who laid the eggs were not mistreated. Keeping hens crammed into tiny cages all their lives does not render the eggs unkosher, but it does make them unacceptable to me. The same goes for using chickens as *Kapporos*; I choose to abstain, and encourage others to do the same. But I leave it as a personal choice.

Assimilating foreign ideas about animals

Ask any rabbi to name the three greatest threats to Jewish survival, and the list will no doubt include "assimilation." In Jewish parlance, "assimilation" means to become so absorbed in the surrounding culture that you lose your Jewish identity. The Yiddish expression is to be *fargoyisht*. This word is difficult to translate exactly, but it definitely has the connotation of something un-Jewish. As writer Ira Steingroot put it, "Engaging in blood sports, having a Christmas tree, and putting mayonnaise on a corned beef sandwich are all *fargoyisht*."

Orthodox and Hasidic Jews pride themselves on being bulwarks against assimilation. Usually this is defined in terms of traditional dress, foods, music, holidays, literature, education, or attempting to "pass" for a gentile. In these areas, they generally succeed in not assimilating. But it is also possible to assimilate un-Jewish *ideas.* Very often, this happens so slowly that the process is not even noticed until the damage is done.

For example: A few years ago, in an online "coffee-house" site,[67] a discussion came up about the conditions seen at local *Kapporos* centers, and whether or not the chickens suffer. And if so, then how much? The topic was debated pro and con, until eventually somebody posted:

> As a vegetarian, I am often criticized in the Orthodox world, the standard argument being that animals were created for our use. I am not going to get into that discussion here, but whether they are here for us or not, we are in no way free to do what we like with them. If we do use them, for purposes either mundane or holy, we must set certain boundaries for ourselves and always remember that animals have nervous systems and can and do experience pain and suffering.

A few comments down, somebody else, with the screen name of "Feivel," countered with:

> Pain and suffering is a function of consciousness not a nervous system. Animals can make motions that appear as pain and suffering. Perhaps it is, perhaps it's not. You can program a robot (ala Steven Spielberg's creations) to appear to experience pain.

The vegetarian then came back with references from Maimonides and Rabbi Samson Raphael Hirsch, stating that animals *can and do* feel pain. The debate went on for, as of this writing, 65 comments, some of which were quite long and detailed.

This discussion took place on a website called "The Yeshiva World," a meeting place for Haredi and other "black hat" Jews. Similar discussions appear from time to time on other Orthodox sites, indicating that there is debate about *Kapporos* in these communities. What made me choose this particular example was "Feivel's" reference to programming robots. Not

---

[67] I have "translated" the spelling, grammar, and "yeshivish" vocabulary for clarity. See http://www.theyeshivaworld.com/coffeeroom/topic/what-kind-of-a-kapora-is-this

only is he scientifically incorrect about nervous systems in animals, he has also assimilated – however unconsciously – the very un-Jewish ideas of a 16th-century philosopher named René Descartes (day-CART), who also thought animals were like robots ("automata" was his word) and incapable of feeling pain.

Known as "the father of modern philosophy," Descartes is famous for his saying: "I think, therefore I am." He was also a brilliant mathematician. But what is not as well known is this: He believed that only humans have the ability to think and feel. *Descartes* could think, he reasoned, therefore *he* was; but since animals did not "think" according to his definition, therefore they were not – at least not beyond the physical.

To Descartes, animals not only did not have souls, they were incapable of feeling any emotions or pain. Animals were mere things, unthinking automatons with no consciousness whatsoever. The cries of an animal in pain, to Descartes, were nothing more that the squeaking of a poorly maintained machine. To prove his point, he once nailed his wife's dog to a board and proceeded to dissect it, ignoring its cries of anguish. History does not record his wife's reaction, but I'm willing to bet she was not pleased.

Descartes was an enthusiastic promoter of vivisection, which soon became widely accepted in scientific and medical circles. Researchers dissected live animals without anesthesia, and were taught to ignore their cries of pain. School children also practiced vivisection in class, and were often ridiculed for showing any compassion for the suffering animals. It was not considered "scientific" to feel sorry for specimens.

Descartes was not Jewish, and his ideas about animals are not in line with Jewish teachings. Nor are they in line with Christianity. The Roman Catholic Church condemned his books and forbade reading them, on the grounds that they degraded God's creation. Nevertheless, his influence continued to grow in scientific and medical circles.

Cartesian influences in the Jewish community

Descartes did not have much influence on Jews at first. At the time he was teaching, Jews in Europe were still ghettoized and not accepted at the universities where he lectured. Nor were Jewish schools interested in teaching children to dissect animals. But ideas will spread across all barriers, so that, by the time you get to the late 1700s, Cartesianism was starting to filter into the Jewish community along with the secular "Enlightenment" *(Aufklärung)* movement. You can see his influence in some of the period Torah commentaries. Belief in animals as conscious beings was gradually being replaced by pseudo-scientific theories of them as controlled entirely by instincts – not unlike the "programming" referenced by "Feivel" above.

This partially explains why Rebbe Nachman of Breslov (1772-1810), told his followers not to study philosophy. I had always been puzzled over this, this, because Maimonides was a philosopher, Nachmanides was a philosopher, so were Ibn Ezra and Luzatto and a lot of other classical Torah commentators – and we study them, right? But after reading about Descartes, I realized that Rebbe Nachman was talking about *secular* philosophy. During his travels he had come into contact with the world of the "Enlightenment," and must have realized that this type of thinking would lead us away from respecting God and the creation. As indeed it has.

Rebbe Nachman was the great-grandson of the Baal Shem Tov who, as we learned in the previous chapter, regarded animals as "comrades in the universe." We can assume that Nachman grew up with this attitude in his family circle. Certainly he enjoyed going out into the forest to be with nature like his great-grandfather did. And he was fond of *Perek Shirah,* the ancient Jewish text that describes how everything in the universe is singing a song to God. When Nachman told his followers to pray in a field or forest because the plants would join in their prayers, he meant it literally. To this day, Breslover Hasidim still prefer to pray and meditate outdoors.

Rabbi Schneur Zalman of Liady, the first Chabad-Lubavitch Rebbe, was a contemporary of Nachman. Some say the two actually met. Others portray them as rivals. Be that as it may, they were definitely different in their approaches to serving God. The mysticism of the Baal Shem Tov, and subsequent Hasidic masters, including Nachman, emphasized cleaving to God through *devekut* (from the root *davak,* "to cleave" or "cling to,") an ecstatic state of being with God that is evoked through fervent joy. The intellectual approach of Schneur Zalman, continued by six successive Chabad-Lubavitch Rebbes, emphasized the mind as the route to the inner heart.

The Chabad school of thought requires deep knowledge of Hasidic philosophy to establish mystical faith. The very word "Chabad" is made up of the initials for *Chochmah* ("wisdom"), *Binah* ("understanding") and *Da'at* ("knowledge"), all of which are functions of the intellect. Schneur Zalman's system plays down the emotions and tends to suppress them — so much so, that he was accused by some early Rebbes of over-intellectualizing Hasidism. Rabbi Zusya of Hanipol, upon reading Schneur Zalman's masterwork, the *Tanya,* sarcastically marveled at how the author had managed to put such a big God into such a little book.[68]

In the *Tanya,* Schneur Zalman defines the "animal soul" part of humans *(nefesh ha-behamit)* as coming from the *yetzer ha-ra,* the "evil inclination," which must be conquered by the "Godly soul" *(nefesh elohit).* This, in turn, tends to affect the way Chabad Hasidim relate to actual, living animals. Rather than seeing animals as "comrades in the universe," they tend to view them merely as dumb beasts. And that, in turn, has had profound effects on Chabad education about living things. An online search for "animals in Chabad" brings up mostly material on *kashrut* and sacrifices. Very few Chabadniks have pets, either, so there is seldom an opportunity to get to know individual animals as living, sentient beings.

Schneur Zalman himself does not seem to have been much interested in animals or nature. Once, during his youth, he was traveling with Rabbi Pinchas of Koretz, an older Hasidic Rebbe, to visit Reb Dov Ber of Mezeritch, the Great Maggid (preacher). Along the way, Reb Pinchas offered to teach him the language of birds and plants, but young Schneur Zalman refused. "There is only one thing men [people] need to under-

---

[68] Ironically, Chabad Jews today *embrace* this opinion of their founder's work, even posting it on their websites. They completely miss the sarcasm. Zusya was an emotional ecstatic of the old school, not an intellectual philosopher. Therefore, I think it highly unlikely that he meant his statement about the *Tanya* as praise. That is certainly not the way I first heard it over 40 years ago.

stand," he replied.[69] Presumably he meant the fear of God, which even at that age came to him through the intellect. Whatever the secrets of nature that Reb Pinchas knew, they were not passed down into the Chabad-Lubavitch line.

Unlike the Breslovers, Chabad Hasidim are not encouraged to spend time outdoors, nor is there any talk of trees and plants joining in one's prayers. During the 1970s and early 80s, when I lived in Minneapolis, I sometimes spent the Sabbath and holy days with Chabad-Lubavitch in Saint Paul. In those days, the Lubavitcher Rebbe was not so right-wing politically, nor were his disciples claiming him to be the Messiah. The mood was more contemplative. For a while, I thought I might fit into Chabad. We would eventually part ways over politics, but I still have good memories of my experiences there. Never before had I danced with such ecstasy on Simchat Torah!

At the same time, I was deeply disappointed that these 20th-century Hasidim no longer had any real connection to nature like the Hasidim of old. The Lubavitchers always hurried everywhere, oblivious to any trees or flowers along the way. The sidewalk was merely a way to get from one building to another. One person told me he did not want to take the shortcut through the golf course because *it was too hard to walk on the grass!* If I pointed out a bird or a butterfly, they glanced with little interest. They actually considered me strange for spending time alone in the woods, and were suspicious of my need for solitude. When I brought up Rebbe Nachman's meditation techniques, they waved it away or changed the subject.

We shall return to this question in Chapter 7 when we discuss humane education and the value of nature study in understanding certain aspects of Torah. For now it is enough to note that the Chabad attitude toward nature is one of the reasons I ultimately chose to follow Breslov teachings instead. Unlike the Lubavitchers, the Breslovers have never criticized me for living away from the urban community, nor do they shake their

---

[69] Buber, *Tales of the Hasidim,* Vol. I, pp. 266-167. Understanding the language of animals was regarded as a saintly skill, attributed to Solomon, the Baal Shem Tov, and others. The old stories take this literally, as actually talking in a language, but it is more likely that people who had this skill were like the "horse whisperers" of today. See Bibliography for recommended reading on animal communication.

heads at my love of nature. "Bloom where you're planted" describes the Breslov attitude. A Jew can serve God anywhere. And sometimes God sends us to remote places for a specific reason. After all, if Moses had remained in the cities of Egypt, he would never have seen the Burning Bush.

Stewardship not "dominion"

The Jewish view of Genesis has traditionally been one of *stewardship,* based on God's instructions to Adam and Eve to *tend* the Garden and *guard* it (Genesis 2:15). They were to rule as benevolent caretakers, not despots. Indeed, the dominant image of God in the Hebrew Scriptures is that of a good shepherd caring for his sheep. Many of our great leaders, including Moses and King David, spent time as shepherds. Christianity later adopted this image for their founder as The Good Shepherd, but originally it was and still remains authentically Jewish. A good shepherd cares for the sheep, making them "lie down in green pastures" and leading them "beside the still waters" (Psalm 23).

In *The Splendor of Creation: A Biblical Ecology,* Ellen Bernstein makes the following point:

> In all the biblical commentaries over the last two thousand years, the rabbis rarely even mentioned dominion; undoubtedly because Jews rarely owned their own land for most of history, and consequently were not in a position to dominate nature. What little the rabbis did say about dominion — most rabbinic commentary focuses on the "be fruitful" half of the verse — was framed in the context of the governance of nature, never control... Humanity's charge was to preserve the order and integrity of creation, maintaining all the diverse kinds of organisms. The prototype of dominion was Adam's stewardship of the Garden of Eden (Genesis 2:15).[70]

A classic example of Adam's stewardship comes from the *Midrash Rabbah,* a major collection of oral traditions, inter-

---

[70] Bernstein, *Splendor of Creation,* p. 142.

pretations, and parables dating from the talmudic (Greco-Roman) period:

> "Look at the work of God, for who can rectify that which has been damaged?" (Ecclesiastes 7:13). At the time when the Blessed Holy One [God] created the first human being [Adam], He took him around to see all the trees of the Garden of Eden and said to him: "See my works, how beautiful and excellent they are! Everything that I created, I created for you. Do not ruin and destroy My world, for if you ruin it, there is no one to repair it after you."
>
> (*Ecclesiastes Rabbah* 7:28)

A Hasidic teaching cites this midrash in the following parable. A coat has two pockets: In one pocket are God's words to Adam, "All of this I have created for you." In the other pocket we have the words of Abraham to God, "I am but dust and ashes." Both of these we carry with us. When we are feeling lost and hopeless, we draw upon the promise to Adam that God cares about us as the "crown of creation." But when we are feeling arrogant and all-powerful, then we must remember the humble "dust and ashes" words of Abraham. Between them is the balance of the human heart.

So yes, Judaism places humanity above the animals, but with this privilege comes a great responsibility *to care for* the earth and its inhabitants, not plunder it. However, interfaith dialogue did not exist back in the 1700s when Cartesianism was spreading. By and large, Jews were excluded from the universities and other intellectual circles, so they had very little say in how Scripture was publicly interpreted in the Western world. Judaism was regarded as having been "replaced" by Christianity, and post-biblical writings like the Talmud and Midrash had long ago been rejected by Christian theologians. So it was the idea of "dominion" over nature, as expressed in such translations as the King James Version, that ultimately prevailed.

This attitude resulted in the extinction of the Passenger Pigeon, the Dodo Bird, The Great Auk, and numerous other species that were over-hunted without any moral restraint. The American Bison (buffalo) barely missed extinction; by 1906 only about a thousand were left. It is difficult to determine how much of this wanton slaughter was influenced by Cartesianism, but it certainly did not help.

The Writings of Samson Raphael Hirsch

By the time we get to the mid-1800s, Cartesianism was having an impact on the Jewish community. This rising insensitivity to God's creation is probably the reason that Rabbi Samson Raphael Hirsch, the foremost Torah scholar in 19th-century Germany, devoted considerable space in his *Nineteen Letters* and *Horeb* to our relationship to animals and nature. He writes:

> There are probably no creatures that require more the protective Divine word against the presumption of man than the animals, which like man have sensations and instincts, but whose body and powers are nevertheless subservient to man. In relation to them man so easily forgets that injured animal muscle twitches just like human muscle, that the maltreated nerves of an animal sicken like human nerves, that the animal being is just as sensitive to cuts, blows, and beating as man. Thus man becomes the torturer of the animal soul.[71]

Clearly, this is the exact opposite of what Descartes taught, regarding the ability of animals to feel pain. Hirsch also re-emphasized our responsibility to be kind to animals and lessen their suffering:

> Here you are faced with God's teaching, which obliges you not only to refrain from inflicting unnecessary pain on any animal, but also to help and, when you can, to lessen the pain whenever you see an animal suffering, even through no fault of yours.[72]

---

[71] Samson Raphael Hirsch, *Horeb*, Chapter 60, Section 415

[72] *Ibid*, section 416

Rabbi Hirsch was one of the primary founders of what is now known as Modern Orthodox Judaism, a movement that attempts to synthesize Jewish values and the observance of Jewish law with the secular, modern world. Yeshiva University, for example, is a Modern Orthodox institution. Unfortunately, few Modern Orthodox congregations today offer classes on Rabbi Hirsch's compassionate teachings about nature and animals. The movement is now more interested in Zionism and right-wing politics, and tends to ignore – or even deny – the importance of animal welfare and environmental issues. But that does not negate the teachings of Rabbi Hirsch.

Although he does not discuss Descartes by name, he is clearly opposing Cartesianism in this passage about having compassion (a quality that Descartes, in his callous disregard of animal suffering, clearly lacked):

> Compassion is the feeling of sympathy which the pain of one being awakens in another; and the higher and more human the beings are, the more keenly attuned they are to re-echo the note of suffering, which, like a voice from heaven, penetrates the heart, bringing all creatures a proof of their kinship in the universal God. And as for man, whose function it is to show respect and love for God's universe and all its creatures, his heart has been created so tender that it feels with the whole organic world... mourning even for fading flowers; so that, if nothing else, the very nature of his heart must teach him that he is required above everything to feel himself the brother of all beings, and to recognize the claim of all beings to his love and his beneficence.[73]

However, "compassion" here is not *ahimsa;* it does not mean never kill anything. Literally, it means, "to feel with." In cases where it is deemed necessary to slaughter animals for food or other purposes, this should not be done callously. One should always be aware of the pain involved. The Baal Shem Tov himself used to shed tears when he had to slaughter. Those

---

[73] Hirsch, *Horeb,* Chapter 17, Section 125

who say that the suffering does not matter because "they would be killed anyway" (as has sometimes been heard at *Kapporos* centers) should consider the following story from the Talmud.

Rabbi Judah ha-Nasi was once walking to the House of Study when a calf, which was being driven to slaughter, broke loose and ran up to him, hiding behind his robes and pleading for him to save its life. Rabbi Judah said to the calf, "Go to your fate, for this is what you were created for."

It was proclaimed in Heaven that since the rabbi had not shown any compassion for one of God's creatures, then he should be punished with suffering himself. So for thirteen years this holy rabbi suffered in great pain.

Then one day, a maidservant in the rabbi's house found a nest of newborn baby weasels in one of the rooms. She wanted to sweep them out the door, but he restrained her. "Leave them be," he said, "for God has mercy on all His creatures." At that moment, it was decreed in Heaven that since he had shown mercy, he should be cured of his pain. And he was.[74]

Interestingly, Rabbi Judah is the same Sage who said, "One who is ignorant of Torah is forbidden to eat meat." (Pesachim 49b) This does not mean he became a vegetarian. But perhaps the punishment he received for his callousness towards the calf helped him to see that eating animals is not a matter that should be treated lightly. Rabbi Judah is regarded as the primary compiler of the Mishnah, the earliest part of the Talmud. He was, therefore, a master scholar of Jewish law. But until the incident with the calf, he was lacking in compassion, which is *also* part of Torah. It was *that* kind of ignorance that, he felt, made one unworthy of eating meat. Rabbi Judah learned his lesson. Sadly, a lot of Jews today still have not.

The rise of factory farming

Sincere as he was, Rabbi Hirsch simply could not hold back the rising tide of Cartesianism that spread across Europe to the Americas and eventually around the world. In a chapter

---

[74] Retold from Talmud, Baba Metzia 85a.

called "From Living Soul to Animal Machine," Roberta
Kalechofsky writes:

Descartes' view of animal life is the antithesis of Maimonides' view, who wrote: "With respect to the joys
and sorrows the animal feels for its young, it is no different from the human being." But the medical world,
and later the agricultural communities, had much to
gain from Descartes' philosophy of the animal machine: It relieved them as it relieves them now of moral
responsibility for their actions... Western philosophy
denied the animals the capacity to suffer." [75]

Descartes' thesis opened the way for factory farming
and the mass production of today. If animals were only machines, people reasoned, then what would be wrong with cramming them into tiny cages or overcrowded filthy barns and feed-
lots? What would be wrong with slaughtering them on assembly lines? "Farm animals," write Kalechofsky, "which, even
when eventually eaten, were often regarded as near members of
the farming family as long as they lived, were relegated to the
same category as research animals. They became solely objects
to be manipulated for human gain."[76]

The kosher meat industry, in turn, gradually adapted itself to this rising industrialization. It was either that or go without meat, something the Jewish community was not prepared to
do. Rabbis became focused on the moment of slaughter only,
with little regard as to how the animals were treated beforehand.
Today they rationalize that the "human need" for meat trumps
the suffering of the animals, becoming more and more enmeshed in the system.

In a 2014 article entitled "The Significance of Eating
Meat,"[77] Rabbi Eliezer Melamed, headmaster of Yeshivat Har
Bracha in Israel and a prolific writer on Jewish law, discusses

---

[75] Kalechofsky, Roberta, *Vegetarianism Judaism: A Guide for Everyone*, Micah Publications, Marblehead, Massachusetts, 1992. p. 37.

[76] *Ibid*, Kalechofsky, p. 37.

[77] http://blogs.timesofisrael.com/the-significance-of-eating-meat/

the question of whether or not it is permissible to starve chickens for 10 days in order to force them into a premature molt and renew their egg production. Common sense would say that starving a bird for a week-and-a-half is cruel. But in Jewish law, the issue is more complicated than that. As we discussed earlier, one must balance the suffering against human needs.

Chickens normally shed their feathers and grow new ones a few at a time, over a period of a month or two. During this time, they stop laying eggs. In a natural life cycle with the older breeds, this molt happens after their chicks have hatched and are now following their mother around, learning to scratch and peck for food. It would not be practical for her to be incubating another clutch of eggs at this time, so she stops laying.

Commercial egg breeds, on the other hand, don't hatch chicks. In fact, the instinct to go broody (sit on a nest) has been selectively bred out of them, because a broody hen is not a profitable hen for egg farmers. The new breeds will lay steadily for 20 weeks or more before beginning to molt, at which point they stop laying. Usually the hens are then sold as meat. But egg producers have figured out that if the birds go without food for a week or more, this will speed up the molt and get production back on line. The hens drop all their feathers at once, grow new ones, and then resume laying. This is a common practice in the egg industry, but is it permitted according to Jewish law? Rabbi Melamed writes:

> Some *poskim* [Jewish law arbiters] were stringent in this issue, because in their opinion it involved immense sorrow and cruelty (*Shevet HaLevi* 6:7). Others were lenient, because such an act is taken for the benefit of the farm — this being the purpose of raising the hens in the first place — and in the long-term, the starvation even adds to their health, seeing as they live longer lives (Rabbi Goldberg, in the book *Haaretz v'Miztvotey'ha'*, pg.437)… In practice, whenever there is an extremely great need to support farmers and reduce food prices, we are lenient. [Underlining is mine]

Melamed then goes on to explain why he accepts Goldberg's more lenient opinion: "The opinion of Rabbi Goldberg can be relied on to a greater extent, because he served as the rabbi of the agricultural village Kfar Pines, and was familiar with the livestock and all its considerations, as opposed to Rabbi Wosner, who was not familiar with the issue up close."

In other words, Goldberg was part of the factory farm system and Wosner was not. Which becomes a case of the fox guarding the henhouse. All things being equal, I prefer to rely on Rabbi Wosner's stricter opinion (that it is forbidden) precisely because he is *not* directly involved with the egg industry. He would, it seems to me, be more objective than somebody serving as rabbi for a community that produces factory farm eggs, where there might be a conflict of interest.

Another argument that is commonly used in this debate says that if something is the "usual practice," then we do not regard it as excessive cruelty. Originally this referred to things like keeping a dog on a leash, saddling a horse, or hitching oxen to a plow. But as things have become more and more industrialized, and the factory farm system has become the standard, some people now justify it as "the usual practice." I have more than once been told that there is nothing wrong with stacking chickens in cages at *Kapporos* centers, because this is the way all chickens are raised nowadays. It becomes a circular argument that is very hard to break.

It is also not so clear that factory farming "reduces food prices" as Rabbi Melamed claims. In the short run this may sometimes be true, but when we consider the overall impact of meat production on our planet, the costs are very high. In 2006 the United Nations Food and Agricultural Organization (FAO), published a landmark report called "Livestock's Long Shadow," estimating that livestock production globally is responsible for more greenhouse gas emissions (GHGs), in CO^2 equivalents, than the emissions from all of the world's cars, planes, ships, and all other means of transportation combined.

The FAO asserts that: (1) the production of animal products causes about 9 percent of total CO^2 emissions, from the production of pesticides and fertilizer, use of irrigation pumps, extensive refrigeration, and other processes; (2) nitrous oxides are emitted from animals' manure and from chemical fertilizer used to grow feed crops and these gases are almost 300 times as potent as CO^2 in producing global warming; and (3) when rainforests are burned to create grazing land and land to grow feed crops for animals, substantial amounts of CO_2 are released, and trees that would absorb CO_2 are destroyed.

We can already see the negative results of this pollution in the weather changes happening right now as I write: stronger hurricanes, increased numbers and strength of tornados, vast floods in Texas, drought in California, more earthquakes and erupting volcanoes, etc. Not to mention the bird flu epidemic currently spreading through Minnesota poultry farms that has cost billions in cleanup, created an egg shortage, and driven the prices up, not down. All of which indicates that the cost of that "cheap" bucket of chicken wings is very expensive for all of us in the long run.

Rabbi Melamed, in the same article cited above, completely dismisses the concerns of animal welfare advocates in this debate. He considers them unqualified to define "cruelty" because they are not Torah scholars who, in his words, must be "knowledgeable and familiar with raising animals and the laws of *shechita* (ritual slaughtering)." By "raising animals" I'm pretty sure he means factory farm methods, not hatching baby chicks under mother hens like I do. He also cites some political reasons for disqualifying vegetarian activists that I won't go into here.

Suffice it to say that I consider it absurd to claim that the starving process *benefits* the chickens because they might live longer. Is a longer life in a factory farm cage even worth living at all? The only reason they are kept alive is to harvest their eggs for profit. That is "for the benefit of the farm," not the chickens. When they stop laying again, it's off to the soup pot. The hens are nothing to the farmer but egg-making machines.

Which brings us back to Descartes. When it comes to chicken farming, we have become assimilated, *fargoyisht* Cartesians, right along with the gentile world. We consider it normal to raise chickens in ways that would have horrified the pious rabbis of old. It happened slowly, over a century or more, so slowly that most of us did not notice at first — but it happened. Like the proverbial frog in the slowly heated water, we have gradually adapted to cruelty until now we are fully cooked.

Most Jews do not realize the horrible conditions under which chickens are raised nowadays. They have been taught that kosher means "humane." Partly this is true: even PETA and the ASPCA have upheld *shechita* as humane if done properly.[78] But little thought is given to the way the animals are raised, which is often abominable.

Some rabbis also argue that since most animals are raised by non-Jews, and since non-Jews are not required to keep the same strict religious laws as Jews, we therefore need not worry about how they treat the animals before the *shochet* slaughters them. Originally this distinction between Jews and non-Jews was meant to say that the whole world does not have to become Jewish. The Rainbow Covenant made with Noah after the Flood, which has only seven basic ethical laws, applies to everybody. The Covenant at Sinai where the Torah was given, on the other hand, has many more laws that are only binding on the Jewish people. Non-Jews may voluntarily take on Jewish observances and traditions, and many do. But this is not required of them to be "saved."

In a sense, this Dual Covenant theology was an early form of multiculturalism, one that promoted tolerance toward one's gentile neighbors in regard to dietary laws, lifestyle, observing the Sabbath, etc. All well and good. But to use it as an excuse to turn a blind eye to animal cruelty in factory farms is, in my opinion, morally wrong. It also violates the mandate in the *Shulchan Arukh* to "relieve the pain of any creature, even if it is ownerless or belongs to a non-Jew," that we cited at the beginning of this chapter.

One possible benefit of the public *Kapporos* centers is that people can actually see how chickens are routinely treated nowadays. Those stacks of cages are what millions of chickens endure every day on the way to market. If you eat chicken, the likelihood is that the meat on your plate – whether kosher or not – came from birds who are treated the exact same way as the ones you see at *Kapporos* centers. This is not some sort of

---

[78] In fact, the ASPCA was responsible for designing the more humane restraining pen that replaced the cruel shackle-and-hoist method formerly used during *shechita* for cattle. Shackle-and-hoist was never required by Jewish law, but rather, by the U.S. Department of Agriculture, which mandates that the blood of one animal cannot touch that of another for health reasons. The ASPCA pen solved this problem. The animal is first killed in the pen while standing upright, then hoised onto the processing line.

"Jewish cruelty" – it is the reality of the modern meat industry for everyone who is not a vegetarian.

The wrong way to handle a bird

There is also the question of how the birds are being handled. As I mentioned before, Rabbi Hecht claims that the way he holds the chickens by the wings calms the birds. He also claims it does not injure them or cause them pain. However, I have never heard him cite any sources as to why he believes this to be true. From *where* does he get this opinion? Has he actually made a study of chicken physiology, or is he relying on Cartesian-influenced ideas from the past? Or did he simply see his father do it that way?

As we noted in earlier chapters, the chickens raised today are not as sturdy as the older breeds our ancestors knew. They have been bred to grow and gain weight so fast that their bones and muscles do not keep up with their growth. My free-range bantam chickens can fly up into trees; the commercial breeds can hardly get off the ground, especially if they have been confined all their lives with no exercise. Many cannot even walk or stand properly. One of the reasons that *Kapporos* practitioners have begun using such young birds is that the older ones are often so crippled in their legs as to be ruled unkosher.

When Dr. Amir Kashiv, a member of the Royal College of Veterinary Surgeons, reviewed videos of *Kapporos* rituals, he reported that:

> The wings of the "modern industrial" chicken aren't strong enough to support its body and therefore it is largely flightless. In broiler chickens, even the legs can hardly carry the intentionally bred-for-increased-bulk body, resulting in very common lameness problems. Lifting the bird by its wings places an unnatural tension on ligaments, tendons and bones. Swinging the bird in the air can cause dislocations, tears, ruptures and broken bones. The manner in which chickens are

handled during the ritual of *Kapporos* is, in my view, painful and harmful and thus inhumane.[79]

Other veterinarians have expressed the same opinion:

Shown pictures of chickens being held with their wings pulled back by *Kapparot* practitioners, Dr. Ian Duncan, Professor Emeritus of Poultry Science at the University of Guelph in Ontario, wrote that "holding a domestic fowl with the wings pinned back as shown will be painful. It will be extremely painful if the bird is held in this position for some minutes."

Dr. Nedim Buyukmihci, Emeritus Professor of Veterinary Medicine at the University of California, observed that "the manner in which the man is holding the chicken, with the wings pulled back, puts the chicken at risk for ligament and tendon injury, possibly even bone fracture."[80]

In his paper "Pain in Birds," Dr. Michael Gentle of the Institute of Animal Physiology and Genetics Research in Edinburgh, cites the "widespread nature of chronic orthopedic disease in domestic poultry," and Dr. John Webster, professor of animal husbandry in the University of Bristol School of Veterinary Science, points out that these birds "have grown too heavy for their limbs and/or become so distorted in shape as to impose unnatural stresses on their joints."

So I must ask you, dear reader: Whom are you going to believe? Expert professors of veterinary medicine who understand chicken physiology, or misinformed practitioners who rely on word of mouth that "this does not hurt the bird"? The page on *Kapporos* at chabad.org clearly states:

---

[79] http://www.endchickensaskaporos.com/vet.html

[80] "Why Chickens Should be Eliminated from Kapparot Ceremonies," http://www.jewishjournal.com/yom_kippur/article/why_chickens_should_be_eliminated_from_kapparot_ceremonies_20090925/

It is of utmost importance to treat the chickens humanely, and not to, G-d forbid, cause them any pain or discomfort. Jewish law very clearly forbids causing any unnecessary pain to any of G-d's creations.

The *Shulchan Arukh* also says that "it is forbidden to tie the legs of a beast or bird in a manner that causes pain." While this sentence refers specifically to tying the legs, it would seem to me that holding the wings in a painful manner would also be included, since the purpose of the law is to avoid restraining the bird in a way that causes suffering. And given the testimony of veterinarians cited above, who are experts in the field of animal science, it seems beyond a doubt that Rabbi Hecht and his followers are wrong. Holding a bird by its wings is very painful and should be stopped.

If you insist on using a chicken, then please at least hold it humanely. Given the weakness in the legs of modern breeds cited above, holding it by the legs is no longer a humane option, either, even though this was once a common way to carry chickens and other fowl. With older breeds who got lots of exercise, the leg muscles were strong enough; but with birds raised under commercial conditions, the likelihood is you could tear the muscles or dislocate the leg joints. Best would be to hold the chicken upright, supporting the body by tucking it under your arm to control the wings, and restraining the legs to prevent kicking. That's how I carry my chickens. But keep the bird away from your eyes; they do sometimes peck. However, a peck on the hands might be a very good reminder that this is a living creature you are holding. If you don't feel you can deal with that, then using money is a better option.

If you are worried about getting your clothes dirty, then wear old clothes and change into your good clothes later. That's what our ancestors did. There is no requirement to dress up for this ritual. Early accounts describe people doing *Kapporos* in the early morning, often before sunrise. Only afterward did they go to the *mikveh* to purify themselves, then put on their good clothes and *kittel* (white robe) to prepare for the holy day.

Again I must emphasize: Holding chickens by the wings is not something "Jewish." Nor is it required by the ritual. In fact, all the old drawings of *Kapporos* show the birds being held upright by the legs or cradled in the arms as I described above. This dangling them by the wings is a recent phenomenon. The first time I saw someone hold a bird that way was by a gentile farmer back in the late 1980s. Since then, I have seen videos of other farmers doing the same thing. So we must ask ourselves if this method of handling chickens is also something *fargoyisht* that we have assimilated from the surrounding culture.

Hopefully people seeing this mistreatment of God's creatures for what it is will be moved to compassion, as indeed was the case in the "Yeshiva World" debate I mentioned earlier. Not everyone in that thread saw animals as robots like "Feivel" did. Several people said they no longer use chickens, including this Orthodox mother:

> My children used to insist on bringing along food and water for the chickens when we went to do *Kapporos.* Then they refused to go. I have seen children chase and abuse kittens and dogs; my daughter once saved a kitten from being attacked by a crowd of boys. My husband just does it for us with money. The only way I could do it is if I raise my own chickens and bring them to the *shochet.* Just chickens are so noisy and messy.

Indeed they are noisy, especially if you try to raise them in the city, but not necessarily as messy as the ones you see sitting in their own excrement in those tiny cages. Free-range chickens take dust baths, preen their feathers, and generally keep themselves neat and clean. Still, given her children's' sensitivity to animals, it is unlikely this woman's family would kill birds they raised themselves. Realistically, this is a family that will not be using chickens in the future. I encourage others to also think hard about what they see, and understand that those birds are neither robots nor machines. They are, as Rabbi Hirsch and others before him have taught, living beings who do indeed feel pain and suffer.

Chapter 6:

Using Money Instead of Chickens

As the title of this chapter indicates, we will now discuss the option of using money for *Kapporos* instead of chickens. There are numerous good reasons for making this substitution, which we shall explore in some detail. But first, a few words about how change takes place in traditional communities, which is not always by the same processes as in the secular world – and the need to respect and understand this difference. The first part of this chapter will therefore be directed primarily at activists, while the second half is directed at my fellow Orthodox Jews. But course, it is good for everyone to read both sides of the issue in order to understand each other better.

Animal rights activists see the question in very simple terms: Since money can be substituted for a chicken, they feel that everyone should do that, period. As for those who don't make that substitution, the activist approach thus far has been to try and shame the Jewish community with bad publicity. Unfortunately, as we shall see later in this chapter, that approach ends up evoking negative stereotypes. Social prejudices against Orthodox Jews abound in the mostly-secular activist world, and this gets in the way of any real communications.

The first time I posted a comment on the Alliance to End Chickens as Kapporos Facebook page, as well as on other activist and vegetarian sites, I was greeted with stereotyped hostility based on my profile picture. Apparently they were seeing only the beard and *payos,* and did not even recognize *the very same face* that is on some of the protest posters they carried and in the slide show they were passing around online. Instead, I was immediately seen as the face of the enemy. Interestingly, I did not get this reaction when I used only my name without a photo. So it was not my ideas they were reacting to; it was my appearance. If this had happened with any other group, it would be blatant racism. People have been fired over less. But when it comes to Hasidic Jews, it's open season for taking potshots.

Alliance spokesperson Karen Davis, when asked in an interview on the Patheos "Friendly Atheist" blog about why the *Kapporos* practitioners use chickens and not money, replied:

"Hasidic communities/members will rarely depart from/defy what their specific rabbis tell them to do. Even if a member personally winces or objects, he or she won't speak up publicly. These communities live strictly defined lives like the Amish, Jehovah Witnesses, and other extremely insular groups. Women are not respected as persons in their own right. Fear of being shunned/ostracized, having no other options or imaginings but to conform, stay, and obey, are motivations."[81]

This is the opinion of a hostile outsider who has no real understanding of Hasidism or much social interaction with the community. It doesn't really answer the question of why Hasidim use chickens; it merely rants against what she perceives as an oppressive culture. Davis is hostile to all religions that allow meat eating, which pretty much rules out most of the world for most of human history. This is the problem with one-issue politics. There is a strong tendency to judge everything based on one particular point. It's an approach I try to avoid.

In the same interview Davis stated: "For the record, I am not Jewish or religious. I grew up in a family that attended the Methodist Church down the street from us, but religion never influenced me as a worldview. No religion even if proven 'true' would reconcile me in the slightest to the way things are (concerning slaughter and meat-eating)."

---

[81] Mehta, Hermant, "The Kapporos Problem," October 1, 2014, http://www.patheos.com/blogs/friendlyatheist/2014/10/01/the-kapparot-problem/

From my conversations with her, I would say that "ethical veganism" is her religion, although it was never clear to me if she actually believes in God or any other authority beyond herself. Davis tends to see things in terms of bullying, coercion and "male domination" – words that frequently appear in her writings. Notice all the negative buzzwords in her statement about Hasidism: "Rarely depart/defy," "strictly defined lives," "no other options," "extremely insular," "fear," "conform," "obey" – my goodness, she has practically recited the whole anti-Hasidic dictionary, with a dig about feminism to boot! I'm surprised she didn't reference the movie *Yentl*.

This is a very stereotyped view of Orthodox Judaism. She is probably getting these opinions from secularized or "cultural" Jews who are themselves hostile toward the religious. Jewishness *(Yiddishkeit)* is not just about religion per se. It also includes many cultural aspects. Although "secular Christian" would be an oxymoron, it is possible to be a Jewish atheist, and some people are. Such a person will probably connect with the Jewish community through ethnic foods, music, culture, and supporting Israel, but not "the religion."

There is often deep hostility between those Jews who are religiously observant and those who are not. And the gate swings both ways on this issue. Secular Jews can be just as intolerant as the ultra-Orthodox. People outside the Jewish world do not always understand the various quarreling factions within it, or the negative stereotypes that are thrown back and forth. Davis' language may be "politically correct" in the secular activist world, but it is totally ineffective in the world where the *Kapporos* ceremony is actually practiced.

Hasidim are not Luddites, nor are they as "insular" as Davis claims. Many are very tech savvy and regularly use the Internet. Chabad Hasidim, especially, are active online, with numerous websites, blogs, Facebook pages and discussion groups. And they are just as capable of doing a search for articles on *Kapporos* as anyone else. Finding remarks like the one above does absolutely nothing to promote the Alliance cause.

My own wife was deeply offended by Davis' stereotypical remark about Hasidic women, and insisted I state here that she is indeed a "person in her own right." And she is. However, she does not like to be photographed and sees no need to appear with me everywhere I go, or to have her face plastered all over Facebook. It is *because* she is a person in her own right that we are not joined at the hip as a public couple.

I am reminded of a scene in *The Right Stuff,* where Vice President Lyndon B. Johnson throws a fit because Annie Glenn, the wife of astronaut John Glenn, refuses to appear on national television with him. This is based on a true incident, and was not about Johnson per se: Annie had a severe stutter, and presumably did not want to be embarrassed in public, not even for the Vice President of the United States. Just because her husband was famous did *not* mean she had to go on TV. Astronaut Glenn went against the NASA director's orders to solve "the problem with his wife" and backed her up in her right to refuse. So did the rest of the Mercury Seven astronaut team.

I, too, respect my wife's right to make her own decisions and not appear with me in photographs or TV interviews. This is not about being "strictly defined" or "extremely insular." It is about her choices as an individual human being.

It is also untrue that there is no dissent within Hasidic communities. But this dissent rarely takes the form of marching up and down the street shouting slogans. Like most people in human communities everywhere, Hasidic Jews prefer to live in peace with their neighbors. It is relatively easy for outsiders to show up once a year, wave their protest signs, and then disappear again until the following year. It is much more difficult to challenge the people living on your own block. For the sake of *shalom bayit* – peace in the family – even hard-core activists will often tone down their rhetoric at home.

However, this does not mean there is no dissent. People may not "speak up publicly" at the Alliance protests, especially if the rhetoric is as anti-religious as the examples I have cited. I myself ended up dropping out of the Alliance because its primary spokesperson was so negative about my core Hasidic beliefs – and I was already against using chickens. But rest assured, there is indeed discussion behind the scenes or within study circles, not to mention the anonymity of the Internet. In traditional communities, change often happens by processes that are not always visible to outsiders. This book itself is a form of dissent, one that will hopefully arouse a lot of discussion.

The power of internal debate

Let's look at an example from another culture, one that is generally more respected in "progressive" circles than Hasidism, but where the processes of change are often similar. When nine-year-old Kinlichiinii Ashkii John, a Navaho Indian Cub Scout, discovered that there was no Native American religious emblem he could earn for his uniform,[82] he set out to change that. When it was suggested that he could join a church and earn their emblem instead, he said no. He wanted something authentic from his own people.

A non-Indian might organize a protest outside the Boy Scout headquarters, go on national TV about it, cry discrimination, bring a lawsuit, and/or try to embarrass the Boy Scouts into doing his will. But that is not how things work in Navajo communities. John and his parents first did some research, and learned that the emblems and requirements for earning them do not come from the Boy Scouts directly, but from the various religious denominations. John's tribal religious leaders would need to submit a proposal, which would then be reviewed and approved by the national Scout council. And there would need to be at least 25 Scout units chartered by Native organizations, which meant getting other tribes involved.

A non-Navajo would probably write the proposal himself, collect a lot of signatures, and then submit it. But again, that is not how Indian community decisions are made. So John and his family began meeting with tribal elders and medicine men from many tribes across the country, working to find a consensus on what the requirements for earning the Native religious emblem should be. It is a slow, quiet process that has been going on for several years now. John's project has received very little media coverage, but in the Native world it is working, and there will be such an emblem in the near future.

Similar internal processes often take place within the Jewish community, which is more like a tribal culture than a

---

[82] Fonesca, Felicia, "Native Cub Scout on quest to create Scout emblem for American Indians," Online at: *Albuquerque Journal,* August 14, 2007. http://www.abqjournal.com/news/state/apcubscout08-14-07.htm

"religion" per se. Anthropologists often use a five-point check-list for what constitutes a tribe, and Jews fit the bill:

1. Common origin story (Abraham and Sarah)
2. Common land of origin (Israel)
3. Common language (Hebrew)
4. Common festivals and foods (kosher laws)
5. Common religion or mythology (Judaism)

I should also clarify here that "tribal" does not necessarily mean primitive or barbaric. Human beings – even very "modernized" ones – naturally form into tribes, whether they are based on families, clans, neighborhoods, ethnic groups, social clubs, sports teams or Boy Scout troops. The tribe is a basic unit of human society, rooted in the deep-felt need of all people to belong somewhere.

As you can see from the above list, religion is only *part* of being Jewish. Not everything is handed down by the rabbis like Davis claims. There is also a very strong cultural component that works more like community consensus than a conference of theologians. This is especially true of a *minhag,* or community custom, which is often established not by the decree of a single rabbi, but by long-standing agreement in the community that "this is how we do things among us."

How traditions sometimes change

All communities, even very secular ones, have their own traditions. Take, for example, wedding rings. In Jewish law, a man does not have to give the bride a ring; he merely needs to give her an item worth the smallest coin in the land, which in America would be a penny. A plastic toy ring would do. In the Nazi concentration camps, people got married with loaves of bread – a very valuable commodity at the time. Still, people have come to expect wedding rings, and a man who *really* gave his bride a toy would be seen as the ultimate cheapskate. This would be true even in the secular world – perhaps even more so, because there would be no religious law to fall back on. It just would not feel like a real wedding without the ring.

Traditions and rituals play an important role in group identity, and change does not happen overnight in any community. I am old enough to remember when artificial Christmas trees were just coming on the market. Most of my Christian neighbors refused to buy them because they were fakes. They felt that a plastic tree would cheapen the holiday. It has taken a couple generations for artificial trees to catch on, and there are still people today who want real ones. Cutting down a fir tree might not seem as traumatic to some as slaughtering a chicken, but the principle is the same. It is very hard to suddenly change a centuries-old tradition.

I can also remember a time when grape juice was rarely available at Jewish religious functions as an alternative to wine for *Kiddush* and Passover – so much so, that when I published an article called "The Chemically-free Seder" in 1984, it was considered radical. In terms of Jewish law, both grape wine and juice are "fruit of the vine" (*pri ha-gafen)* and interchangeable in terms of ritual. But it just never occurred to anybody that there were people who, for various reasons, abstained from alcohol. Nowadays, with a rise in awareness, it is much more common to have grape juice on hand.

Here is a third example: Since meat is traditionally served on the Sabbath, it is forbidden to butter the bread, because meat and dairy are never served together in a kosher home. When we became vegetarians, my wife Caryl, who prefers buttered bread in general, began buttering her *challah* (a traditional bread) at the Sabbath table. There is absolutely no reason not to do this if no meat is being served. Yet it took me a very long time before I was able to do it without feeling strange. I'm willing to bet that for some Jews, even *reading* about buttered *challah* will seem like a sacrilege. This may be hard for secular people to understand, but for those who come from long-standing traditions, making ritual changes – even positive ones – can create a certain cognitive dissonance.

Nevertheless, changes can and do take place. In the fall of 2014, just before Rosh Hashanah, a Chabad Hasid called from California to thank me for putting my materials online. He had first found my videos on YouTube, and then spent *three hours* reading my blog. The result? He said it "changed his thinking." He also said the materials he found on PETA, The

Alliance, and other sites did not move him because it was "all politics." I was the only one he had found who came at it from the standpoint of Jewish spirituality. As a result, he does not use chickens for *Kapporos* anymore, and is eating far less meat.

It is very likely that this man will refer others to my blog. He will also discuss his change of heart, perhaps around the Sabbath table with his family, or in a Torah study group at his synagogue, where debates are traditionally hot and heavy. He will probably explain that his decision was not made because of the Alliance protests or the PETA website. It was made because I was arguing *from within the Hasidic worldview,* and I did it with knowledge and respect. It might even happen that his rabbi will eventually address the issue from the pulpit.

But little, if any, of this will ever appear in the media, even though change is happening. And for every person who contacts me, there are many more who read the blog but never tell me about it. As of this writing, my blog gets almost 4000 "hits" per month. That's well over 100 people per day.

As I said before, Orthodox rabbis do not speak with one voice on *Kapporos*. Hasidic Jews may "all look alike" to outsiders, but they do not all *think* alike. There is no "pope" in Judaism who rules for everyone. Hasidic Rebbes each hold authority over their own branch of Hasidism, but not over everyone else.[83] Even in communities where *Kapporos* is usually done with chickens, the individual is free to use money instead, should he or she so choose. Nor would their rabbi forbid doing so. Even the Chabad Hasidim – the very group to which Rabbi Hecht's *Kapporos* centers belong – even they recognize on their official website that money is an acceptable alternative.

While it is true that sometimes rabbis do rule on issues for their whole congregation, it is also true that individuals can make individual choices, often voting with their feet. People may not choose to join Davis at the barricades, but individually they can and do choose not to use chickens.

---

[83] Chabad Hasidim are fond of referring to their late leader as "the Rebbe" as if he were the only one. And some Chabadniks do make the claim that their Rebbe speaks for all Jews. Because Chabad is tech savvy and widespread, many people assume that "Hasidic" and "Chabad" are synonymous. However, there are other groups, each with their own Rebbe and traditions.

However, the reasons that Jews give for substituting money may not be the same as those advocated by the activists. This can become a barrier to working together for change. Jews often reject vegetarian arguments because of groups like PETA, while activists reject Jewish arguments because they are not vegan enough. Meanwhile, the chickens continue to suffer.

There is an old Yiddish saying that "where you find two Jews you will have three opinions." Judaism stresses *actions* rather than defining dogmatic reasons for *why* we do something. For example, it is clearly stated in the Torah that Jews do not eat pork. No reason is given for this rule; it just is. In Jewish law this is called a *chok,* a religious decree with no apparent logical reason. But since human beings tend to look for meaning in things, numerous explanations have been offered over the centuries, ranging from "it's God's will" to "pigs carry trichinosis" and everything in between. Jews are free to adopt any personal explanation they want, as long as they obey the prohibition and don't eat pork.

My approach is equally pragmatic. Use the argument that is most effective, even if it's not what you personally believe, as long as there is some truth in it. In the end it does not really matter whether somebody quits using chickens out of veganism, a desire to give money to the poor, concerns about Jewish law, concerns about wasting meat, concerns about bad publicity, or some other personal reason. To the chickens the results will be exactly the same; they get to live. In the following sections, I will present a number of reasons to use money instead of chickens, *and they are all equally valid.*

The biblical/halachic basis for substituting money

In the days of Moses, all sacrifices – indeed, all slaughtering in general – took place at the *Mishkan* (Tabernacle) in the center of the camp. Because everyone was living close together around the *Mishkan,* transporting animals was not a problem.

However, once the people crossed the Jordan and began to spread out and settle down in various communities, the problem arose of how to bring sacrifices to the *Mishkan* (and later the Jerusalem Temple) without undue suffering on the part of the animals. For secular purposes, local slaughtering was now permitted (Deut. 12:15). But there was still the problem of how to bring religious offerings, which had to be perfect without any blemish. The reality of traveling long distances on foot often meant injuries along the way, which would disqualify the animals as offerings, as well as cause fruits to spoil.

Therefore, the Torah states that people who lived too far away to bring their tithes in animals or produce could "turn it into money" and bring that instead: "Then shall you turn it into money, and bind up the money in your hand, and shall go to the place which the Lord your God shall choose." (Deut. 14:24-26). From this came the current *Kapporos* custom of taking money, perhaps the value of the fowl or a symbolic multiple of 18, wrapping it in a handkerchief or other cloth ("bind up the money in your hand") and waving this instead of a fowl.

In the light of what we have already discussed about transporting chickens in cramped cages, it would seem that the same principle regarding long distances applies today as it did in biblical times, and giving money is a better option. This substitution maintains the tradition of giving charity to the poor (with money instead of a chicken), has been endorsed by many rabbis, and is mentioned in many prayer books, including the *Artscroll Siddur* used in many Orthodox synagogues.

There is also the additional problem, already raised in the *Shulchan Arukh* in the 16th century, of animals experiencing fear during slaughtering from seeing other animals slaughtered in front of them, which is forbidden. This fear can even cause the lungs to shrivel and render the meat not kosher (*Shulchan Arukh* Yoreh Deah 36:14).

The *Yad Ephraim,* commenting on this ruling, refers specifically to the problem of many people standing in line side-by-side with fowl to be slaughtered for *Kapparos,* saying, "And this [slaughtering of one bird in the sight of another] is not correct for this is a violation of *tsa'ar ba'alei chaim…* and there is no greater infraction of animal cruelty than this. And we do not say that fowl do not have feelings, for behold it was just described that sometimes their lung is shriveled due to the sight of slaughter before them" (*Yad Ephraim*, Yoreh Deah 34:14).

The author of *Yad Ephraim*, Rabbi Ephraim Zalman ben Menachem Margoliot (1762-1828), was writing just as Cartesianism was beginning to influence the Jewish community (see Chapter 5). Hence the need to clarify that "we do not say that fowl do not have feelings." This opinion is in line with Maimonides, Nachman of Breslov, and Samson Raphael Hirsch, all of whom we have previously quoted as affirming that animals feel fear and pain. Unfortunately, these teachings are not as well known today – a subject we shall explore further in Chapter 7 under "humane education." For now, let us look at some recent rabbinical opinions about the suffering of chickens during *Kapporos* under modern conditions.

Rabbis who endorse using money

In chapter 2 we discussed several rabbis who opposed *Kapporos* as a pagan superstition. But recently there have also been many rabbis who, while they did not condemn the ceremony as such, nevertheless felt, for various reasons, that using money is a better option. These rabbis include but are not limited to:

Rabbi David Rosen, International Director of Interreligious Affairs for the American Jewish Committee and Former Chief Rabbi of Ireland, wrote: "Those who wish to fulfill this custom can do so fully and indeed in a far more halachically acceptable manner by using money as a substitute, as proposed by many Jewish authorities."

The renowned Haredi kabbalist, Rabbi Yitzchak Kadouri (died in 2006) wrote that one should abstain from using chickens for *Kapparos* due to "the cruelty to animals, which is prohibited by the Torah, and *kashrut* problems."

Rabbi Shlomo Zalman Auerbach (1910-1995), a leading authority on Jewish law and head of the Kol Torah yeshiva in Jerusalem, also cited halachic problems and stopped using animals for *Kapparos,* giving money to charity instead.

Rabbi David Stav of the Tzohar Rabbonim organization came out against performing the ritual with chickens in 2014. He concedes that the *minhag* dates back quite some time and those who perform *Kapporos* have a legitimate source for their custom. However, he feels that even with this being the case, it is preferable to do *Kapporos* with money, not with a chicken, because the realities that exist today lead to unacceptable suffering for the chickens as well as concerns regarding the integrity of the slaughtering under far less than optimal conditions.[84]

Rabbi Yonah Bookstein, an Orthodox rabbi in Los Angeles, pleaded with the Jewish community in 2014, "Today's travesty of *Kapporos* transgresses major Torah prohibitions and needs to be changed." He concedes that in a case where the ritual can be done properly, then *halachah* says it is permissible. But all too often the ritual is being performed improperly, and the *minhag* is distorted. Then many serious sins are committed. Therefore it is better to use money.[85]

The late **Rabbi Ovadiah Yosef**, a spiritual leader of Israel's Shas party (very Orthodox) expressed serious concern that the volume of chickens being slaughtered would cause overworked *shochtim* to be careless and not do it properly, rendering the chickens unkosher. He did not go so far as to forbid using chickens, but he did remind his followers that Rabbi Joseph Caro was "against this thing," referring to Caro's belief that it was a pagan custom.[86]

Rabbi David Lau, newly elected Ashkenazi Chief Rabbi of Israel, in 2013, warned *Kapparos* organizers that the failure to treat animals decently is a violation of religious law.

Rabbi Meir Hirsch, a member of the Neturei Karta community in Jerusalem (about as "ultra-Orthodox" as one can get) began having second thoughts when he noticed chickens squawking in distress in plastic cages near his house. "Butchers bring the chickens from the farm at night, and they spend all day in the sun without food or drink," said Hirsch. "You cannot perform a

---

[84] *Ibid.*

[85] http://thejewishlink.com/archives/7113#sthash.gaPYKInD.dpbs

[86] http://www.haaretz.com/print-edition/news/shas-spiritual-leader-calls-for-caution-with-kapparot-ceremony-1.229467

commandment by committing a sin." Hirsch said he now waves a $10 bill above his head instead of a chicken.[87]

Rabbi Natan Slifkin, the "zoo rabbi" whose specialty is animals and biology, does not outrightly forbid using chickens. However, he does say the following about *Kapporos* under modern conditions: "While it is permitted to cause suffering to animals for material or spiritual benefit, the suffering in this case is quite needless. It would seem that causing needless suffering to animals is a Biblical prohibition that far outweighs the value of a custom. Furthermore, it would seem to fundamentally negate much of the significance of the *Kapparos* ritual... On the eve of the Day of Judgment, when there is a special need to earn Divine mercy, it is surely counterproductive to inflict needless suffering upon creatures."[88]

In 2010, **Rabbi Steven Weil,** CEO of the Orthodox Union of Rabbis in New York City, told the Alliance to End Chickens as Kaporos that the OU opposes using chickens due to the ritual's "insensitivity" to the birds and the lack of historical foundation.

Shlomo Aviner, head of Jerusalem's Ateret Yeshiva, rabbi of the settlement of Beit El, and one of religious Zionism's most influential leaders, issued a religious ruling that, rather than slaughtering an animal, giving money to the poor is a better method of absolving oneself of transgressions, stating in a letter to the SPCA: "Because this is not a binding obligation but a custom, in light of problems related to *kashrut* and the suffering of animals, and given the edicts of the aforementioned rabbis, a recommendation must be made to favor performing *Kapparot* through money, by performing the great mitzvah of providing for the needy."[89]

---

[87] http://www.vosizneias.com/post/read/92696//2011/10/06/jerusalem-ap-report-neturai-karta-gets-on-the-bandwagon-to-rethink-kaparot-yom-kippur-ritual/

[88] Slifkin, *Man and Beast,* p. 207.

[89] http://www.haaretz.com/news/national/leading-rabbi-joins-animal-rights-group-s-campaign-against-kaparot-1.313459

The late **Rabbi Chaim David HaLevy,** former Sephardic Chief Rabbi of Tel Aviv, similarly wrote in his well-accepted series of Halachic works, *Aseh Lekha Rav*: "Why should we, specifically on the eve of the holy day of Yom Kippur, be cruel to animals for no reason, and slaughter them without mercy, just as we are about to request compassion for ourselves from the living God. (He is the same Rabbi HaLevy who issued the decree against wearing fur that we cited in chapter 5.)

* * *

The list goes on, with new names added every year. Note that most of these rabbinic authorities (all of whom are Orthodox, by the way) have cited the cruelty and suffering of the birds *under modern conditions* as a violation of *tza'ar ba'alei chayyim*. That is currently the most acceptable argument among Orthodox Jews according to Jewish law.

This is one reason why I called this book *Kapporos Then and Now*. Back *then* the ritual may well have had some spiritual validity; but *now* any benefit is canceled out by the modern cruelties involved. This fits with the statements I cited above. Not one of these rabbis has said it is morally wrong to kill a chicken. Not one of them has condemned their ancestors for having used chickens in the past. All have focused, in one way or another, on the specific problems of today.

Also note that most of these rabbis are not vegetarians – as for example, the CEO of the Orthodox Union, which certifies kosher meats, but who nevertheless said his organization does not endorse *Kapporos* with chickens, thus indicating that one does not have to be vegetarian in order to oppose this particular ceremony. I know many vegans believe that slaughter of any kind is and always has been cruel, and they may be right. Some animal rights activists, like Gary Francione, go so far as to say that any compromise with using animals is wrong, and that a total "abolitionist approach" is the only way to address animal issues. But if protesters take this "all or nothing" approach, they get into the very sticky issue of whether the Torah itself is cruel because it allows meat eating. And if you say that, then Orthodox Jews will shut down and the dialogue is ended. So everyone in the "End Chickens as Kapporos" movement needs to stop and ask themselves: Which is more important, to be politically correct in the vegan world, or to be effective in the Hasidic world where the ceremony is being practiced?

You cannot commit a sin to do a mitzvah

In chapter 4 we went into considerable detail about the mystical doctrine of "raising holy sparks" in order to do *tikkun olam,* repairing the universe. I therefore will not repeat myself here, except to point out what has already been said by some of the rabbis above: *You cannot commit a sin to do a mitzvah* – or a *minhag* for that matter. Not only does one cancel the other out, it can make things *worse* than if you did nothing at all.

Recall the story about Rabbi Isaac Luria (the Holy Ari) and the man who forgot to feed his chickens that I told in Chapter 4. This story comes from *Shivchei Ha-Ari,* a classical text – and yet few Jews are even aware of it today. *Kapporos* practitioners are quick to point out that Rabbi Luria did the ritual with chickens, but are seldom aware of this *other* side of Luria; namely, that he was very sensitive to the suffering of animals and recommended that his disciples eat a minimum of meat. His closest disciple, Rabbi Chaim Vital, wrote: "My master was careful never to kill any insect, even the smallest and least of them, such as fleas, lice and flies – even if they were causing him pain." *(Sha'ar HaMitzvot,* section on Noah)

We certainly do not see this level of sensitivity at today's *Kapporos* centers, where chickens are often roughly handled without much thought. Rabbi Luria was not a vegetarian, and he endorsed *Kapporos,* but he also took "raising holy sparks" very seriously. If he avoided harming even insects unnecessarily, then surely he must have been careful with chickens. As for *Kapparos,* he prescribed a complex set of kabbalistic meditations *(kavannot)* that the *shochet* must have in mind:

> The *shochet* should slaughter the chicken immediately after the individual swings it around his head; the chicken should not be left in a box to be slaughtered later. While slaughtering the chicken, the *shochet* should have in mind that he seeks to "sweeten" the five *Gevurot* [judgments] in the *Yesod ha'Malchut* [a level

121

on the Kabbalistic Tree.] He should also have in mind to repair the human souls that are reincarnated in the chicken, and to repair the soul of the individual for whom he slaughters the chicken.[90]

How many of the *shochtim* at modern *Kapporos* centers even know of this teaching, let alone have the proper spiritual focus to carry it out? Or enough time to center themselves before slaughtering each individual chicken? Recall what I said in Chapter 3 about the Chabad rabbi who told me that it was not necessary for the *shochet* to have *kavannah* when he slaughters. Rabbi Luria would not have agreed. Neither would the Baal Shem Tov. *Kavannah* has traditionally been part of the ritual.

In a recent discussion on Amazon, when I brought up the topic of human souls reincarnated in animals as mentioned above, I was taken to task by another Orthodox Jew who accused me of being outside the mainstream, saying: "The very fact that you wrote 'The Baal Shem Tov himself talked to human souls reincarnated as animals' tells me how out of touch you are with mainstream Orthodox Judaism. Not only are you on the fringe, you are on the fringe of the fringe."

This heckler even went so far as to suggest that I should *remove my photo* from my Amazon profile, claiming that my Hasidic appearance would "mislead" people into thinking my remarks were a legitimate part of Judaism. He was that unfamiliar with the teachings of both the Ari and the Baal Shem Tov! Yet the stories I was referring to are in *Shivchei Ha-Ari* (about Luria) and *Shivchei Ha-Besht* (about the Baal Shem Tov), both classic texts which are available in English for those who don't know Hebrew (see bibliography).

If people are going to be citing these teachers in support of doing *Kapporos* with chickens, then they should at least be familiar with the rest of their teachings to put it into proper context. The Safed Kabbalists, and later the Hasidic masters, did indeed believe that human souls sometimes reincarnated as animals, and that releasing these souls was part of the *tikkun*

---

[90] As explained by Rabbi Eli J. Mansour on the "Daily Halalcha" series at: https://www.dailyhalacha.com/displayRead.asp?readID=2384

process.[91] Many Hasidim and kabbalists still believe this, even if it is no longer common knowledge among modern Jews.

There is an old Hasidic story that goes like this: When there was danger threatening the Jewish community, The Baal Shem Tov would go to a certain place in the forest, light a fire, say a prayer, and the threat was averted. In the next generation, his disciple, the Maggid of Mezeritch, no longer knew how to light the fire, but he would go to the place in the forest, say the prayer, and it was answered. Yet another generation, and Rabbi Moshe-Leib of Sasov would go into the forest and say: "I do not know how to light the fire. I do not know the prayer. But I still know the place in the forest and this must be sufficient." And it was. In the fourth generation, it fell to Rabbi Israel of Rizhyn to save his people from misfortune. Sitting at home with his head in his hands, he did not know how to light the fire, or say the prayer, or even find the place in the forest. All he could do was tell the story. And still it was enough.

Today many people have forgotten the story. Oh, they know the words all right, but the story does not resonate with their souls, because *they have forgotten the place in the forest.* I have always felt it was highly significant that the forest was last thing to be lost in this story. As long as we had the connection to God's living creation that the Baal Shem Tov knew so well, the miracles worked. But now we no longer have that connection. Nor do we hold our heads in our hands and mourn the loss. Most of us do not even know what is missing.

Kapporos chicken sellers often unwittingly commit the exact same sin that was condemned by Rabbi Luria in the 16th century, namely, leaving their chickens go without food and water. Practitioners will point out that it is the usual practice not to feed birds before slaughter, because a full crop might prevent making the cut properly. This is true. However, under normal circumstances the birds do not go for *days* without eating as often happens at *Kapporos* sites.

---

[91] See for example *Shiur Komah* by Moses Cordovero and *Sefer HaGilgulim* by Chaim Vital. See also Chapter 5: Animals and Reincarnation" in Rabbi Dovid Sear's *A Vision of Eden: Animal Welfare and Vegetarianism in Jewish Law and Mysticism,"* which cites more sources.

In the *stetl* world, the *Kapporos* chickens were slaughtered in the early morning, often captured before sunrise while they were still roosting. Under those conditions, the chickens did not go hungry any longer than they normally would overnight. However, today's chickens are first packed into crates, then driven long distances to the city, where they are stacked in warehouses or other sites to await their fate.

Since the ritual can be done any time during the Ten Days of Repentance, the birds are likely to sit there for days on end without any food or water. In many cases, one can see dead chickens in the cages that apparently died of hunger and thirst. In 2013, thousands of chickens in New York City died in their crates during an abnormal heat wave.[92] Others have been left to thirst and hunger over the Sabbath or even on Yom Kippur itself. This violates the biblical commandment to feed our animals before we feed ourselves.[93] Clearly it is cruelty to animals, as stated by many of the rabbis I cited above. I shudder to think how many prayers are blocked on Yom Kippur because of this sin. The Holy Ari would have been horrified.

In the Luria story, the cries of the hungry chickens were blocking their owner's prayers and Torah study from rising to Heaven. Now, stop and listen to the voices of all those hungry, thirsty chickens at the *Kapporos* centers. These chickens are suffering just as much as those in the Luria story. In fact, they are probably suffering more, because chickens in the 16th century were not crammed into shipping crates for days on end.

So ask yourself: Are all those thousands of sad cries rising to Heaven and canceling out your Torah and mitzvahs, heaven forbid? Even worse, are they canceling out the prayers of the whole Jewish community? At the very time when we are praying for God's mercy in the coming year? Do you *really* want to take the risk that this is literally true?

---

[92] http://www.bkmag.com/2013/09/13/orthodox-jews-didnt-kill-thousands-of-chickens-in-brooklyn-heat-stroke-did/

[93] Based on Deuteronomy 11:15. Pious people in the past took great care to observe this mitzvah. It is told that Rabbi Aharon Rokeach, the Belzer Rebbe, would buy a share in a horse, just so he could observe this mitzvah. Before eating, he would often check to see that the animal was properly taken care of. Cited in *Rescuing the Rebbe of Belz* by Yosef Israel (Artscroll - Mesorah Publications, 2005).

The sin of wastefulness

In addition to the sin of animal cruelty, there can also be the sin of *bal tashchit* – wanton wastefulness. As I explained in previous chapters, it was the normal practice to give the chicken or its value to the poor. Nowadays, however, many of the *Kapporos* chickens are ending up in the city dump. There are a number of reasons for this:

- In the past, Jews took their chickens home, to clean and kasher them for the pre-Yom Kippur meal, but today few people do this anymore;

- Many of the chickens have blemishes that render them unkosher in the first place. Recall what we said earlier about weak legs and broken bones in modern breeds. If an animal cannot walk, it is considered too sick to be kosher;

- Many of the *shochtim* at these centers are either inexperienced or too overworked to carefully examine their knives or to slaughter properly, rendering the chickens *neveila* (not kosher);

- There are no on-site refrigeration facilities to prevent the chickens from spoiling before they can be delivered to food shelves or other facilities.

- Some people consider the act of slaughtering to be the most important aspect of the ritual, and do not want the dead chicken or care what happens to it.

To be sure, there are some practitioners who do take their chickens home to eat, and some centers that process them properly and give them to charity. But all too often, the dead birds are just dumped into garbage bags and hauled off to the landfill. This kind of wanton destruction would *never* have happened a hundred years ago. It is purely a modern phenomenon that makes a travesty of the tradition.

In addition, it makes the Jewish community look bad in the eyes of the non-Jewish world to be wasting food when people in their own city are going hungry. Under online articles about chickens ending up in the dump I found numerous comments asking why they were not given to the local food shelves. The answer was often that the chickens were not kosher. But non-Jews do not *care* if the meat is kosher. In fact, meat that is declared unkosher after slaughter is routinely sold to the non-Jewish market in the commercial industry. So why, these commenters ask, are the *Kapporos* chickens sent to the dump instead of going to soup lines for the homeless?

Public scandals and antisemitism

There is a Yiddish expression, *shanda fur di goyim,* which translates roughly as "a scandal for the nations" (that is, the non-Jews.) In other words, don't do something that will arouse hatred and/or violence toward the Jewish community. Like other minorities, Jews have learned the hard way that when one member does something wrong, the whole community gets blamed. This is especially true of highly visible Jews like Haredim and Hasidim, whose mode of dress makes them recognizable as easy targets. Antisemitism is deeply engrained in Western culture, with a tendency to judge Jews more harshly for actions similar to those in the gentile community.

Kapporos practitioners have accused the animal rights activists of doing exactly that. They see the protesters as singling them out, stirring up hatred against their communities, and making trouble for Jews in general. Angry accusations of antisemitism fly across the protest barriers and abound on the Internet. I myself have gotten hate mail accusing me of "stirring up trouble" and creating a *shanda* by getting publicly involved in this issue. Nor are Hasidim the only ones who have second thoughts about supporting the anti-*Kapporos* campaign.

Sherry F. Colb, Professor of Law and Charles Evans Hughes Scholar at Cornell Law School, in a critique of the anti-*Kapporos* campaign, expresses concern that singling out *Kapporos* for protests will attract the wrong people:

126

The reason is that perhaps what makes the *Kapporos* ritual objectionable to some people who learn of the campaign against it may have as much to do with its apparent primitiveness as it does with the fact that it hurts animals. Stated differently, the *Kapporos* cere- mony, for many, will look different from other in- stances of animal cruelty because it is "weird," because it is seemingly pointless and irrational, and because it involves people who may be wearing unusual, Hasidic garb. Protests that highlight *Kapporos,* even when ini- tiated in good faith, can easily attract people whose opposition to the practice is frankly rooted in prejudice rather than in concern for animals.[94]

Colb goes on to say that labeling *Kapporos* as cruel without also objecting to similar conditions in the secular meat industry is prejudiced. Therefore, although she is both a Jew and a vegan who cares about animal suffering, she does not feel she can wholeheartedly endorse the Alliance campaign.

Animal activist Gary L. Francione, who is both a vegan and a full professor at Rutgers University School of Law, goes further. After taking part in a panel discussion on *Kapporos* at the New York City Bar Association, he outrightly urged his fel- low vegans not to support Davis' campaign:

Why? Nothing Karen showed in her presentation is behavior that does not occur as part of the process of slaughtering all chickens. For example, she showed pictures of what appeared to be Hasidic men holding the chickens in ways that caused them pain. But the only difference between how chickens are often held and handled at slaughterhouses, and how they are held or handled at the *Kapporos* event, is the fact that in the latter, it is Hasidim or other Jews doing the holding and handling. If these poor birds were not used in the *Kapporos* ritual, they would have been sent to the slaughterhouse and would have had the exact same

---

[94] https://verdict.justia.com/2014/10/01/singling-jewish-kaporos-criticism

fate. This is a perfect example of what is wrong with single-issue campaigns: they encourage the idea that what some group does is worse than what the rest of us do... I think that the *Kapporos* campaign enables and facilitates antisemitism.[95]

Francione requested that Davis post a disclaimer on her site and in all future mailings, stating that "the Alliance does not maintain that anyone involved in the *Kapporos* event is engaged in conduct that is morally more odious than those who engage in the slaughter of chickens in non-religious contexts," as well as state that the Alliance believes veganism to be the answer. After Davis failed to do this, Francione stated in an addenda to his original article: "I have come, reluctantly, to the conclusion that this campaign is deliberately exploiting and promoting antisemitism." He therefore urged people not to support it.

Having worked with Davis myself, I can attest that Francione is wrong; she is not deliberately intending to arouse hatred or exploit antisemitism. She is simply ignorant of Hasidic culture, or the Jewish community in general, as we noted at the beginning of this chapter and in several other places in this book. She is also naïve about how her words can be twisted and misused by those who do have prejudices against Jews.

However, she does sincerely believe that what she is doing is for the good of the chickens and not an attack on Jews as such. Unfortunately, neither anthropology nor Jewish theology is her area of expertise, and she often misinterprets what she sees or reads. Frankly, I think she is now in way over her head on this issue. She barged in like a runaway tank in a minefield, and it all blew up in her face.

As for Francione's demand that the Alliance preach veganism, I disagree. In this area he, too, is ignorant of Hasidic culture. As I have pointed out several times in this book, "ethical veganism" is *not* an effective way to get Orthodox Jews to listen. I myself have encouraged Davis *not* to mix in veganism, especially since she goes way beyond diet toward making it al-

---

[95] http://www.abolitionistapproach.com/the-kapparos-campaign-a-good-example-whats-wrong-single-issue-campaigns/#.VS_BO_nF-q8

most a religion. Those who insist that Veganism Is The Only Way are not going to be very effective in this campaign.

Refer back to the list of rabbis I cited earlier; *not one of them* used veganism as the reason for not using chickens. Francione may not like that – he considers veganism to be the absolute baseline for everything, and rejects any kind of compromise on that position. So he probably won't like this book very much, either. But then again, I'm not writing it for him.

To her credit, Davis has disabled the "comments" option on the Alliance's YouTube channel in order to stop the posting of hateful comments about Jews. At my suggestion, a disclaimer was also added to the "About" section of their Facebook page, stating:

> "We are opposed to this particular ceremony, not Hasidic culture in general. We recognize that there is much that is beautiful in the Hasidic way of life. Comments attacking or expressing prejudice against Hasidic Jews will not be tolerated."

Unfortunately, this statement is somewhat buried on the page, due to Facebook's tendency to truncate things. You must go to "About," click "Mission," then "see more," and scroll down a ways to find it. If it were my choice, it would be on the homepage. But at least it now exists and can be invoked as needed. However, the very fact that this was necessary at all should tell Davis she is sending the wrong message. She herself might not be antisemitic, but some of her readers and viewers definitely are. I have encountered some pretty prejudiced people within the animal rights movement over the years.

It is also true that the practice of *Kapporos* itself arouses antisemitism in people who are anything but animal lovers. One need only spend time reading the comments under online articles about *Kapporos* to see their horrified reactions to the public slaughter of chickens. In some cases, the comments are obviously made by neo-Nazis or other hate groups. Indeed, the articles – both pro and con – seem to attract such people, many of whom have nothing better to do than troll the Internet posting canned hate speeches about Jews. In that sense, Francione is right: the campaign does stir up antisemitism.

But there are also many others who are not antisemites at all, just ordinary people who are shocked at seeing videos and photos of what they perceive as unnecessary cruelty. For many, this is their only awareness of Hasidism, and it is very, very negative. It is these people that we should be the most worried about. If their first impression of Orthodox Jews is one of cruelty, it will be difficult to change that opinion later.

As I stated in Chapter 1, part of the problem is the rise of modern technology, enabling everyone to "air dirty laundry" in public. Anybody with a camera can now post anything they want online, and it can go viral overnight. People who, in the past, might have read about *Kapporos* as a quaint custom in a book can now see it on YouTube in living color. Many Jews see this as a *shanda* and are concerned about the bad publicity, as well as the impact on their own neighborhoods.

A man named Daniel Schwartz[96] wrote in an online discussion with Rabbi Natan Slifkin about *Kapporos*:

"Where I live (Monsey), there is a far more serious issue: *chillul Hashem* (desecration of God's Name). Every year, there is a big *Kapparot* center set up. The people who run it routinely violate local ordinances, leaving blood, innards, feces, feathers etc. strewn about. The stench is awful. Chickens literally die in the crates from dehydration. Every year, the local non-Jewish population looks upon this with sheer and utter disgust (who could blame them? It is disgusting). The health department levies fines, which are not paid but resolved politically, and people become more and more resentful of the Jewish community."[97]

There are those who will dismiss this man's opinion – and mine – by calling us "self-hating Jews," a catchall phrase used nowadays to shoot down anybody whose opinions they don't like. But my concerns are not out of self-hate, whatever that means. They are based on my love of Judaism and the Jewish

---

[96] No relation, as far as I know, to Professor Richard H. Schwartz.

[97] http://www.rationalistjudaism.com/2010/09/kapporos.html

community. And my love of our Heavenly Creator. I have a genuine concern that we are committing a *chillul Hashem,* defaming the name of God in public. People see the bloody slaughter and come to the conclusion that "the God of the Jews" is heartless and cruel. This is hardly serving as "a light unto the nations." *Chillul Hashem* is a serious sin, one that in previous centuries was punishable by ostracism or worse.

Nowadays, however, there is a certain "devil may care" attitude among many Jews that says we shouldn't give a damn what the non-Jews think. Partly this is a reaction to the Holocaust, the reasoning being, that the world did not care about the Jews back then, so why should Jews care what the world thinks now? This is especially true among Israelis. The early founders of Israel rejected what they saw as "ghetto Judaism" in favor of developing a tougher, more assertive type of Jew. In discussing possible reasons why Israelis seem to care less about animals than Americans, Rabbi Slifkin writes:

> "It is difficult to determine whether the rate of cruelty to animals in the Orthodox Jewish and/or Israeli community than in the wider community. But one thing is clear — it is definitely higher than it should be. There are cultural factors that perhaps account for this... Life in Israel is a tough struggle, and Israelis often have less sensitivity than Westerners used to an easier world. Regardless of the causes, however, it is a problem that should be addressed.[98]

Those who do care about public opinion are often painted as the Jewish equivalent of Uncle Toms. Others go out of their way to heckle activists with insults and foul language, especially on the Internet. But this is not only unfair; it is dangerous, both spiritually and socially. We Jews do not live in a vacuum. We are part of a global community, and what we do is only a mouse click away for all to see. And that goes for comments we make online. We should indeed care what the general public thinks about the mass slaughter of chickens that often end up in the city dump. When we reply with callousness

---

[98] Slifkin, *Man and Beast,* pp. 159-60.

end up in the city dump. When we reply with callousness and harsh profanity, we desecrate the Name of God.

The law of the land is the law

There is also another consideration, namely, "the law of the land is the law" *(dina malchus dina)*. In Jewish law this means that when it comes to secular issues, we obey the local rules and ordinances. Most cities have laws against animal cruelty and public slaughter, as well as prohibiting health hazards. Madison, Wisconsin, for example, allows residents to keep up to four backyard hens, but no roosters and no slaughtering.[99] Permits are required, and there are regulations regarding shelter, noise, smells, cleanliness, etc.

Judaism also has laws against animal cruelty but, unfortunately, they are not often taught in much depth today. Partly this is because urban Jews don't have much contact with animals, so the laws of *tza'ar ba'alei chayyim* remain in the realm of theory for many people. However, this is no excuse. All of Torah is important, even those things that we cannot personally carry out. As our Sages taught: "Be as careful with a minor mitzvah as with a major one, for you do not know the value of a mitzvah" *(Pirkei Avot)*. It may well be that in the eyes of God animal cruelty is a much bigger sin than people today normally regard it. "Major" and "minor" are relative terms.

Then there is the issue of health hazards, which also come under the category of *dina malchus dina.* With current concerns about bird flu (a major outbreak of which is happening on Minnesota turkey and chicken farms as I write this) people living near *Kapporos* centers are understandably worried about unsanitary conditions, as well as seeing blood and feathers on the public streets. Chicken blood can also carry salmonella. While it is not illegal to kill a chicken, it is indeed against the law to treat it cruelly or create a public health hazard.

The *Kapporos* practitioners have countered that this is a religious practice and protected by the First Amendment. Which is true. But just because we *can* do something does not necessarily mean we *should* do it. The First Amendment does

---

[99] http://www.backyardchickens.com/a/madison-wisconsin-chicken-ordinance

not necessarily protect those people who abandon chickens to starve or leave a foul mess behind. "Freedom of religion" is not a blank check to behave however you want. As we have said before in this book, you cannot commit a sin to do a mitzvah.

Animal rights groups, most notably Karen Davis's United Poultry Concerns, have tried to shut down *Kapporos* centers by filing lawsuits and invoking the health department and other agencies. Most of these efforts have failed. Davis claims that nothing is being done because the Jewish community has a lot of money and political clout. That may be true, but it is more likely that the police do not want to get embroiled in a First Amendment controversy. Given the amount of violent crime in any large city, they would rather put their resources elsewhere besides shutting down a religious ceremony that will end in a few days anyway.

So it is up to us to police ourselves. To those Jews who feel they must do this ceremony with chickens, I say: You should also take into account the public reactions. Jewish law might interpret "human need" as permitting the practice, but local laws and public opinion often define "animal cruelty" more strictly, taking into account the health regulations and public opinion. If "the law of the land is the law," then we should obey it, if only to avoid looking bad to the rest of the world. We should ask ourselves: Is it really worth it to arouse the hatred of our neighbors against us, when there is a perfectly acceptable, more compassionate alternative? Do you really want to be responsible for creating a public *shanda?*

Using money avoids all these problems

The High Holy Days liturgy says, "Repentance, prayer, and *charity* avert the evil decree." Giving money to charity before Yom Kippur has a long and honored history. According to Menachem Friedman, an expert on Jewish religious society in Israel, replacing chickens with donations to charity is a rising trend in Israel and around the world. "There is also a very accepted custom in synagogues that in the afternoon, people bring their money for *Kapparot,* and everyone chooses the charity he wants to support," he said.[100]

Giving money to charity instead of using a chicken eliminates all the questions of cruelty and *kashrut.* Plus, you can avoid absorbing negative spiritual energies *(klippot)* into your life and that of your family. Instead, you will be raising the "holy sparks" by caring for your fellow human beings and showing compassion to God's creatures. There are sparks in money as well as chickens; everything in the material world can be elevated in the service of God. And you can be sure that the monetary value of the chicken really is going to the poor and not to the city dump.

As for those organizations that use *Kapporos* as a fundraiser, they, too, would benefit by eliminating the cost of the chickens and transporting them, the overhead of renting space, and the need for cleanup afterward. Plus they would avoid any fines from the city for violations. Instead, all of the money would go directly to their specific causes.

You can also be more certain that your prayers are not being blocked from rising to Heaven because of cruelty to animals. You can be certain that you are making a real *tikkun:* the act of charity that averts the evil decree. Instead of arousing antisemitism, you will be demonstrating that Jews are generous people who feed the poor and care about others. In short, you will be helping the world instead of possibly adding to its burden of sin. For all these reasons, I believe it is time for us all to stop using chickens and give money instead.

---

[100] http://www.vosizneias.com/post/read/92696//2011/10/06/jerusalem-ap-report-neturai-karta-gets-on-the-bandwagon-to-rethink-kaparot-yom-kippur-ritual

Chapter 7:

Beyond Kapporos:

Re-connecting with God's Creation

When Rabbi Yaakov Yitzhak, the Seer of Lublin, was still a young boy, he loved going alone into the forest. His father asked him what he was doing out there, wasting his time wandering among the trees. "I am looking for God," the boy replied. His father then asked, "But isn't God everywhere, and isn't He everywhere the same?" The young Seer replied, "He is, but I am not." – Hasidic folktale

I did not grow up Hasidic. There are those who immediately discount me for that reason, arguing that I am "tainted" by the secular world and therefore not a "real" Hasid. However, I would quote back to them the old adage that "The *baal tshuvah* ("one who has returned" to Judaism) stands in a place where the perfect *Zaddik* (saint) cannot stand." Both places are good, and each has much to teach the other. Besides, I've been observant for decades now, so that should count for something.

All too often, returning to Judaism is expected to be a one-way street. Not so with me. I have learned a great deal from my fellow Hasidim, and for that I am very grateful. But there is also a great deal that I can teach them.

Growing up outside the community gave me some unique experiences that I can share to help enrich the understanding of those parts of Torah that relate to animals and nature. I will also cite the common Hasidic belief that every Jew is a "letter" of the Torah, and if even one letter is missing, the Torah is not complete. My special "letter" — as eccentric as it may seem to some people — is nevertheless important. Rabbi Ben Bag-Bag said in *Pirkei Avot:* "Turn the Torah over and over, for everything is in it." And that includes ecology, animals, and the environment.

Born in 1947, I went to public school, spent part of my summers at Scout camp, and otherwise participated in the world at large. I was what is now called a "free range kid," roaming the neighborhood on my bike, playing in the nearby woods, and spending a lot of time alone in nature. For part of my early childhood we lived on the edge of what my father called a "game preserve," where deer and pheasants were a common sight in the backyard. The exact location was long ago lost to urban sprawl, but the memories are still with me.

When I was in 5th grade we moved to a suburb outside Philadelphia. My father and I would often go to Longwood Gardens, where we marveled at the amazing diversity of flowers and plants, especially the orchid collection. This love of gardening and the outdoors shaped me for life. To this day, I think of my father whenever I see a new flower blooming. All of this gave me an experience of God's magnificent creation that is sadly lacking in the Jewish community today.

In 2005, journalist and author Richard Louv published a book called *Last Child in the Woods: Saving our Children from Nature Deficit Disorder.* "Nature deficit disorder" is not a medical diagnosis; it's a term he made up to describe what he sees as a very serious lack in childhood experience nowadays. The book examines some recent psychological research and concludes that direct exposure to nature – and especially unstructured solitude – is essential for healthy childhood development and for the physical and emotional health of children and adults. He is credited with helping to found an international movement to re-introduce children to nature.

Louv makes the point that, as parents have become more and more worried about child abductions, accidents on playgrounds, lawsuits, etc., the lives of children have become overly controlled and, more and more, their playtime is all happening indoors. With many housing developments and condos having covenants forbidding tree houses, playhouses, even gardens in some areas, kids who do have a backyard have only dull, boring places to play. Everything is being so tightly organized by adults, there is little or no free time for children to develop their own creativity. Kids no longer explore the woods free range like I did, learning from personal observations. As my friend Lee Weissman recently put it, "Nowadays you would have to take a Forest Appreciation seminar." In some places it is actually *illegal* to let your children walk or play outside alone.[102]

And we Jews are not immune to this. In fact, I would venture to say that within certain segments of the community, we have a *worse case* of nature deficit disorder than the general population. Partly this is because most Jews today are urban people. Although Jews were shepherds in biblical times, and even up until the High Middle Ages they worked farms and vineyards, the majority today are urbanized. True, there are Jewish farmers in Israel and a few other places, but by and large, whenever I speak of being "connected to the land," I get a political response about supporting Israel, rather than appreciation of nature.

In this chapter, I will go beyond the specific issue of *Kapporos* to examine nature deficit disorder in the Jewish community; how we got there, and how we can heal it. As Richard Schwartz[103] explained in his Foreword to this book, Judaism has many beautiful teachings about kindness to animals. It is his opinion – and I concur – that if these teachings were better known among Jews today, many problems of animal cruelty, including *Kapporos,* would resolve themselves.

Although this chapter is directed primarily at my fellow Jews, secular activists can also learn from it. As I have said numerous times in this book, you cannot change something without first understanding it. Keep in mind that as strange as the Hasidic world may seem to you, the world you live in is equally alien to Hasidim. Each side needs to respect the other.

---

[102] See freerangekids.com for more on this controversy.

[103] Professor Emeritus Richard H. Schwartz, College of Staten Island.

The parable of the spaceship

The Sages of *Pirkei Avot* spoke wisely: We should be careful of every mitzvah, major or minor, even those that we do not understand or see as relevant to our own lives. Consider the following parable: A spaceship filled with colonists takes off from Earth to settle on a planet circling a distant star. The people on board do not yet have "warp drive" like on *Star Trek,* so this journey is going to take several centuries. Generations will be born, live, and die aboard the ship, knowing nothing else but its interior as their entire world.

On board the spaceship are all the things the colonists will need to survive when they get to their destination; seeds for planting; frozen embryos of animals to grow upon arrival, and the laboratory equipment to do it; shelters to erect; machines for mining and manufacturing; instructions stored in the computer for how to farm, how to build, etc. In short, all that is necessary to make a home on their new world is right there on board their ship. And along with these things are very strict rules about how to care for everything during the long journey.

But as the generations go by, the practical knowledge about what these things are for begins to get lost. The people have the videos, the photos, the diagrams and instructions – but now it all seems like a fairy tale. And it also seems like a big bother to go through all those time-consuming, detailed protocols necessary to keep these things in good condition. The new generations begin to wonder why they are wasting time and valuable space. Insects? Birds? Trees? What are they? And why would we need them anyway, they argue. We have everything we need already, including replicators to manufacture food and other goods. So let's just throw this useless junk out the airlock, delete unused files from the computer, and free up more room for us in the here and now.

Upon arriving at their destination, the colonists soon discover that they are missing vital instructions and materials for building their community – the very stuff they had jettisoned along the way. How then can they survive outside the ship? Some people don't even want to leave the ship for the planet below. All their lives they have lived inside familiar steel walls.

138

Now the wide-open sky, fresh air, and endless horizons are just too big and frightening. So they remain inside.

Like the space colonists, we Jews are also on a centuries long, intergenerational journey. Our operation manual is the Torah. Every mitzvah has a purpose in the end – if we are far-sighted enough not to throw it overboard because it does not seem to have any value in the here and now.[104]

And that, my dear fellow Jews, is exactly what many of us have done with the Torah's teachings about animals, nature, and the environment. Living for generations within the confines of urban ghettos – the "ships" of our centuries-long history – we have come to regard nature as something alien to our experience. Now that we are free to walk in the open air once more, the vastness and unfamiliarity of the great outdoors is too frightening. And so, we remain trapped inside cement walls, cut off from the very Eden we had hoped to reach.

But unlike the people aboard the spaceship, who threw away material things and instructions that they could never replace, we haven't really thrown away the nature-oriented mitzvahs in the Torah. We have simple forgotten how to study them properly. The instructions about how to relate to God's creation are still there, if we are willing to retrieve them. Let us now look at some ways that we can do that.

Our alienation from the natural world

With few exceptions, the mystical connection between human beings and God's creation is rare in the Hasidic communities of today, even though the Baal Shem Tov, 18th-century founder of Hasidism, loved nature. He was said to have been a rather poor student, always wandering off into the forest instead of sitting in the classroom all day. Historians debate whether he actually knew the Hebrew texts, or simply preached on what he

---

[104] Take note of that, my secular friends, who are all too fond of telling me that my way of life is "medieval" or "outdated." The Kabbalah Tree diagram, which first appeared in 9th century manuscripts, strongly parallels the left and right brain functions that were not discovered by modern science until the mid-1970s. Not to mention that psychologists now recommend "unplugging" from our electronic gadgets one day a week – something Orthodox Jews already do every Sabbath!

picked up orally. Others question whether he was ever ordained as a rabbi. Elie Wiesel writes in *Souls on Fire:* "Some sources claim he was a saint who fled the limelight; others describe him as a harmless dunce; still others endow him with enough learning and wisdom to make him a judge of the rabbinical court."[105] We have many scholarly books written about him, but nothing that he actually wrote himself. And yet the zeal of his love for God and the whole creation set the European Jewish community on fire with ecstatic devotion.

But that was generations ago, and much of the reality has been forgotten. Hasidism eventually became institutionalized, and few people in the community today go to the forest like the Baal Shem Tov did. Chabad Hasidim actually get annoyed when people portray him as "that guy living out in the woods." Then again, Chabadniks pride themselves on being the intellectual branch of Hasidism. As such, they are probably embarrassed to admit that the founder of Hasidism was an unlettered nature lover who spent his early years wandering alone in the Carpathian Mountains.

We have the texts and stories, but have lost the practical knowledge and experience that creates a real inner connection with God and his creation. Consider Psalm 148, where everything in the universe — sun, moon, stars, oceans, fire, snow, and hail — is praising God. Or Psalm 150: *Kol ha-neshamah te'hallel Yah* — "everything that has breath is praising God" and similar lines in Psalms. I like to think that King David, the sweet singer of Psalms, acquired this sensitivity to nature during the years when he was a shepherd boy. Those formative years spent outdoors shaped his awareness in a way that he never forgot. Years later, it influenced his prayers, songs, and poetry.

Unfortunately, most Jews today are so urbanized that they no longer have that direct experience. If you have never looked up at a starry sky or listened to a chorus of birds singing at dawn, how can you make any real connection with the texts that describe such things? How can you picture God as a mother eagle sheltering her nest if you've never seen a bird nesting, and know eggs only as something in Styrofoam boxes that you buy at the supermarket? In many of our yeshivas, even

---

[105] Wiesel, Elie, *Souls on Fire,* Random House, New York. 1972. p.12.

the teachers often lack these firsthand experiences with nature. So they focus on stuff that is familiar to them, namely, the rules of *kashrut* and using animals as food. The environmental Torah laws are not seen as important.

In some circles, spending time in nature is actually discouraged as a waste of time or worse. Rabbi Yisroel Ber Odesser (1888-1994), the founder of the Na Nach sub-group within the Breslov movement, tells in his autobiography how, after he became a Breslover Hasid, neighbors in other Hasidic groups tried to dissuade him from this path. Failing that, they tried to convince his father that this nature-oriented way was actually dangerous. Rabbi Odesser writes:

> When they saw that their words had no effect on me, they went to my father, who was already blind at the time, and said, "Your son has become a Breslover Hasid, one who wanders in the mountains speaking to G-d. All the rabbis [in his community] are against this way; it could cause your son to lose his mind. Now there is still time to save him. But later on he will be in the category of 'all those who enter will never return' [from evil ways]..." When my parents heard these menacing words from the other Hasidim, they became very frightened.[106]

That story left me scratching my head, wondering how anyone could possible believe such a thing. Go insane from hiking in the woods? Surely that is in itself a crazy idea!

Here is not the place to go into detail about Jewish history and how this attitude came about. Suffice it to say that for a thousand years or more, Jews in many parts of Europe were forbidden to own land. In some places it was even forbidden for Jews to walk in a field or forest, because superstitious peasants believed that the very presence of a Jew would cause the milk to curdle and the crops to fail. Violating that prohibition could result in death, and there was no punishment for those who killed Jews. Consequently, Jewish folktales are filled with

---

[106] Odesser, Yisroel Ber, *The Letter from Heaven: Rebbe Nachman's Song*, Netzach Yisrael, Jerusalem, 1991, 1995, pp. 42-43.

stories of peasants beating Jews and robbers attacking Jews along the roads through the forest. The wilderness, in the Jewish experience, was not a friendly place to be. The result is a cultural fear of the outdoors that continues to this day. It is understandable, but also very sad. We have such a severe case of nature deficit disorder that it has completely skewed the way we relate to God's world and the creatures in it.

Re-Connecting with God's Creation

No, I don't think being with nature makes you go insane. Quite the opposite is true: It restores your sanity and opens you up to connecting with God in a very real and personal way, because when you spend time in God's creation, everything around you is alive. When you spend time surrounded by nothing but asphalt and cement buildings, everything is dead. Even the Talmudic rabbis recognized the value of being with nature, ruling that: "It is forbidden to live in a city that has no garden or greenery" (Jerusalem Talmud, Kiddushin 4:12). Many centuries before the Industrial Revolution and today's urban sprawl, the Sages recognized the therapeutic value of "green spaces."

However, that greenery is of no use if people don't spend any time in it. Lately there has been a series of public service ads running on TV about "discover the forest." When I was a kid, there would have been no need for such an advertisement. You could hardly keep me out of the small suburban woodlot we called our "forest." I feel sorry for children today who are deprived of that free-range experience.

Hasidic mothers do sometimes take their babies and toddlers to the park, but once the kids enter school, the primary focus is on Torah learning, often to the detriment of other activities. School days in yeshiva are long, and there is very little focus on spending time outdoors. And even when the kids are outdoors, there is little appreciation of nature as such.

Richard Schwartz tells how once, while at a Sukkot celebration, some children noticed ducks in a nearby backyard and said, "Let's *shecht* (slaughter) them." Already at that young age, the children saw ducks only in utilitarian terms, as something to eat. As one Hasidic mother put it to me, "We can't really know the purpose of wild animals, but for a chicken it's obvious. Its purpose is to be the meat on your plate." With an attitude like that, her children are going to grow up to have no appreciation of chickens as living things with feelings.

Nor is this attitude limited to Hasidim. One summer during my college years, I was hired as the very first nature study instructor at a well-established Jewish summer camp — but only because none of the staff could recognize poison ivy. This camp was not Orthodox; it wasn't even all that religious. Nor was it a wilderness experience. It was more like a resort, a place where parents sent the kids while they went off traveling to Europe or Israel. Getting these fellow Jews to see any beauty in the forest was the most frustrating camp job I ever had.

Nevertheless, there were a few small victories, such as the time we all watched in awe as a Luna moth emerged from its cocoon, or the night when we marveled at thousands of fireflies reflected in the lake. At the end of the summer, one of the counselors thanked me, confiding that although she had attended that camp since childhood, she had never before seen anything there but "a bunch of trees and a dirty old lake."

Perhaps some of those campers grew up to have more interest in the outdoors, because there have been some real advances in environmental education at Jewish schools, at least among the non-Orthodox. But Jews in the yeshiva world still regard nature study as *goyim naches,* a gentile pleasure that is a big waste of time. Recently a Torah teacher told me about a Sabbath retreat in the Catskills where, throughout the entire weekend, he was the only one who bothered to go out and look at the night sky. Nobody else was even interested.

And yet Isaiah clearly tells us to "lift up your eyes on high and see: Who has created these?" What would it be like, I wondered, to lead the students outside into the night and read them this verse? Would having the actual experience of seeing stars make this ancient quotation come alive? It certainly did for me. The first time I saw a clear night sky was on a road trip through South Dakota in 1968, where we camped in the Badlands and had a 360-degree view of the horizon. Suddenly I understood what God meant when he told Abraham that his descendants would be "as numberless as the stars."

Unfortunately, lack of interest in nature and animals not only causes many Jews to miss these types of insights, it also causes them to reject legitimate Torah sources on these topics. In a recent discussion about *Kapporos,* when someone referred to the writings of Rabbi Samson Raphael Hirsch as proof that animals feel pain the same as humans, one heckler replied, "Where did you get this stuff? Off some animal rights website?" In his mind, if it was quoted by PETA or Jewish Vegetarians, then it was automatically bogus. Obviously he had never studied Hirsch's writings on God's creation.

Now it is true that Rabbi Hirsch is often cited by environmental and animal activists, precisely because he was an Orthodox rabbi who wrote on these topics. But the activists did not invent the teachings. Hirsch was writing in the mid-1800s, long before there was an animal rights movement. And he was basing his rulings on even earlier Jewish sources, as well as the common knowledge of Jews who worked with animals on a daily basis. To dismiss the writings of a 19th century scholar as something made up by PETA is absurd. Torah is Torah, no matter who may choose to quote from it.

The need for humane education

One of my fondest childhood memories is Be Kind to Animals Week. This was a nationwide event sponsored by the American Humane Association, with posters and essay contests, public service announcements on TV by celebrities, and local animal-oriented events. I hadn't heard much about it lately, and got to wondering if it still existed. Yes, it does, and this year (2015) is the 100th anniversary! In fact, Be Kind to Animals Week is the oldest commemorative week in all of U.S. history.

Next I wondered if it is observed in Jewish schools. Do yeshiva students ever enter posters in the contest? I found a lot of older references to Jews participating, but very little about it in today's curriculum. This is not to say that no Jewish schools observe it, but it doesn't seem to be much of a priority nowadays, at least not enough to write about it on their websites. That's too bad. It would be wonderful to see some Jewish kids design posters about kindness to animals, which is, after all, a Jewish teaching as well as a secular one. It would be a great opportunity to teach the greater society about *tza'ar ba'alei chayyim*. As I sit here writing this, I can picture posters of Jewish boys in yarmulkes feeding stray cats or dogs. And why not?

It was suggested to me that the reason this event is no longer celebrated as much among Jews is because environmental issues have gotten linked to the Jewish holiday of Tu B'Shevat, the New Year for Trees, which has become a sort of Jewish Earth Day. That is possible. In recent generations American Jewish schools have moved toward finding Jewish equivalents of various activities, rather than join in national events. But Tu B'Shevat focuses more on trees, pollution, and recycling rather than on animals. Still, there is no reason why animals could not be more actively included in it. You might consider showing Karen Davis' excellent 10-minute video, "Chickens at Play," to start a discussion. (See Bibliography.)

There is also a recent movement to make the first day of the Hebrew month of Elul, which the Talmud calls the New Year for Animals,[107] into a humane education event. This seems a bit topsy-turvy to me, since this was originally the day that Jewish farmers tithed their flocks, so it was hardly "Animal Rights Day." But this would not be the first time that a Jewish holiday got re-defined after the Temple was destroyed. Shavuot, the "Feast of Weeks," was originally celebrated with processions of people bringing their first fruits to the Temple. Today it focuses on receiving the Torah at Mt. Sinai, which also took place on the same date. So it would not be out of line to transform "Rosh Hashanah for the Animals" into a day for teaching kindness.

However one may choose to approach it, there is definitely a need for more humane education. During my research for this book I found some appalling stories about Jewish children poking sticks at *Kapporos* chickens, throwing stones at stray cats, harassing squirrels and pigeons in the park, and behaving badly at zoos. Not all Jewish kids do this, of course, and gentile children also misbehave. Still, there were far more such stories than there should be. Kids will be kids, and wearing a

---

[107] See Talmud, Rosh Hashanah 1a. There are actually four "new years" on the Jewish calendar. Three are fiscal years and one is Rosh Hashanah, the actual Jewish New Year as we commonly know it.

145

yarmulke does not transform them into saints. However, it does make them visible as Jews and their misbehavior reflects badly on the whole community. We have a responsibility to see that our children treat God's creatures with kindness. Rabbi Natan Slifkin writes:

> Mocking organizations like PETA and people such as [Peter] Singer[108] has become almost a sport in some circles. It makes people feel good to scoff at those who claim to be morally superior. But many of those who do so should realize that there are many genuine problems of cruelty to animals within the Orthodox community that we need to address. Public discourses by Orthodox spokesmen on the Torah's attitude to animals tend to comprise of mocking the extremist views of fanatical animal rights activists such as PETA and Peter Singer, and then triumphantly describing the Torah's sensible laws of sensitivity to animals. But they usually fail to discuss whether the Jewish community today lives up to the Torah's ideals...
>
> In general, it is a regrettable fact that kindness to animals in the Orthodox Jewish community, especially in Israel, is far from what it should be.[109]

I myself have run across the mocking attitudes that Rabbi Slifkin describes, and it makes me sad that people can be so ignorant. We Jews have beautiful teachings about kindness to animals, as well as inspiring stories about great rabbis and teachers who put them into action. These teachings should be studied and taught more often, not because of PETA or animal rights or the anti-*Kapporos* protests, but because they are an essential part of our own tradition. If you really believe that *all* of the mitzvahs are important, then you should not neglect this area of study and practice. "Be as careful with a minor mitzvah as with a major one, for you do not know the value of a mitzvah." *(Pirkei Avot)*

---

[108] Peter Singer: Author of *Animal Liberation* and a major founder of the animal rights movement. Note: PETA is actually an animal welfare org, not animal rights.

[109] Slifkin, *Man and Beast,* p. 159.

The Lubavitcher Rebbe and animal toys

The Seventh Lubavitcher Rebbe, Menachem M. Schneerson (d. 1994), leader of Chabad , was opposed to Jewish children playing with toys or pictures in the shape of non-kosher species of animals. This, I believe, has greatly exacerbated the nature deficit problem among Chabad Hasidim. Although I do not believe that the Rebbe meant to create generations of children who were emotionally cut off from relating to animals, that has been the result. In his edict he wrote: "Because what one sees leaves lasting impressions, especially on young children, the toys that a child plays with, and the pictures that he looks at, should not be of impure animals."[110]

"Impure" *(tameh)* means animals that cannot be eaten in a kosher home and/or offered as sacrifices in the Jerusalem Temple. Rabbi Schneerson believed that playing with such toys or looking at such pictures would somehow damage the child's innocent soul, or lead him or her to idolatry. Since then, many Chabad Jews have provided their children with stuffed toy Torah scrolls or plush lambs and chickens to hug instead of teddy bears. This in itself is not necessarily bad, but how do you avoid seeing Tony the Tiger on cereal boxes?

My first reaction to all this was, "What? No more Noah's Ark models? No Garden of Eden coloring pages?" My mind flashed back to third grade and the Noah's Ark that I made out of a shoebox. I was very proud of that artistic creation. Why would the Rebbe have forbidden it? The answer I got was that if kids played with these toys, they might eat forbidden species later in life. Which is absurd. I have never in my life wanted to eat bears because I had a teddy bear.

I later learned that this answer was not quite accurate. The concern was not so much about *eating* non-kosher animals

---

[110] He based this on a belief dating back to Talmudic times, in which the first thing a woman sees after she leaves the *mikveh* (ritual purification bath) will affect the nature of the child she conceives with her husband that night. During the Middle Ages this was known as the doctrine of "maternal impressions." In those days embryology and the nature of birth defects were not understood. Birthmarks, physical and mental deficiencies, personality traits, or even miscarriages were often attributed to seeing an animal or being frightened by it. Barking dogs, especially, were often blamed for this.

as about *seeing* them and becoming influenced by the images. Instead of "you are what you eat" it was "you are what you see." On one level this is true; that's why we have ratings on movies and TV programs. Certain images can be very disturbing to young children, and we all know the debate about playing violent video games. For that matter, some segments of the evening news are inappropriate for children. So it is probably best not to let toddlers see films of lions killing prey. The same would go for animals mating. But to ban all pictures of non-kosher creatures, even the gentle ones, seems overly extreme.

However, the Lubavitcher Rebbe did make exceptions for pictures or models of animals that were mentioned in the Torah if this would help children learn the structural differemcees between the species, both kosher and non-kosher, or to understand references to animals in the Psalms, etc. So I guess a Noah's Ark model isn't really so out of bounds. Still, this struck me as a rather utilitarian approach that doesn't really encourage an appreciation of God's creation for its own sake.

The Rebbe's objection was originally triggered by a cartoon mouse named Mendel in a Jewish children's magazine called *Olameinu* ("Our World") that first appeared in 1945 and remained in print for three generations. Mendel was an obvious take-off on Walt Disney's Mickey Mouse. This was a common form of Jewish humor back then, to take an icon from the dominant culture and then give it a Jewish twist. In the case of Mendel, he wore a yarmulke, was a good Jew, and taught his friends about various mitzvahs. In other words, he was a wholesome role model. And a favorite character loved by Jewish kids.

However, the Lubavitcher Rebbe found the cartoon strip offensive because it personified a mouse – an animal the Torah considers "unclean" – as a Jew. Mendel was later replaced with the more kosher "Duvi the Duck." (By the way, Chabad Hasidim are not the only ones concerned with the unclean status of Mickey Mouse. According to Palestinian television, Mickey Mouse has converted to Islam and is now "Mohammed Mouse." Will Porky Pig soon follow?)

In general, the Rebbe objected to cartoons, toys and books that personified animals in human roles. It is possible that he was reacting to antisemitic cartoons and other portrayals of Jews as rats and vermin that the Nazis had circulated in

Europe. At the very least, I do not think he understood the modern mediums of cartooning and animation. No doubt he would also have objected to the award-winning graphic novel, *Maus,* by Art Spiegelman, where Jews during the Holocaust are portrayed as mice and the Nazis are cats.

I have never read anywhere that the Rebbe was familiar with *Maus.* Since it appeared only shortly before the Rebbe had a debilitating stroke in March of 1992, I rather doubt he read it. But it does seem to fall into the parameters of the Chabad prohibition, as an example of animals depicted as Jews, so it deserves a mention here. Spiegelman used these cat-and-mouse metaphors to emphasize the predator-prey relationship between Germans and Jews during the Nazi regime. This is a common technique in political cartooning. *Maus* has proven to be an excellent educational tool about the Holocaust for young people who might not otherwise read a history book.

The Rebbe expanded his ruling beyond cartoon mice to include all non-kosher species, animated or not, unless directly connected to illustrating Torah texts. It became a general prohibition among his followers that continues to this day. This includes cartoon cats like Garfield and Daniel Tiger, puppets like Big Bird (although, if Big Bird is supposed to be a chicken, then he would be kosher, so maybe he's OK?) as well as teddy bears and other animal-shaped toys. Some people take this idea about "not seeing" non-kosher animals to extremes and won't even visit the zoo. Others argue that it only refers to toys and artwork, not live animals.

This is an unfortunately narrow view of nature, but it is not mainstream Judaism! It is not even typical Orthodox Judaism. It is simply a *khumra* (extra strictness) taken on by Chabad. And not all of them follow it strictly. You can find some pretty heated discussions about it on the Internet. Personally, I think it has produced a whole generation of Chabadniks with a serious case of nature deficit disorder. If you can't learn about the different kinds of animals in our world, then how can you learn to appreciate God's creation?

In Brooklyn there is a small museum called Torah Animal World, whose curator, Rabbi Shaul Shimon Deutsch, has tried to fill this educational gap with a taxidermy collection of all the animals mentioned in the Bible, both kosher and not.

Since the Rebbe permitted looking at "unclean" animals for Torah education purposes, viewing this collection is permitted.

The place looks like something out of the mid-1800s. It consists of glass cases full of specimens, displays of dead animals mounted on fake rocks, and trophy heads on the walls. "The zombie version of Noah's Ark" is what one writer called it.[111] Oddly, there is no specimen of a pig, even though Leviticus 11:7 clearly says, "The swine you shall not eat." The same section of Leviticus goes on to say "you shall not touch their carcasses" so maybe he doesn't want people touching a stuffed pig. Still, he could have put it behind glass.

Rabbi Deutsch claims that all the animals in his exhibits died naturally and were not hunted. That's rather hard to prove if you are collecting taxidermy specimens from various sources. Be that as it may, this is an outdated way to teach children about animals. At least the ones in the zoo are alive.

The zoo as a modern Noah's Ark

Perhaps this is the place for me to address the issue of zoos in general. I know that many animal rights activists are against all zoos, on the grounds that animals should never be kept in captivity. It is true that zoos of the past were often horrific, and there are still many roadside menageries that ought to be closed down. But I do not condemn all zoos based on the sins of the worst. Modern, accredited zoos are more like Noah's Arks, helping to save endangered species like the white rhino that would otherwise be extinct by now. Busch Gardens, for example, has an extensive behind-the-scenes program for raising and releasing endangered animals into the wild.

It should also be noted that the human idea of freedom as "wandering wherever you want whenever you want" is not necessarily what animals want or need. In *The Secret Language of Animals,* an excellent manual for zoo-watching, biologist Janine M. Benyus writes:

---

[111] http://www.religionnews.com/2014/01/02/brooklyn-museum-every-biblical-animal-money-stay-open/

The truth is animals are not really free to go anywhere they want in the wild. They operate within strict limits imposed by the seasons, the paucity or richness of their habitat, and their territorial status. How much energy can they afford to spend also restricts them. Notoriously thrifty animals are constantly balancing their energy checkbooks, and if they don't have to travel far to eat or to find a mate, they won't. A squirrel, for instance, may spend its whole life in a few hundred feet of forest, as long as it can harvest enough nuts, find a mate, and hide from predators there. Wolves, on the other hand, travel long distances, not because it's fun, but because moose are lot harder to locate than acorns are.[112]

But if those wolves have plenty to eat and the right habitat, then they don't wander very far from it. Benyus goes on to say that it is the quality of habitat in a zoo exhibit that counts, not necessarily the size. Modern zoos try, as much as possible, to create enclosures that duplicate the animal's natural environment. The Minnesota Zoo, for example, keeps Siberian tigers because the winters there are similar to Siberia, so the big cats can go outside and feel at home in their naturalized enclosure. In short, if a zoo exhibit has the right habitat and meets all the animal's needs, then the animal will feel comfortable there. Benyus gives a list of criteria for evaluating your own local zoo, as well as actions you can take if it is not up to par.

To me this is a far better approach than condemning all zoos outright. "Zoos are often the only place where most people encounter animals that are not pets, food, or considered urban or rural pests," writes Benyus. Many zoos also have hands-on programs where children can, for example, touch a snake and find out that it really isn't slimy. Of course, it is important to teach our children how to behave properly at the zoo or other live animal events, which means moving slowly and watching quietly, so they do not upset the animals.

---

[112] Benyus, Janine M., *The Secret Language of Animals,* Black Dog & Leventhal Publishers, 2014. p. 460.

One animal rights activist suggested to me that children can learn just as well from watching nature documentaries. True, these allow us to see the activities of animals in the wild that we would otherwise miss. But a movie does not create the same emotional response as seeing a live animal in person. Not to mention that many of the habitats where those documentaries were filmed are rapidly disappearing. The zoo might not be the perfect place for an endangered species to live, but it sure beats going extinct.

On a spiritual level, we should consider what I said in Chapter 4, about possible ways that the "holy sparks" in animals might progress without them being eaten. Maybe those zoo animals really are ambassadors for their species. It could be that the captive snake benefits spiritually from having helped a child learn more about the world. In the long run, a little reptilian inconvenience might well save that snake's wild home in the future. Who knows the effect a child's animal encounters can have? When we used to go to the Philadelphia zoo, there was a favorite peacock who would come right up and eat out of my hand. I'll never forget the day his mate came out of the bushes followed by four adorable peachicks. Those birds were friends that I looked forward to seeing on each visit. To this day, peafowl are among my favorite birds.

Koko the gorilla, who was born in captivity, has taught us a great deal about her species. The story of her love for a cat named All Ball, told in a book called *Koko's Kitten,* has been distributed to people in areas where wild gorillas still live. Children who read this touching true tale are much less likely to grow up to be gorilla hunters. Would it not be fair to say that Koko's "holy spark" is elevated through this sharing?

Kosher homes and synagogue cats

A while back I spoke with a woman in Brooklyn who told me that the most difficult thing for her becoming religious was giving up her cat. Why did she have to do that? Because the community pressured her, even though there is no prohibition against owning a cat. So not only does the ultra-Orthodox world have little or no contact with nature or animals, they expect people who do have those connections to give them up when they join the community. To me, this is a step backwards. It's like taking a free bird and cramming it into a cage for the rest of its life.

Why did she have to get rid of her cat? The answer she got was that a Jewish home is like a temple, and in the Holy Temple they did not have cats, so Jews should not keep any animal in the house that was not allowed in the Temple. Which is halachic nonsense, and, in my opinion, taking symbolism too far. It is true that our table is *like* an altar and the home is *like* a temple, but in the days when the Temple actually existed, nobody tried to make the home literally as pure as the Temple.

In fact, the priests *(kohanim)* had to go to the *mikveh* and put on clean robes every time before entering the Temple precisely because, in the ordinary world outside, they came into contact with things that were *tameh,* not ritually pure. And as the Talmud states, "While they [the priests] are clothed in the priestly garments, they are clothed in the priesthood; but when they are not wearing the garments, the priesthood is not upon them" (Zevachim 17b). We are also told how, after Yom Kippur, the Kohen Gadol (High Priest) took off the sacred garments and put on his own clothes to go home. So there was a clear line between sacred space and ordinary space, and the people understood where that line was.

But nowadays, some people are trying to maintain a Holy Temple level of purity at home, and it has become overly restrictive. Going back to the cat story again, when I worked as a nursing home chaplain back in the 1980s, I met elderly Jews from Eastern Europe who told me that it was common to have a *shul katze (*synagogue cat) to protect the books from mice. In fact, it was very common in general to have bibliocats on patrol in libraries. Books were leather-bound back then, with glues made from animal hide, so they were very tempting for rodents to chew. Now, if our great-grandparents had no problem with letting a cat roam among the holy books in shul, why should there be a problem with keeping a cat in the house?

That troublesome line in *Pirkei Avot*

Another objection to nature study that is often quoted in these discussions is *Pirkei Avot* 3:9, which says: "If someone studies

[Torah] while walking along the road, and interrupts his studying to say, 'How beautiful is this tree! How beautiful is this field!' it is as if he has forfeited his life." This is meant spiritually, of course; nobody was actually put to death for looking at a tree. Other translations read: "sinned against his soul." The Hebrew word used is *nefesh,* which, as we learned in Chapter 4, means both the life force of the body and a level of the soul.

Much has been written on this saying, and from many different viewpoints. I myself have balked at it every time, looking for a way to understand this line that does not negate my appreciation of God's creation. So over the years, I've studies a lot of commentaries, both classical and modern. Not that I'm a big expert, but I have given it a lot of thought.

Maimonides explains that although the beauty of nature may lead a person to God, this is a more primitive way than learning Torah, and thus a spiritual step backwards. Rashi says that studying Torah protects the mind from wandering into sinful areas and temptations. The Baal Shem Tov interprets it mystically, as admiring the "tree" of one's own ego and the "field" of one's knowledge, thereby succumbing to pride. Rabbi Herbert S. Goldstein, writing in the early 20th century, saw in it the conflict between science and religion: "Revealed religion is exact and certain, whilst the natural is speculation, therefore inexact and uncertain."

The bottom line is, most interpretations of this saying regard nature study as a frivolous waste of time. I've heard stories of kids who took this warning so much to heart, that they refused to go on nature hikes at Jewish summer camps. But I doubt this was the original intent, because we have so many other teachings telling us to appreciate God's creation. We even have a special blessing to be recited during the month of Nissan when one sees the trees starting to bloom. Obviously, in order to do that, one must first stop and look at the trees! If you don't notice the blossoms and focus your attention on them, then how can you make the blessing properly?

The Chofetz Chaim (Rabbi Israel Meir Hacohen, 1838-1933) was of the opinion that this line in *Pirkei Avot* applied in ancient times, when all learning was done orally through memorization, and it was usual for students to recite their lessons while walking along the road. In those days, interrupting the recitation to admire the scenery could mean losing the text altogether. But now that we have books available, and learning usually takes place in the House of Study, the Chofetz Chaim recommended providing oneself with printed volumes to learn from. (Chofetz Chaim *On the Torah,* Deuteronomy section.)

However, I prefer the interpretation of Rabbi Samson Raphael Hirsch. He says that the problem is that the person in question *stopped learning* in order to admire the tree, whereas in reality, *admiring a tree should be part of his Torah learning.* In other words, the tree should elevate his religious consciousness, not distract from it. Rabbi Zalman Schachter-Shalomi used to say a similar thing when I studied with him in the 1980s: "Bring it all back to Torah, bring it all back to Torah." Admiring the tree should enrich our understanding of Torah, and draw us closer to God.

This can apply to all the wonders of nature. When I was in Montreal a number of years back, I visited this amazing museum called the Insectarium that has collections of bugs, live and mounted, from all over the world. There is also a butterfly room where you can walk through and see all kinds of free-flying butterflies. Visiting there was an amazing experience. But my fellow Jews simply did not get why I would want to go there. Only one person understood, because she had been to the museum herself. She said, "When I saw all those amazing bugs, I understood how beautifully HaShem [God] had made the world." However, she was the exception. To most Orthodox Jews, bugs are just something *trayfe* (not kosher) that we must remove from our vegetables.

Years ago, when I still lived in Minneapolis, on Yom Kippur I sometimes went to a Modern Orthodox synagogue named Knesset Israel. Behind the building there was a wooded ravine. During the afternoon break between services I would go there to make *hisboddidus,* the Breslov form of pouring out your heart in spontaneous prayer, preferably in the outdoors. There were hundreds of people who attended that shul, but I never saw anyone else back there in the woods.

There are, of course, some Orthodox Jews who do have a connection to nature and the environment. Several years ago, on a trip to New York, I stayed in Brooklyn with a young man and his family who had previously lived on a farm. He was now growing horseradish (for Passover) and a willow bush (for Sukkot) in big pots on the fire escape, and the children were planting bean seeds in cups on the windowsill. "I want my children to know where these things come from," he told me.

He also had a bird feeder, which, although it attracted mostly sparrows and pigeons, nevertheless made a connection with other living things. I fondly remember his children telling me about a trip to the Arboretum where, the oldest boy exclaimed, "We actually saw tomatoes and corn growing!" Country people may laugh at this, but for inner city kids, it can be a thrill to see how vegetables grow. And, I must add, this family did not use chickens for *Kapporos*.

We can't all be shepherds and farmers like our ancestors. But I think we can all make a greater effort to develop a better connection with nature in whatever circumstances we might find ourselves. Being "too busy" is not an excuse. There is a Hasidic story about a poor wagon driver who came to the Baal Shem Tov, distressed that he always had to hit the road before dawn and could never attend weekday morning prayers. The Baal Shem Tov told him to look up at the stars in the pre-dawn sky and recite the words of Isaiah 40: "Lift up your eyes on high, and see: Who has created these?"

I am very lucky to live in an area where I can actually do this. On a clear night I not only see the stars, I can see the Milky Way and, in the proper season, meteor showers and lunar eclipses. But even for city dwellers whose view of the sky is obscured by bright lights and air pollution, it is still possible to feel the awe of God's creation in other ways. As we go about our daily activities, we can open our eyes and *really see* the things around us. We can learn to pay attention. As the saying goes, "Stop and smell the flowers." Even if you have to grow them yourself on the windowsill.

In conclusion

At the beginning of this book, I said it would not be a vegetarian manifesto, and I shall keep to that promise. Obviously I would like to see people stop using chickens as *Kapporos,* and I have given numerous reasons why using money is a much better option. But ultimately it is up to each individual to make his or her own decisions. Hopefully this little volume has given you the right tools to do so. For those of you who are activists, the Appendix outlines some positive actions you can take to help save the chickens.

I will end with lyrics (in translation) from "The Rooster is Crowing," a song by Rabbi Eizek Taub, the first Kalever Rebbe (1744-1828), whose story we told in Chapter 3. In this song, the rooster – a bird "of golden beak and golden feet" – is heralding the coming of the Messiah,[113] as the dawn of a new day:

"The rooster is crowing, dawn brightens the sky
In the green forest, in the verdant meadow,
A little bird skips around.
Who are you, little bird?
Who are you, little bird?
Of golden beak and golden feet that waits for me?
Just wait, dear little bird!
Just wait, dear little bird!
If God destined you for me, I will be one with you.
The rooster sings his morning song,
The sun is slowly rising--
Yibaneh hamikdash, ir Tzion temalei
(May the Temple be rebuilt, [114] the City of Zion replenished) --
When, O when will it be?
Vesham nashir shir chadash uvirnana naaleh,
(There shall we sing a new song, with joyous singing ascend),
It's time, O let it be!"

---

[113] The rooster awakens us to a new day, and begins to crow at the very beginning of dawn, about an hour before the sun is actually up. (As a keeper of roosters, I can personally attest to this!) He is therefore seen in Jewish folklore as the herald of the Messiah, announcing that the New Day will be here soon.

[114] "May the Temple be rebuilt": Not necessarily with animal sacrifices. Rabbi Abraham Isaac Kook (d. 1935) was of the opinion that offerings in the Third Temple would be made up of fruits, vegetables, and grains. Since Original Eden was vegetarian, many Jews believe that New Eden will be vegetarian also.

Epilogue

Writing this book has been a difficult journey for me personally. It has forced me to examine my own beliefs and my reasons for being a vegetarian, as well as my commitment to the Torah way of life. In seeking to balance the two worldviews, I have come to the conclusion that I am basically an animal welfare person, not an animal rights activist.

Having said that, I fully expect certain segments of the animal rights movement to write me off as a hypocrite or worse. On the other side, there will be Jews in certain circles who will try to discredit me for attacking *Kapporos*. That comes with the territory when you take a controversial stand on anything nowadays. Luckily my computer has a "delete" button for hate mail.

I must live with my own integrity, and I cannot claim to be something that I am not. I love animals and prefer not to eat them, but I do not consider animals and humans to be created equal. I deplore the factory farm system and will continue to preach against it, but I cannot go so far as to become an "ethical vegan" and declare it murder to kill an animal. I do not wear fur or leather, but I see nothing wrong with using feathers that my birds shed naturally

Nor do I have a problem with eating eggs from my own chickens, who get to run free and will never be slaughtered. I see that as taking full responsibility for the source of my eggs. Karen Davis told me she boils the eggs from the chickens at her sanctuary and feeds them back to the hens. The Woodstock Farm Sanctuary says on their website that they feed the boiled eggs to their pigs and dogs as a protein supplement. In either case, they are still taking them away from the hens. So why is it so wrong for me to eat the eggs instead?

After doing all the research for this book, in the end I found the animal rights movement to be too obsessive, to dogmatic, and far too anti-religious for my taste. Their insistence upon being the one and only true moral position for everyone on the planet has turned me off to the whole idea of ethical veganism and all that it implies. Labeling myself as an animal welfare person, on the other hand, allows me to care about animals and work to help them without becoming a fanatic. And frankly, I think it helps the animals far more in the here and now than preaching to the vegan choir.

During my research I ran across a story about how Ingrid Newkirk, founder and President of PETA, had once sent out a letter asking people to oppose some cruel legislation that would have permitted slaughterhouses to stop watering the cattle at specific intervals during transit. The reasoning was, that it would save the industry some time and money, since the cows would soon be killed anyway. To her shock, Newkirk got back replies from certain activists that because this was about slaughter, any cooperation with the industry would be wrong. In short, they would rather have the poor cows suffering from thirst than violate their own "ethics." This has come to be known as the "thirsty cow" scenario. Should you offer water to a cow on the way to the slaughterhouse?

Newkirk says yes. I agree. Her argument goes like this: If you were sitting on death row, facing execution soon, and somebody offered you food and water, wouldn't you be grateful? Of course you would. And would you appreciate somebody refusing to give you food or water because you would ultimately be killed? Probably not. Yet that is exactly what the opponents of animal welfare are advocating: Do all or do nothing. Which all too often ends up as nothing.

Over and over, I found evidence that animal welfare organizations, such as the ASPCA and Friends of Animals, were accomplishing more genuine, down-to-earth improvements for the lives of animals than the hard-liners in the "abolitionist approach," which often does nothing more than make its adherents feel self-righteous.

"The abolitionist" people are fond of comparing human slavery to animal exploitation. In some cases this is valid. But even human slavery abolitionists recognize the value of intermediate measures. In the USA, the 1807 Act Prohibiting Importation of Slaves did not completely stop slavery – that would take another half century to accomplish. But meanwhile the 1807 Act did help stop the terrible suffering aboard slave ships. (The *Amistad* case was based on this law, and it was won against the slavers.) This early legislation was only a step in the right direction, not the end of the struggle itself. But for those who were no longer being shipped across the ocean in chains, it was a very big step indeed.

Similarly, although I would prefer that my fellow Jews not use chickens for *Kapporos* at all, I would also support measures to treat the chickens better for those who still do. Holding the chickens properly would at least eliminate a lot of pain.

I have respect for those people who choose to follow the vegan path, and I have met some very loving, caring people within that community. But if you force me to choose between veganism and Hasidism, then I must choose Hasidism. I can find plenty of room within Hasidic thought for a vegetarian diet, but I cannot find any room in ethical veganism or "deep ecology" for the Hasidic mysticism at the center of my beliefs.

This does *not* mean I don't care about the suffering chickens and other abused animals, as certain activists have accused me. I most certainly do care. And I still strongly oppose using chickens as *Kapporos*. But my *reasons* for caring are not those of the animal rights people. I am a religious Jew, not a "deep ecology" person. It's a difference in my philosophy, not necessarily in my day-to-day actions.

Over and over throughout this project, my mind kept returning to the following Hasidic story: Rebbe Nachman of Breslov once got so caught up in an obsession about getting rid of *chometz* (leavening) before Passover that it almost drove him crazy. During Passover, not only is it forbidden to eat *chometz,* it is forbidden to own it or derive any benefit from it at all. So he started worrying about whether or not there would be *chometz* in the water used during the festival. What if someone had dropped a piece of bread down the well? That could taint the whole water supply. Even the tiniest bit of *chometz* would render the water unusable. (That's similar to how using the tiniest bit of animal product would render a person completely unvegan in some people's eyes.)

After much deliberation and minute examination of every possible halachic detail, Rebbe Nachman finally came to the conclusion that the only way to be absolutely, positively sure there was no *chometz* in the water would be to camp out next to a spring in the woods where the water bubbled up fresh and uncontaminated. The problem was, the only such spring was a long way from his home. If he went there, then he would be away from his family, his friends, his disciples, and the whole Jewish community. Was that any way to celebrate a festival? In the end, he decided that such ultra-strictness was unnecessary, even on Passover. Being overly rigid killed the joy and led to depression. Don't be a fanatic, he taught, and do not worry yourself sick with unnecessary restrictions. "The Torah was given to human beings, not the ministering angels."[114]

That's good advice. And lest you think this obsession with "the letter of the law" is limited to Orthodox Jews, let me assure you that it occurs among secular people also. Rebbe Nachman's lesson came to mind when I received an email essay by Karen Davis (later published in her *Poultry Press* magazine) about a vegan woman who had decided to take her practice to the ultimate ethical vegan level and refuse to eat anywhere meat was being served. Basically, this meant hanging out only with other vegans in vegan restaurants or at vegan events. It also resulted in her walking out on a reunion of family and friends that she had really been looking forward to. Davis praised this behavior as heroic, touting it as the level of commitment that is needed by everybody in the animal rights movement.

But if I were to do that, it would mean never eating with anyone but my wife, because most of my family, neighbors and associates are not even vegetarians, let alone ethical vegans. If I followed Karen's advice to the letter, I would end up living as "insular" and "strictly-defined" as she accuses the Hasidim of being[115] – maybe more so.

Granted, there is intolerance in some Hasidic communities. But there is also serious intolerance among secular vegans. Consider the story of Jordan Younger. Her blog, "The Blonde

---

[114] *Rabbi Nachman's Wisdom (Shivchei Haran),* section 235.

[115] See beginning of chapter 6.

Vegan," had over 70,000 followers. But behind the scenes she was developing an eating disorder called "orthorexia nervosa," defined as a "fixation on righteous eating," that made her seriously ill. Orthorexia is usually first motivated by goals to achieve health through diet, but turns into an unhealthy obsession with food quality, quantity, and purity.

Younger had declared herself a vegan after doing a "juice cleanse," and at first this seemed to improve her health. So she started an Instagram account and later a blog to document and share her recipes and lifestyle. Soon she had her own brand, testing and endorsing various health food products. But as time went on, she became more and more obsessed with making sure everything about her diet was absolutely perfect. She would stand in front of the fridge for 20 minutes or more, debating what to eat that would be OK. Ordinary veganism was no longer enough; she moved on to become a raw foods vegan. Of course, this cut out major protein sources like soybeans and lentils unless you could find them fresh – not an easy task. Soon she was eating mostly juices and salads. And her health suffered. Like Rebbe Nachman and the Passover water, the Blonde Vegan came to the conclusion that, for her own health and sanity, she had to get rid of the obsession.

In June 2014 she announced on her blog that she was giving up the vegan lifestyle. But unlike Rebbe Nachman's disciples, some of her followers did not take it positively when she admitted this. She began to receive anonymous death threats – yes, *death threats!*

"Certain leaders in the raw vegan community turned their back on me so violently," Younger says. "People I know personally, who I have collaborated with. One blogger began lashing out and leading an army, commenting hateful things in the middle of the night. Some vegans have this cult-like mentality — it turned me off of the lifestyle."[116]

If you think it is incongruous for people who claim to have renounced all killing to make death threats, you are not

---

[116] See http://wellandgood.com/2014/07/08/what-happened-when-the-blonde-vegan-wasnt-vegan-anymore/ Younger's memoire, *Breaking Vegan: One Woman's Journey from Veganism and Extreme Dieting to a More Balanced Life,* is due out November 1, 2015. See Bibliography.

alone. Reading the comments and discussions about this woman's story revealed quite a few other stories of people who tried veganism, found it was not working for them, and were then deserted and reviled by former "friends" in the vegan community. Which only goes to prove my point: Intolerance can be found everywhere.

Of course, not all vegans are like this. It is possible to lead a balanced, sane lifestyle without eating animal products, and many people do. In the same vein, it is also possible to lead a balanced, sane lifestyle as a Hasidic Jew, and many people do. I have met religious Jews who are every bit as obsessive about keeping kosher as Jordan Younger was about veganism, but I have *also* met religious Jews who are loving, caring, tolerant people for whom Judaism is life-affirming and positive toward both animals and humans. It is from them that I take my cues.

I keep kosher and I am a vegetarian, but I do not insist that everyone else around me be the same. I recognize that there are people with serious physical conditions such as rapid metabolism due to endocrine disorder, people with Crohn's disease, diabetics who have difficulty digesting plant proteins, people allergic to soybeans and nuts, etc., for whom it's very difficult to maintain their health while avoiding all animal protein. For people with kidney disease, a meal of nuts, beans, and other legumes is way too high in potassium to be a major source of protein on a daily basis.

For every rule there are exceptions, and a wise person makes room for the needs of others. Judaism itself says that in cases where life is threatened, we set aside the dietary laws and follow the doctor's orders. In practice, this can mean using serums or medications that are not kosher if no other options are available. In that area, Orthodox Judaism is more flexible than some segments of the vegan community.

Every path has the potential to become an unhealthy obsession, but that should not be the sole criterion by which we judge it. So let's all set aside our fanaticisms and unite in our common desire to end chickens as *Kapporos* – for whatever reasons that work within our own individual worldviews. And with that, I will close, wishing you all peace and blessings on whatever path you chose to take. Amen.

APPENDIX A:

A Manual for Anti-Kapporos Activists

By Yonassan Gershom

People who are concerned about the treatment of animals and who want to end using chickes as *Kapporos* should try to engage *courteously and respectfully* with Jews who perform this ritual. Here are some suggestions for how to do that. A PDF version can be downloaded at rooster613.blogspot.com. Feel free to pass it around.

Activist, educate thyself

First of all, you should recognize that *Kapporos* practitioners are performing what they regard as an important religious act, even if you do not agree with it or understand it. Before you go to a protest, write letters to the editors, or leave comments on the Internet, take the time to find out about the beliefs, history, and cultural significance of this ceremony, so you can write respectfully and be more convincing. I wrote this book to help you learn not only about *Kapporos* itself but also something of Hasidic spirituality, to help you dialogue from within the tradition. Religious people in general (not just Hasidim) are more willing to listen if it is clear that you are not condemning their entire way of life. Here are a few questions you can ask:

- Do you know that holding a bird by its wings like that can tear the muscles and cause a lot of pain?

- Do you know that the loud peeping/crying sounds you hear are not normal, they are the distress call of a frightened baby bird calling for its mother?

- Do you know that a chicken is as intelligent as a three or four year old child, and can feel just as much pain and fear as your own children?

- You cannot commit a sin to do a mitzvah; what if the suffering of these chickens is blocking your prayers from rising to heaven?

Be prepared for skepticism; these are new ideas to many urban Jews, who may be ignorant about live chickens. Don't be offended if people laugh at you — laughter can be a cover for discomfort at new ideas. More than likely, you have laughed that way yourself in the past. Be loving and patient.

Don't condemn everyone for the actions of a few

Even among "the Orthodox," only a small minority actually do this ceremony with chickens. It may seem like everybody is doing it when you visit a *Kapporos* center, but there are plenty of Orthodox people who stay home and don't participate. They just are not as visible as those who do.

There are over a million Jews in New York City, and, according to recent polls, 40% of them identify as Hasidic or Orthodox. So even if 20,000 chickens were sacrificed, that is only 5% of the entire Orthodox community. It is important to keep this statistic in mind, and not paint all religious Jews with the same angry brush. As I have explained throughout this book, there is diversity among Hasidic communities, even if they do "all look alike" to you. So it is best to say *"some* Orthodox Jews" do this, not all of them.

In the same vein, not all of these guys are rabbis, either, even if they do have beards and dress in black. This is standard dress for all Hasidic males, even total ignoramuses. Wearing the clothes is no guarantee of sainthood! So please, unless you actually know that a particular person really is a rabbi, don't refer to him as such in your articles and blogs. In many cases, the smart-alecks mouthing off across the barricades may be no more than teenagers acting out — and every community has those! (In some news photos they don't even have beards yet, proof positive that they are still youngsters, because Hasidic men do not shave.) Not that I approve of profanity or sexist remarks, but it is usually not "the rabbis" making them. And the guy slaughtering the chickens is probably not a rabbi, either — just a butcher trained in kosher slaughtering.

Respect, not insults, please

For outsiders to call any traditional culture "barbaric" or "medieval" or "primitive" or whatever never really works. It only causes the traditionalists to close ranks against you. And it goes without saying that sending nasty, obscene, anti-Jewish and/or personally insulting messages to various rabbis is not going to win any converts to your cause. Also be aware that using death threats or vandalizing synagogues and places of business is illegal and could land you in jail. The same goes for stealing chickens, even if you think you are rescuing them. Keep it clean in thought, word, and deed, please.

If you yourself are Jewish but not Hasidic, please keep negative stereotypes and in-house politics out of the dialogue. Stick to the specific issue at hand and don't go dragging in feminism, gay marriage, dress codes, Israeli politics, the Palestinians, "who is a Jew" or references to the movie *Yentl*. In other words, don't use the opportunity to dump everything you always wanted to yell at an Orthodox Jew. Hasidim are human beings just like you, even if you think they dress funny.

Speaking of dress, do it modestly at the protests or when meeting with people in the Orthodox/Hasidic community. This does not mean you must wear dark colors, but it does mean cover your body. For men: no shorts or tank tops, and wear a hat or yarmulke if you are Jewish. (If you are not Jewish but are invited into a synagogue or someone's home, you'll be asked to cover your head regardless. Please comply.) For women: no bare arms above the elbow, no low-cut tops or tight clothes, no shorts, and skirts should be below the knee. Although it might feel uncomfortable to wear clothing that is different from your norm, remember that you are going into *their* neighborhood. Dressing modestly shows that you respect the community and people will be more willing to listen.

Ridicule does not work

In a recent dialogue with an animal rights activist, he told me the best way to handle this would be to use rubber chickens to make fun of the ceremony ala Mark Twain, so that it would be rendered ridiculous through satire. He even made a reference to Borscht Belt comedians. (Did I mention he wasn't Jewish?) But that is exactly the *wrong* way to go about it. Most Hasidic Jews have probably never read Mark Twain (if they even know who he is) and won't see this as satire. They will see it as "a bunch of ignorant *goyim* ridiculing the Jews again." Hasidim and other Orthodox Jews already endure enough ridicule and rude comments on the streets without you adding to the load. So forget the street theater. Just as you would not go to a civil rights march painted up in blackface, don't use humor in offensive ways at *Kapporos* protests.

Watch your language!

And I don't just mean profanity. It has become common in animal rights groups to compare the suffering of animals to the Holocaust. I explained in Chapter 1 why this is a very bad idea politically. Beyond that, there are personal issues as well. Many Hasidim are themselves Holocaust survivors or children and grandchildren of survivors. For these communities, the Holocaust is not just something you learn about in school, it's personal family history. Comparing animal abuse to the Holocaust will be heard as saying that Grandma's death was worth no more than a chicken. It will also be heard as disrespecting the dead – *never* a good idea. So please, keep the Holocaust out of it. And avoid using "murder" and "genocide" to refer to animals. As I explained in chapter 1, this is counterproductive.

Also, don't throw around Yiddish/Hebrew terms or make references to Jewish law unless you really know what you are talking about. Some of the early protest signs read, "Is this a mitzvah from the Torah?" implying that since it was not in the

168

Bible, it was bogus. I found these signs confusing and asked about the intent. The person who designed them was not aware that in traditional Jewish communities, a long-standing custom is regarded as a mitzvah, and that "Torah" is more than just the Five Books of Moses. "Learning Torah" means studying all of Jewish writings, commentaries, rulings, etc, from the entire 5000+ years of our history. To a Hasid reading those signs, they made no sense. A perfect example of how a little bit of knowledge can be a dangerous thing. And an ineffective one.

And keep veganism out of it, too.

If you have read this book in its entirety, then you should understand by now why mixing radical veganism into the cause is counter-productive. Real political change means a willingness to make alliances with people who might not follow your entire lifestyle or philosophy, but who can agree with you on a specific issue. The most successful politicians are those who can reach across the aisle and negotiate a compromise. (A lesson that the U.S. Congress often forgets.)

Let's put the shoe on the other foot: How would you feel if I insisted you adopt the whole Hasidic way of life before I would even consider working with you or using any of your materials? What if I kept sending you emails and pamphlets telling you to "Go Hasidic"? Most likely you would file them in the trash. Which is what I do with all missionary tracts.

Most Hasidim are not vegetarians and are not likely to be so in the near future. That's the reality. If you insist on pushing "meat is murder" as the one-and-only acceptable doctrine, then you will make it impossible for people to consider giving up the use of chickens without betraying their entire belief system. And that simply will not work. If you force people to choose between "ethical veganism" and Hasidism, they will choose Hasidism. So please don't push that all-or-nothing choice.

Heed the feedback

One of the most frustrating experiences for me – and the one that ultimately led me to leave the Alliance and write this book – was the unwillingness for leaders in the anti-*Kapporos*

169

movement to listen to me as an expert when I tried to tell them what does or does not work.

When I took a public stand on this issue, my name and image were suddenly posted all over the Internet by animal rights groups, and my blog articles are still being cited in the media. All well and good. But when it came to educating activists about the positive things in Hasidic culture, and how to be more effective in the dialogue, nobody listened because I was not vegan enough (I am a ovo-lacto vegetarian.) Everything I tried to explain was put to the vegan test and then flunked. I was hailed as a hero, but only a token one. Heaven only knows how I would have been treated if I still ate meat.

People were more willing to believe things they read in academic books about Hasidism (sometimes not accurate) or on non-Hasidic websites (often hostile) than listen to the experiences and advice of a living, breathing person who knows his own tradition. This is rather like a bunch of white people trying to tell African Americans what the black experience is like by quoting *Uncle Tom's Cabin*.

Rule #1 in cross-cultural dialogue is that you always let members of a culture define their own worldviews. You never, ever define their culture for them. And Rule #2 is this: There is no "of course" in traditions. Never assume that you, as an outsider, understand what is going on just by looking at it. Rituals are never that simple. God gave you two ears and one mouth for a purpose: To listen twice as much as you lecture.

Suggestions for actions you can take

Here are some of the points that might be respectfully brought up in dialogues, letters to the editor, or blog posts:

1. As explained in Chapter 6, there is a substitute *Kapporos* ceremony that is widely practiced by many Torah-observant Jews. Here's how to do it: Money, perhaps equal to the price of a chicken or a symbolic multiple of 18, is substituted for the rooster or hen. The money is put into a white handkerchief, which the person then waves three times around his or her head while reciting a modified version of the prayer: "This money

shall go to charity, and I shall go to a good, long life, and to peace."

2. Hold a reverent, respectful alternative *Kapporos* ceremony, using the above-described formula. Set up a "mitzvah table" and teach people how to do this. Explain that by substituting money for a fowl, the heightened sense of repentance can be kept, and perhaps even enhanced, since no bird has to lose its life or suffer for our sake. Have a charity box *(pushke)* available for people to give to the local food shelf.

3. Go to my blog at rooster613.blogspot.com and download my printable flyer entitled, "Don't lose the merit of your Torah and mitzvot!" which discusses how animal cruelty cancels out the value of *Kapporos* with chickens, written in a "yeshivish" style aimed at Hasidic/Orthodox Jews. (No, it is not vegan in approach, but I did not write it for vegans.) Fill in your own contact information at the bottom of your printout and then make copies to hand out at protests or your information table.

4. If you are Jewish, work to increase the knowledge of your fellow Jews with regard to Judaism's beautiful and powerful teachings concerning compassion to animals. In order to do this, you must, of course, first educate yourself. I have already explained some of these teachings in this book. Richard H. Schwartz's *Judaism and Vegetarianism* has a good introductory chapter on kindness to animals. Rabbi Natan Slifkin's *Man and Beast* goes into more detail about animals in Jewish law. Rabbi Dovid Sear's *The Vision of Eden* also includes the mystical teachings. Plus there are many excellent materials from Jewish Vegetarians of North America (JVNA) on their website at JewishVeg.org. Further suggestions are in the Bibliography.

5. Here are some teaching you can cite. (This section is adapted from a list by Richard H. Schwartz. Used with permission):

Based on the enormous weight of Biblical, Talmudic, medieval, and modern sources commanding the prevention of animal suffering, it can be argued that one way that Jews can accomplish repentance and other goals of Rosh Hashanah and Yom Kippur is by moving away from the unnecessary exploitation of animals toward greater respect for God's creation. Many of the observances and values of this holiday period are more consistent with practicing mercy toward all of God's creatures:

- Prayers on Rosh Hashanah and Yom Kippur for God's compassion during the coming year are most consistent with acts of kindness to both other people and animals.

- Consistent with Rosh Hashanah as a time when Jews are to "awaken from slumber" and mend our ways, using money for the *Kapporos* ritual shows that we are putting Torah teachings about compassion into practice.

- Acts of kindness and charity, such as giving money to the poor, are consistent with God's "delighting in life" on Rosh Hashanah, because, unlike the version of the *Kapporos* ceremony using chickens, such acts don't involve the potentially cruel treatment and death of animals.

- It is consistent with the High Holy Days theme in general to change old behaviors. The season itself makes this easier than at other times of the year, because God "wipes the slate clean" and lets us start over. Moving from the use of chickens to the use of money can be part of this "reboot."

6. If you are not Jewish, work to educate yourself and your fellow non-Jews about the history, culture, and spirituality of Hasidism (and Judaism in general), so that you will know more about the culture than just chicken slaughter. This will help you see religious Jews as individuals and not "the enemy." Condemning an entire culture by one act or tradition that you disapprove of is morally wrong.

7. Check rumors and accusations you receive by email against the facts before passing them on to others. Remember: Spreading *lashon hara* (evil gossip) is forbidden, and this includes materials you receive by email. Or those you send out. Never put anything on the Internet that you would not want your friends

and family to see on a billboard in your neighborhood. Hiding behind a screen name is no excuse for bad behavior. What you post on one website becomes accessible to the entire world.

8. Inform others about the issue. Write timely letters to editors of publications. Use this book as a reference. Set up programs and discussions. Wear a button. Make and display posters.

9. Ask rabbis and other religious leaders to give sermons and/or classes discussing Judaism's teachings on kindness to animals. If you get no response, then educate yourself enough to offer such a course. A good time in the Jewish community is at the all-night study vigil on Shavuot, when many congregations offer a variety of programs and lessons throughout the night.

10. If you live near or belong to an Orthodox synagogue where *Kapporos* is practiced with chickens, present the rabbi with a copy of this book. Give a print copy; a physical book will be taken more seriously than a computer file. In addition, it can be read and studied on the Sabbath and Jewish holy days, when discussions often take place around the table. (Observant Jews do not use computers or other electronic devices on these days.)

11. Present copies of this book to synagogue libraries, even the non-Orthodox ones, as well as your local public library and your organization's library. The more the information is available, the more that people will become informed and make better decisions. Knowledge is power.

12. Review this book on Amazon, Barnes & Noble, etc. and/or your own blog. Suggest it for a local book club or reading circle. Have copies available for sale at your public events. You can get quantity discounts by ordering directly from Lulu.com.

13. Encourage your school or congregation to participate in Be Kind to Animals Week and other similar events. Make humane education an ongoing part of your daily life. Become a living example of the teachings.

14. Include animals and humane education in your observance of Tu B'Shevat ("Birthday of the Trees," or Jewish Earth Day.) Learn about animals in Israel and ask such environmental questions as; Why are there no lions there today, even though they are mentioned in the Bible?

15. Consider adopting the First of Elul as "New Year for the Animals" for humane education, and make the month of Elul (which comes right before Rosh Hashanah) a time to study the laws concerning *tsa'ar ba'alei chaim* (animal cruelty).

16. Become a vegetarian, or at least sharply reduce your consumption of animal products. Even if you don't feel you can give up meat right now, try having a Meatless Monday (or other day each week) when you try new recipes at home or eat out in a vegetarian restaurant. There are many good vegetarian recipes online.

17. Ask respectful questions about animal welfare and relate them to factory farms, etc. during Torah study groups when the laws about animals are studied. Strive to make a connection between then and now.

18. Before taking any of these actions, examine your own heart and motives. Take some time to pray and meditate about why you are protesting a Jewish ritual. Make sure you are not carrying unrecognized prejudices against Jews. Western society is filled with negative stereotypes, such as "letter of the law," or "an eye for an eye," or "Jews only care about money," etc. that are gross distortions of real Judaism. Antisemitism, like racism, is deeply engrained in our society. To be effective you must first confront your own prejudices. If you claim to be nonviolent, this means in *words* and *thoughts,* too, not just physical violence. Please keep that in mind.

Shalom u'vrachah, Peace and blessings!

Appendix B:

A Brief History of Hasidism

Hasidim is a revivalist Jewish movement that began in mid-18th century Ukraine. The Jewish community of that time had become dispirited by two major events in the previous century; (1) The massacre of thousands of Jews by Bogdan Chmielnicki and his Cossacks as they burned and pillaged across the countryside; and (2) disillusionment with the false messiah, Shabbetai Zevi, who had claimed that the year 1666 would be the beginning of the Messianic Age. When the promised redemption failed to materialize, the rabbis retreated into their studies and a gap emerged between the scholars and the common people.

Enter Rabbi Israel ben Eliezer, later to be known as the Baal Shem Tov, "Master of the Good Name," or "Besht" for short.[114] Born around 1700 in the Ukrainian town of Okup, he was orphaned at an early age, growing up as a lonely and friendless youth, who lived off a meager subsidy from the town and a variety of odd jobs. Historians debate whether he actually knew the Hebrew texts, or simply preached on what he picked up orally. Others question whether he was ever ordained as a rabbi. Elie Wiesel writes in *Souls on Fire:* "Some sources claim he was a saint who fled the limelight; others describe him as a harmless dunce; still others endow him with enough learning and wisdom to make him a judge of the rabbinical court."[115]

---

[114] Besht: Made up of the initials for **B**aal **Sh**em **T**ov. This is a common Jewish practice in referring to sages and rabbis.

[115] Wiesel, Elie, *Souls on Fire,* Random House, New York. 1972. p.12.

We have many stories, legends and scholarly books written about him, but nothing that he actually wrote himself.[116]

Nevertheless, he was exactly what the Jews of Eastern Europe needed at the time. Legend says that he secretly studied kabbalah with a mysterious "Rabbi Adam," and that the spirit of Ahiyah the Shilonite, teacher of Elijah the Prophet, appeared to him between two mountains outside of town and initiated him into its mysteries. Whatever the source of his inner knowledge, at the age of 36 he "revealed himself"[117] and began to publicly teach his mystical approach to life.

His followers became known as "Hasidim" (also spelled "Chasidim")[118] derived from *Chesed,* or "lovingkindness," one of the levels on the Kabbalistic Tree of Life. There was strong opposition to his movement at first. The Besht was suspected of trying to revive the false messianic Sabbetianism of the previous century, and some rabbis actually excommunicated him. But unlike the Sabbetians, who sought to do away with Jewish law and who indulged in forbidden foods and activities, the Baal Shem Tov stressed strict adherence to Torah and mitzvahs. Only he gave it a kabbalistic twist, revealing the inner meanings of the outer rituals.

The new movement shifted the emphasis from Talmudic study to prayer, ecstasy, storytelling, and sanctifying every action in daily life. "Of every good deed we do," the Besht taught, "a good angel is born. Of every bad deed, a bad angel is born. In all the deeds of our daily life we serve God as directly as though our deeds were prayers. When we eat, when we

---

[116] There are some letters reputed to be by him, but scholars debate whether or not they are authentic.

[117] This has mystical significance. The number 36 is twice 18, which stands for *chai,* "life" in Hebrew numerology. It is also a reference to the *Lamedvavniks,* the 36 hidden *Zaddikim* (saints) who are always present somewhere in the world at any given time. Some people believe the Besht was one of these, who chose to go public because the spiritual needs of the community were so great at the time.

[118] The word begins with a guttural as in German "Ach." I prefer to write it with an "H" in English, both because most English speakers cannot make the guttural, and because they tend to see it as the "CH" sound in "church."

work, when we sing, when we wash ourselves, we are praying to God. Therefore we should live constantly in highest joy, for everything we do is an offer to God."[119]

"Holy sparks" were everywhere, the Besht explained, and even the most unlearned person had many opportunities to raised them back to the Creator.[120] Many of the best-known Hasidic stories center around a common person whose sincere prayers are accepted above those of an aloof Talmudic scholar. Kabbalah, which had been a secret doctrine among the elite, became common knowledge and was integrated into the daily practices of Judaism.

As a traveling itinerant preacher, the Besht had no synagogue, and was often unwelcome at the ones in the towns. Many of his gatherings took place in local taverns, which were not only drinking places but also a sort of social club where Jews came to hear the latest news and a *dvar Torah* (a "word of Torah") from anyone passing through. Because "tavern keeper" was one of the few occupations open to Jews under the Tsar, the food and drink was kosher and so was the atmosphere. To this day, Hasidic teachings are more often given around the table over food and drink than preached from the pulpit.

* * *

The Baal Shem Tov had 60 disciples, each of whom founded his own school of thought. The disciples, in turn, had their own disciples who also had disciples. Hasidism spread like wildfire over the next century, with each town having its own Hasidic leader, or "Rebbe," who was much more than a rabbi. The Rebbe might indeed be ordained as a rabbi, but his main function was what is now known as a "spiritual director." Central to the movement was the *Yechidus,* or "one-on-one" with the Rebbe for personal advice. The Hasidic Rebbes were soul counselors, guides on the journey through life and, in some cases, miracle workers. Many could read a person's past incar-

---

[119] As cited in Levin, Meyer, *Classic Hasidic tales, p. 47.*

[120] See Chapter 4 for more on "raising holy sparks."

nations and prescribe the specific *tikkun* (soul correction) that was needed in this life.[121]

By the third generation, Hasidism, like so many movements of its kind, had become institutionalized. Many of the Rebbes founded dynasties. The position became hereditary, with each dynasty named after the place in Eastern Europe where their Rebbe lived or where important events in their history took place. Lubavitcher Hasidim, for example, originally came from Lubavitch, Russia.

Rebbe Nachman of Breslov, great-grandson of the Baal Shem Tov, strongly opposed this institutionalization. He insisted that his greatness was due to his own efforts, and not something inherited from his great-grandfather. "Even if I had been born the most lowly wagon driver," he once said, "I would still have become who I am."

On the other hand, Rabbi Schneur Zalman of Liady, founder of the Chabad-Lubavitch line, believed that a Rebbe was born on a higher level than ordinary people, something like an Eastern Boddhisatva. Thus began a debate that continues to this day: Are Rebbes born or are they made?

Rebbe Nachman never established a dynasty, and insisted that each person should "search for the Zaddik" and find the teacher most suited to his own soul. When asked, "What do we do as Breslovers?" he replied, "Whatever is in the *Shulchan Arukh* (Code of Jewish Law)." He was against adding extra strictnesses as specifically Breslov practices. To this day, there is no required Breslov "uniform" or dress code beyond the normal requirements of modesty for any religiously observant Jew. At Breslov gatherings you will see all types, from men in long black coats and *streimels* to people dressed like hippies.

But Breslov was, and still is, in the minority. Most Hasidic groups today are dynastic and much more conformist. Some people explain this in terms of reincarnation, claiming that the same souls keep coming back in the same family lines, returning to what is familiar. (Rebbe Nachman himself was

---

[121] The Seer of Lublin, for example, was said to read past lives by looking at the person's forehead. Some of his followers took this quite literally, and pulled their hats down over their eyebrows when they went in for their consultations. The Lubliner laughed and said, "Surely a person like me who can see into the soul can easily see through a hat!"

thought by some to be a reincarnation of the Besht, although he himself never made this claim.) For others, it is a matter of preserving tradition and honoring their ancestors.

* * *

It is difficult to know how many Hasidic groups existed before the Holocaust. Probably many hundreds, since each town often had its own local Rebbe. What is known is that the Nazis devastated the Jewish community in Eastern Europe. Rebbes and rabbis were often singled out for "special treatment," in order to break the spirit of their followers. In some cases they succeeded. But in others there was strong opposition of the spirit. A Gerer Hasid named Mati Gellmann led an underground non-violent resistance movement, known as "Mattisyahu's Men," who would not co-operate in any way with the Nazis. They refused to register for work details; continued to dress and live as Hasidim; held underground Torah classes; and in their own words, waged an uncompromising war against evil.[122] Breslov Hasidim, it is told, went to their deaths singing *Ani Ma'amin,* "I Believe," a song with words from Maimonides and a tune from Breslov tradition. This is still sung by Jews the world over at Holocaust memorial events.

After the Holocaust, Hasidic groups were consolidated around those Rebbes who had managed to survive. Although Chabad-Lubavitch is now the best known, there are many others: Belz, Bobov, Breslov, Chernobyl, Ger, Karlin, Satmar, Skver, Vizhnitz, to name a few. Newer post-Holocaust groups have also formed, such as Bostoner, Ashlag, Skulen, etc.

If Hasidism had been institutionalized before the Holocaust, it became even more so afterward. It was a matter of survival. Those who came to America during and after the Holocaust (1940s and 50s) established themselves with new congregations, religious schools, and successful private businesses. But unlike previous waves of Jewish immigrants, who wanted to assimilate into American society, the Hasidim saw them-

---

[122] Prager,. Moshe, *Those Who Never Yielded: The History of the Chassidic Rebel Movement in the Ghettoes of German-Occupied Poland,* Lightbooks, Brooklyn, 1980. A collection of first-hand accounts by survivors.

selves as the last remnants of a culture destroyed by the Nazis. They set about to preserve that culture and rebuild it in America, as well as in other cities around the world where they had settled. Any change of custom, they felt, would be a betrayal of the memory of those who had perished. Everything, from dress to recipes to styles of learning, was seen as the last remnant of a lost civilization. Today, each group has its own "uniform," and it is possible to tell one type of Hasid from another by the style of their hats, the cut of their clothes, and the songs they sing at their gatherings.

During the mid-20th century, many Hasidic texts found their way into the more mainstream Jewish community. In the 1970s and 80s, a lot of people were earning their doctorates by translating these source materials. There was a strong sense of urgency to this work, an understanding that if the stories were not collected and preserved right now, they would be lost forever, as was the pre-Holocaust world that had produced them.

Hasidic music has also had a strong influence in the Jewish community at large. With the invention of recording, it was possible to spread traditional songs beyond the borders of the groups that produced them. New songs were also written in the Hasidic style, and popularized by performers like Shlomo Carlebach (1925-1994), known as "The Singing Rabbi," who was originally Lubavitch but later established his own following. As has always happened with Jews and music, songs from the wider culture also exerted an influence. Hasidic Rebbes in Eastern Europe adapted tunes sung by gentile shepherds; today you can even find bands playing "yeshiva rock" and Hasidic rappers like Matisyahu.

* * *

In the 1990s, many Lubavitcher Hasidim began to believe that their Rebbe, Rabbi Menachem M. Schneerson, was potentially the Messiah. This was partly due to a general Millennial fervor in the world population as the year 2000 approached. Partly it was also due to the establishment of the State of Israel, which many Jews saw as a sign that the Messianic Age was at hand. And it was due to the fact that "Bringing Moschiach" through doing Torah and mitzvahs (which redeems the lost "holy sparks") was a strong theme in the Rebbe's ministry ever since he took office. He was convinced that the Messiah would come in his own generation.

Some of his followers felt that he was making veiled references to himself as Messiah in his speeches and writings. Significantly, the Lubavitcher Rebbe himself never made the claim.[123] At one gathering, when the Hasidim began to sing a song that hailed him as the Messiah, he stopped it quickly and almost left the room. On other occasions, when asked if he was the Messiah, he replied, "I am not." In 1991 he lamented that he had failed to bring the Messiah in his generation and passed the responsibility on to his followers to "bring Moschiach."

This may have contributed to the fervent hope among his followers that he would declare himself Messiah before his death. Then in 1992 he had a debilitating stroke that destroyed his ability to speak or otherwise communicate. Nevertheless, the idea that he was the Messiah persisted, received wide publicity at the time, and continues to influence the public perception of Chabad Hasidism in general.

This messianic fervor may also partially account for the Chabad focus on reviving *Kapporos* with chickens. Chabad Jews believe that when the Messiah comes and the Temple is rebuilt, animal sacrifice will be practiced there again. *Kapporos,* some believe, keeps the idea of sacrifices alive.

After the Rebbe's death in 1994, many Chabad Hasidim continued to believe he was the Messiah, expecting him to rise from the dead. This has been criticized as an un-Jewish influence from Christianity, and has aroused strong opposition from other Orthodox Jews. In 1996, The Rabbinical Council of America, an umbrella organization of Modern Orthodox Rabbis, issued a statement that:

> "In light of disturbing developments which have recently arisen in the Jewish community, the Rabbinical Council of America in convention assembled declares that there is not and has never been a place in Judaism for the belief that Mashiach ben David will begin his

---

[123] See Berger, David, "Did the Rebbe Identify Himself as the Messiah – and What do his Hasidim Believe today?", *Tablet,* July 21, 2014.

Messianic mission only to experience death, burial, and resurrection before completing it."

There are still many messianists among the Lubavitchers today, and you can find this belief in articles on the Internet. But other Chabad Hasidim feel that although he was *potentially* the Messiah as "the Prince of his Generation" (*Zaddik ha-Dor*), now that he has passed away, he was not. Since he left no descendants, the Lubavitch dynasty has ended, but they still study his writings and consider them to be authoritative.

In this they are similar to Breslovers, who also do not have a living Rebbe, since Rebbe Nachman never appointed a successor and established no dynasty. Breslov Hasidim, too, relate to their founder through his writings. It was rumored in Nachman's day that he, too, was the *Zaddik ha-Dor* and potentially the Messiah, but he realized he was not. He later ordered all his books on this topic to be burned, and he was obeyed.

It is important to remember that although Chabad is well known to the general public due to this recent Messianic fervor (the world at large is often overly obsessed with what Jews believe about the Messiah), they are not the only Hasidic group, nor are their beliefs universal among Hasidim in general. There has always been diversity within the Hasidic movement, and this is still true today. There are many different Rebbes, not just "The Rebbe" of Chabad-Lubavitch, each with his own "flavor" of Hasidic songs, stories, and teachings.

This is only a very brief history of the Hasidic movement – given on one foot, so to speak – filtered through my own study and personal experience. There are many good books on the subject, as well as a great deal of material on the Internet. In the words of Rabbi Hillel, "Now go and learn."

Annotated bibliography & further reading

Who is wise? He who learns from all people.
— *Rabbi Ben Zoma (Pirkei Avot 4:1)*

This is a very small sampling of books and other materials that I have found useful. I included authors from a variety of Jewish backgrounds, as well as some non-Jewish and scientific ones, to give a balanced perspective. Classical Jewish texts are not included, since their references are given in the text itself. Links to articles on the Internet are in the footnotes. I do not necessarily agree with everything written in these books – they often don't even agree with each other! – but they are all good reads.

Benyus, Janine M., *The Secret Language of Animals,* Black Dog & Leventhal Publishers, 2014. Designed as a guide for viewing animals in zoos, the author covers various behaviors of 20 animal species that you might see. An excellent resource for urban people to learn about how animals communicate and know what they are looking at. Also contains a history of zoos both good and bad, a section for critiquing your local zoo, and suggestions for actions you can take to improve conditions for the animals if necessary.

Bernstein, Ellen, *The Splendor of Creation: A Biblical Ecology,* Pilgrim Press, Cleveland, Ohio, 2005. Commentary on Genesis relating each of the seven days of creation to being in harmony with nature, from the founder of Shomrei Adamah (Guardians of the Earth), the first Jewish ecology organization.

Bernstein, Ellen, editor, *Ecology and the Jewish Spirit: Where Nature and the Sacred Meet.* Jewish Lights Publishing, Woodstock, Vermont, 1998. Anthology of essays with a wide variety of Jewish perspectives about environmental issues.

Bernstein, Ellen and Dan Fink, *Let the Earth Teach You Torah: A Guide to Teaching Ecological Wisdom*, Shomrei Adamah, Wyncote, Pennsylvania, 1992. Guidebook for teaching Jewish perspectives on the human relationship with nature.

Davis, Karen, *Prisoned Chickens, Poisoned Eggs,* revised edition, Book Publishing Company, Tennessee, 2009. An updated version of the groundbreaking exposé of the horrific conditions under which chickens are raised today. Difficult reading emotionally but an eye opener as to the suffering our "chicken soup" really causes and why it is no longer so healthy.

—— VIDEO: "Chickens at Play." Watch free, happy chickens at the United Poultry Concerns sanctuary go about their daily activities, with brief explanations of what the chickens are doing from dawn until they roost at night. Narrated by a young child. Aprox. 10 minutes long, an excellent opener for a discussion. Watch at http://vimeo.com/13210456 or order the DVD from http://www.upc-online.org/merchandise.

Gershom, Yonassan, *Jewish Tales of Reincarnation,* Jason Aronson, 2000. Annotated re-telling of 70 stories on this topic from both classical and contemporary sources, including many Hasidic stories about human souls reincarnating as animals.

—— VIDEOS: Visit Gershom's YouTube channel for videos on animals, reconnecting with nature, and "raising holy sparks."

—— VIDEO: "A Heartfelt Plea for Mercy," a one-minute slide show narrated by Gershom, explaining that holding a chicken by the wings is painful and advocatng the use of money instead. Produced by the Alliance to End Chickens As Kaporos.

Grandin, Temple, *Animals in Translation: Using the Mysteries of Autism to Decode Animal Behavior,* Scribner, 2005. Excellent, insightful book, exploring the ways in which animals experience the world around them. Also contains case histories of how selective breeding in agricultural programs has resulted in crippled chickens, "rapist roosters" and other distortions of natural animal behaviors.

Heschel, Abraham J., *The Prophets.* Jewish Publication Society, Philadelphia, 1962 (two volumes). Excellent analysis of history's greatest protesters against injustice and their messages.

Hirsch, Samson Raphael, *Horeb*, translated by Dayan I. Grunfeld, Soncino Press, New York/London/Jerusalem, 1962. Analyzes a wide variety of mitzvahs, including those that teach us how to relate to the earth and its creatures.

—— *The Nineteen Letters.* Feldheim, Jerusalem/New York, 1969. Passionate defense of traditional Judaism through eloquent letters to a skeptic.

Kalechofsky, Roberta, ed., *Judaism and Animals Rights: Classical and Contemporary Responses*, Micah Publications, Marblehead, Massachusetts, 1992. A wide variety of articles on animal rights, vegetarianism, and animal experimentation, from the perspective of Judaism.

—— *Vegetarianism Judaism: A Guide for Everyone*, Micah Publications, Marblehead, Massachusetts, 1992. Nice discussion of all the reasons Jews should consider being vegetarians. Includes an excellent presentation of how the philosophy of René Descartes changed the Western perspective of animals from sentient living beings to mere "machines," thereby opening the way for today's abusive factory farms.

Lappe, Frances Moore, *Diet For a Small Planet*, twentieth anniversary edition, Ballantine, New York, 1991. Shows the tremendous wastefulness and inefficiency of animal-based agriculture, and why we can feed more people with plant-based foods.

Levin, Meyer, *Classic Hasidic Tales,* Dorset Press, 1959. A very readable collection of legends and stories about the Baal Shem Tov, including some about reincarnation.

Lorenz, Konrad, *King Solomon's Ring,* 1949. Available in numerous editions. A zoological text for the general reader. The book's title refers to a legendary ring that supposedly gave King Solomon the power to speak to animals. Lorenz claims that he achieved communication with several species by raising them in and around his home and observing their behaviors.

Louv, Richard, *Last Child in the Woods: Saving Our Children from Nature Deficit Disorder,* Algonquin Books, 2008. Compelling examination of how today's children are no longer spending enough time outdoors with nature, and how this is seriously affecting their physical and mental health, as well as the health of our planet.

—— *The Nature Principle: Human Restoration and the End of Nature Deficit Disorder,* Algonquin Books, 2011. Richard Louv explore how, by tapping into the restorative powers of nature, we can boost mental acuity and creativity; promote health and wellness; build smarter and more sustainable businesses, communities, and economies; and ultimately strengthen human bonds.

McEeaney, Bonnie, *Messages: Signs, Visits, and Premonitions from Loved Ones Lost on 9/11,* William Morrow Paperback edition, 2011. A collection of psychical experiences connected to the 9/11 attacks, including the butterfly story on pp. 156-57.

MacGregor, Catriona, *Partnering with Nature: The Wild Path to Reconnecting with the Earth,* Beyond Words Publishing, Simon and Schuster, Inc, 2010. A non-Jewish author presents her personal mystical experiences with nature and animals. Although some if it is too neo-pagan in approach for my taste, the stories are well worth reading and much food for thought.

Mindel, Nissim, *My Prayer,* Kehot Publication Society, 770 Eastern Parkway, Brooklyn, NY. 1972. A primer and commentary on the practice and inner meaning of the Jewish prayers, from a Chabad Lubavitch perspective.

Patterson, Charles, *Eternal Treblinka: Our Treatment of Animals and the Holocaust,* Lantern Books, New York, 2002. Explores how the Holocaust was rooted in the 20th-century automation of slaughterhouses, and how treating people "like animals" leads to dehumanization, desensitization to suffering, and genocide. Includes an in-depth analysis of animal and vegetarian themes in Isaac Bashevis Singer's writings.

Patterson, Francine (author) and Cohn, Ronald H. (photographer), *Koko's Kitten,* Scholastic, 1987. True story of the friendship between Koko the gorilla and her kitten named All Ball. A children's book for all ages. Featured on *Reading Rainbow.*

Regenstein, Lewis, *Replenish the Earth: The Teachings of the World's Religions on Protecting Animals and the Environment,* Crossroads, New York, 1991. A comprehensive discussion on the teachings of the Bible and the world's religions on protecting and preserving animals and the natural environment.

Schwartz, Richard H., *Judaism and Vegetarianism*, third edition, Lantern Books, New York, 2001. Argues that Jewish mandates to show compassion to animals, preserve health, help feed the hungry, preserve the earth, conserve resources, and pursue peace point to vegetarianism as the ideal diet.

Sears, David, *The Vision of Eden: Animal Welfare and Vegetarianism in Jewish Law and Mysticism.* Orot, Jerusalem, 2003. An almost encyclopedic treatment of vegetarianism and all aspects of Jewish teachings on the proper treatment of animals, written by a Breslov Hasidic rabbi. Has many important source texts not prviously translated into English.

[Shivchei Ha-Besht] In Praise of the Baal Shem Tov edited by Dan Ben Amos and Jerome Mintz, Indian University Press,

1972. Earliest collection of stories about the founder of Hasidism, including some of him communicating with human souls reincarnated as animals.

[Shivchei Ha-Ari] Tales in Praise of the Ari, translated by Aaron Klein. A collection of stories about Rabbi Isaac Luria, including the chicken story I re-told in in chapter 4 of this book, and several tales about human souls reincarnating as animals.

Slifkin, Natan, *Man and Beast: Our Relationship with Animals in Jewish Law and Thought,* Yashar Books, 2006. Israel's "zoo rabbi" examines many animal issues from an Orthodox halachic perspective. Also includes many contemporary issues.

—— *Perek Shirah: Nature's Song.* ZooTorah, second edition, 2011. Verse-by-verse commentary on *Perek Shirah,* the ancient Jewish poem that uses verses from Scripture to illustrate the "songs" of the different components and inhabitants of the natural world – and their spiritual lessons for humanity.

Wiesel, Elie, *Souls on Fire: Portraits and Legends of Hasidic Masters*, Random house, 1972. A very accessible, heartfelt entrance into the mystical spirituality and down-to-earth humanity of the early Hasidic Rebbes, told by a Holocaust survivor who heard the tales from his Hasidic grandfather.

Younger, Jordan, *Breaking Vegan: One Woman's Journey from Veganism and Extreme Dieting to a More Balanced Life,* Fair Winds Press, Release date: November 1, 2015. The personal memoire of Jordan Younger, "the Blonde Vegan," who developed onorexia nervosa, an eating disorder centered on "righteous eating," and how she eventually left veganism to find a more balanced life.

GLOSSARY

The following glossary contains vocabulary, biographical and technical terms used in this book. Where possible, I have included cross-cultural references to make unfamiliar terminology more accessible. Hebrew pronunciations are a mixture of Ashkenazic and Sephardic, tending to follow the most common way that American Jews pronounce these words. In some cases, both pronunciations are given. Although I am aware of the current system of Hebrew transliteration used by scholars, I have chosen to use spellings that will be easiest for the English-speaking reader.

Ahimsa (ah-HIM-sa): Literally "harmlessness." An Eastern philosophy, practiced by the Jains and some sects of Hindus and Buddhists, which teaches that it is morally wrong to kill animals.

Alliance to End Chickens as Kaporos (or "the Alliance"): A non-profit animal rights organization run by Karen Davis. It is a subsidiary of United Poultry Concerns, a vegan org dedicated to ending the use of all poultry as food.

Animal rights: A political movement that believes animals should have the same rights as humans under the law, and should not be eaten or otherwise exploited by humans.

Animal welfare: A movement that believes animals can be used by humans for various purposes, but must be treated humanely and cared for properly. The ASPCA is an example of an animal welfare organization.

Antisemitism: hatred or prejudice toward Jews. I prefer this spelling to "Anti-Semitism" which, as Emil Fackenheim has pointed out, misleads people into thinking there is some entity called "Semitism" to be opposed. The newer spelling "antisemitism" has gained acceptance among Jews recently and is very common on Jewish Internet sites.

Ari (AH-ree) or **Arizal** (ah-ree-ZAHL): Rabbi Isaac Luria. See "Luria."

ASPCA: American Society for the Prevention of Cruelty to Animals.

Baal Shem Tov (bahl'-shem-TOVE): Literally "Master of the Good Name," referring specifically to Rabbi Israel ben Eliezer, founder of the Hasidic movement in the 1700s. (Not related to the idol "Ba'al" in the Bible.)

Bet Din (bait DEEN): Literally "House of Judgment." A rabbinical court, made up of three judges, one of which must be an ordained rabbi. Also the Heavenly Court where the soul is judged after death.

Bibliocat: Library cat; a cat whose job it is to guard the books from mice. In Yiddish, *shul katze.*

Breslov, Breslover (BRESS-lov, BRESS-lov-er): A follower of the 18th-century Hasidic Rebbe, Nachman of Breslov. After Reb Nachman's death, his followers did not appoint a successor but have continued to regard him as their leader in spirit to this day.

Chabad: Another name for Lubavitcher Hasidism. Derived from the first letters of **Ch**ochmah, **B**inah, and **D**aat, levels on the Kabbalistic Tree of Life. See Lubavitcher.

Challah (KHA-lah): Traditional braided bread served on the Sabbath and Jewish holidays.

Chayah (KHAI-yah): Literally "living being." The fourth level of the soul, corresponding to the collective unconscious.

Chesed (KHEH-sed): Hebrew word for "loving kindness" of "grace." Sephirah on the Tree of Life associated with the attribute of mercy.

Chillul HaShem (khi-LOOL-ha-SHEM: Literally, desecration of the Name of God. A public act that brings shame upon the Jewish people and diminishes the honor due to God.

covenant: A binding agreement between two parties. There are three covenants in the Bible: (1) the Rainbow Covenant between God and Noah after the Flood, which applies to all people; (2) the Covenant between God and Abraham, which applies to all descendants of Abraham; and (3) the Covenant at Sinai, between God and the Jews for all eternity.

Davis, Karen: Founder of United Poultry Concerns (UPC) and a major spokesperson for the movement to oppose using chickens for *Kapporos.*

Deep ecology: An environmental movement and philosophy that regards human life as just one of many equal components of a global ecosystem. To deep ecologists, animals and humans are equal, and humans hld no special status.

Ethical veganism: A philosophy that takes veganism beyond diet to claim that killing anything is morally wrong, and that any use of animals or animal products is exploitation.

Fargoyisht (far-GOY-isht): Taking on the qualities and customs of non-Jewish culture. Assimilated.

Four Species: A palm branch, two willow branches, three myrtle branches, and an esrog fruit are waved in the six directions on each day during the festival of Sukkot (booths)

G-d: A traditional Jewish way of writing "God." According to Jewish law, there are ten sacred Hebrew Names for the Creator that, once written, may never be erased or destroyed. Although this technically refers to the names as written in Hebrew letters, many Orthodox Jews extend it to other alphabets as well. Leaving out one letter means you are not really writing the Name.

Gentile: A person who is not Jewish. The term "gentile" is not usually used by Jews, but is used by the author in several places because of its familiarity to the non-Jewish reader.

halachah (hah-LAH-khah or ha-lah-KHAH): Literally "the way to walk" or "the path." Jewish law as revealed in the Torah and interpreted by oral tradition through rabbinical authority. (Adj. halachic)

Hasid (HAH-sid) also "Chassid" (KHAH-sid): A follower of Hasidism. (Adj. Hasidic)

Hasidism (hah-SEE-diz-um): A mystical, pietist movement within Judaism, founded by Rabbi Israel ben Eliezer (1700-1762), known as the Baal Shem Tov, and characterized by fervent devotion to God and meticulous observance of the commandments.

Hecht, Shea: A Chabad rabbi and primary promoter of the revival of using chickens for *Kapporos.*

High Holy Days: The ten-day period of repentance, beginning with Rosh Hashanah and ending with Yom Kippur.

Kabbalah (kah-BAH-lah or (kah-bah-LAH): The collective body of Jewish mystical teachings. There is no one book called "The Kabbalah." (adj. kabbalistic (kah-bah-LIST-ik).

Kabbalistic Tree: Also "Tree of Life." A diagram of ten levels of consciousness called, mapping energy flow in the universe and the human soul. Originally Jewish, it is now used by other groups as well, with varying interpretations. See "sefirah."

Kapporos: also spelled kaporos, kaparot, kapparot. Literally "atonements." An atonement ritual before Yom Kippur, in which a chicken, fish, potted plant or coins are waved over the head while a prayer is recited, then given to charity.

Kapporos center: A temporary location set up for the sale and slaughter of *Kapporos* chickens.

karet (kah-RATE): Literally "cut off." Banned or excommunicated from the Jewish people. In practice this means ostracism. Not generally practiced today, except among some Hasidic and Orthodox groups, where *karet* is similar to the Amish practice of shunning an offender.

kavannah (kah-VAH-nah or kah-vah-NAH): Literally "focused intention"; the inner focus of prayer; the "spirit" of the Torah. Also, a kabbalistic form of meditation performed before doing a mitzvah. (plural: kavannot (kah-vah-NOTE).

khumra (KHOOM-rah): An extra level of strictness in religious observance.

Kiddush (KIH-dish): Literally "sanctification." Special blessing said over a cup of wine or grape juice to usher in the Sabbath of other Jewish holy day.

Kiddush HaShem (KIH-dish hah-SHEM): Literally "sanctification of the Name of God." Jewish martyrdom.

Lubavitcher (loo-BAH-vich-er): Also known as Chabad (khah-BAHD). Of or pertaining to the Lubavitch sect of Hasidism; a member of this group. Lubavitchers follow the teachings of the 18th-century Hasidic master, Rabbi Schneur Zalman of Liady, and his six successors. The last of the Lubavitcher Rebbes was Rabbi Menachem M. Schneerson, who died in

1994 in Brooklyn, New York. Toward the end of his life, some of his followers believed him to be the Messiah, others did not, and this caused a split in the movement.

Luddite: Someone who is against new technology. Named after bands of English early 19th century English workers who destroyed machinery, especially in cotton and woolen mills, which they believed was threatening their jobs.

Luria, Isaac: 16th-century Jewish mystic who lived in Sfat, Israel. Regarded as one of the greatest kabbalists of all time – so much so, that Lurianic kabbalah became the basis of most of Jewish mysticism to this day. Also known as "the Ari" (lion).

Moschiach (mah-SHEE-akh): Also spelled "Mashiach." Literally "anointed one"; Messiah.

midrash (MIH-drash or me-DRASH): Literally "from seeking." Torah commentaries of a non-legal nature, taking the form of stories, legends, parables, homilies, and other forms of exegesis from oral tradition. Jesus' instruction to "search the Scriptures" was probably a reference to the process of deriving lessons in this way. adj. midrashic.

mikveh (MIK-veh): A special ritual immersion pool used by women after menstruation, men after nocturnal emissions, and by all Jews for other purification purposes. A convert to Judaism is also immersed in the mikveh. (This is the forerunner of Christian baptism.) verb: to mikveh.

minhag (meen-HAGH): Established custom practiced within a specific community, such as the wearing of black clothing among certain Orthodox groups. Within the group it often takes on the authority of a law.

mitzvah (MITS-vah): Any commandment in the Torah or Jewish law. Colloquially, a "good deed." Plural: mitzvot (mits-VOTE).

National Committee for the Furtherance of Jewish Education (NCFJE): A non-profit organization run by the Chabad Lubavitch movement. It is a division of the Chabad educational arm, Merkos L'inyonei Chinuch.

nefesh (NEH-fesh): The first or lower level of the soul, corresponding to the life force of the body.

Neshamah (neh-SHAH-mah): Third level of the soul, corresponding to the mind/intellect. Colloquially used for the "immortal soul" that survives death.

PBS: Public Broadcasting System. An American TV channel.

PETA: People for the Ethical Treatment of Animals, an animal welfare organization led by Ingrid Newkirk.

pogrom (puh-GROME): A riot against the Jews incited by the government in Czarist Russia.

Prayer shawl: In Hebrew *tallit* or *tallis.* A four-cornered piece of cloth with ritual tassels tied in the corners, worn during morning prayers. Based on Numbers 15:37.

Reb: "sir" in Yiddish. Term of respect used by Hasidic Jews and others, often denoting a teacher. In Yiddish it is traditionally used with the first name but in recent American usage it can be used with the surname.

Rebbe (REB-uh): A Jewish teacher, not necessarily an ordained rabbi; also, leader of a Hasidic sect, considered to be an enlightened master.

Rosh Hashanah (ROSH-ha-SHA-nah): The Jewish New Year, which comes on the first of the Hebrew month of Tishri (in the fall near the equinox.) It is a solemn day of judgment and repentance, on which the ram's horn (shofar) is blown. See "shofar."

ruach (ROO-akh): Literally "wind" or "spirit." Second level of the soul, corresponding to the emotions and conscious ego.

sefirah (sfee-RAH) also sometimes spelled "sephirah." Literally "number" in Hebrew. One of the ten levels of consciousness on the Kabbalistic Tree. Plural *sefirot* (sfee-ROTE.)

sentient: having feelings, awareness, and/or consciousness. Authorities differ on the definition of sentience and whether or not animals have it. In this book, we are assuming that birds and mammals are sentient. (Noun: sentience)

Shabbat (shah-BAHT): The Jewish Sabbath. Begins before sundown on Friday night and ends after dark on Saturday night, when three stars are visible.

Shabbos (SHAH-bus): See "Shabbat."

Shechinah (sheh-KHEE-nah): The indwelling presence of God. Often wrongly interpreted as a "goddess" because the word is grammatically feminine (Hebrew has no neuter). The

194

Shechinah is not a separate "person" or deity from God, but rather, an aspect of the One God representing immanence as opposed to transcendence.

shechita (sheh-KHEE-tah): the process and laws of kosher slaughter.

schecht: To slaughter according to Jewish law. See "shochet." Schecht, schechting, schechted.

shochet (SHO-khet): A Jewish ritual slaughterer, trained in the kosher method of slaughtering animals.

shul (shool): Yiddish for a synagogue. Nowadays usually implies an Orthodox form of liturgy.

Simchat Torah (SIMM-khat TOE-rah): A one-day Festival that comes at the end of Sukkot. On this day, Jews take the Torah scrolls out and dance with them.

sparks, holy: Fragments of Divine Light or consciousness that are trapped or enmeshed in the physical world. "Raising holy sparks" refers to elevating these fragments of Divine Light back to their proper place in the universe, i.e., restoring wholeness. A form of planetary healing.

stetl (SHTET-'l): A small Jewish village in Eastern Europe, such as was portrayed in *Fiddler on the Roof.* Has a nostalgic connotation of "down hominess" and Old-World Jewish culture.

streimel (STRAY-mel or STRIE-mel): A traditional fur hat worn by Jews on Sabbaths, festivals, and other special occasions.

Sukkot (Soo-KOTE): The Feast of Booths or Tabernacles. A seven-day harvest festival in which Jews eat in rustic outdoor booths and wave the Four Species (palm, myrtle, willow and esrog) in the six directions.

Talmud: (TALL-mud): A many-volumed compilation of Jewish teachings, both legal and non-legal, spanning approx. 200 B.C.E. to 500 C.E.

tikkun: (tee-KUN): "A repairing," a reparation for past actions.

tikkun Olam (tee-KUN-o-LAHM): "Repairing the world." New Age equivalents: to clear up bad karma; planetary healing.

Torah (TOE-rah or toe-RAH): Specifically, the Five Books of Moses (same as first five books of the Bible); more broadly, the sum total of all Jewish teachings and commentaries, both written and oral.

tshuvah (CHOO-vah or choo-VAH): literally "returning" to Jewish observance or mitzvahs. In a more general sense, repentance. The correct idiom is "to do tshuvah."

Tza'ar ba'alei chayyim *(TZAR-bahl-ay-KHAI-im):* Literally "suffering of living things." The prohibition against cruelty to animals.

United Poultry Concerns: A non-profit animal rights organization founded by Karen Davis, for promoting the compassionate treatment of domestic fowl. Their ultimate goal is to promote veganism and end the use of all birds as food.

Vegan: A diet that excludes eating any animal products or using feathers, leather, honey, etc. See "ethical veganism."

yahrzeit (YAHR-tzite): Anniversary of a death. Usually observed by lighting a candle and making a donation of sponsoring a feast in memory of the deceased.

yarmulke (YAH-mu-kuh): Also called a kippah (kee-PAH). A Jewish skullcap. Available in many styles, the colors or designs have no religious significance but may indicate a social or political connection with a particular group. Traditional Jews cover their heads to show respect before God.

yechidah (yeh-KHEE-dah): Literally "unity." The highest level of the soul, which is united with the Creation and in touch with God.

YHVH: The unpronounceable most sacred four-letter Name of God. Neither "Yahweh" nor "Jehovah" are true pronunciations and are never used by Jews.

Yiddish (YID-ish): A language spoken by Jews of Eastern European background. It includes many words of Hebrew, Aramaic, and Slavic backgrounds. Based on medieval German, Yiddish was the "mother language" of home and marketplace and is still spoken by many Jews in America and Israel. It is written in the Hebrew alphabet.

Yom Kippur (yam-KIH-per or yome-kee-POOR): The Day of Atonement, holiest day on the Jewish calendar. Yom Kippur is a day of fasting, prayer, and repentance.

Zaddik (TSAH-dik) also spelled "Tsaddik." Literally "righteous one." A holy person. Also a Hasidic Rebbe. (plural: Zaddikim)

About the Author

Yonassan Gershom is a freelance writer and author of *49 Gates of Light, Beyond the Ashes, From Ashes to Healing, Jewish Tales of Reincarnation, Eight Candles of Consciousness, Jewish Themes in Star Trek,* and *Kapporos Then and Now,* as well as many feature articles. He was born in Berkeley, California, grew up in the Philadelphia area, and graduated from Minnesota State University at Mankato in 1975. He received his ordination from Rabbi Zalman Schachter-Shalomi, the B'nai Or Rebbe, in 1986; later became a Breslov Hasid; and currently teaches as a Maggid (storyteller-preacher) through his writings. He lives on a 15-acre a hobby farm in northern Minnesota with his wife Caryl, three dogs, two geese, 13 cats, a flock of chickens and guineafowl, and a bunch of wildlife. His blog, "Notes from a Jewish Thoreau" (rooster613.blogspot.com), explores connections between traditional Judaism, animals, ecology, and his personal nature observations.